Prologue to Revolution

Notes of A. N. Iakhontov on the Secret Meetings of the Council of Ministers, 1915

MICHAEL CHERNIAVSKY

University of Rochester

PRENTICE-HALL, INC., *Englewood Cliffs, New Jersey*

Russian Civilization Series

Editors

MICHAEL CHERNIAVSKY

IVO J. LEDERER

Prentice-Hall International, Inc., *London*
Prentice-Hall of Australia, Pty. Ltd., *Sydney*
Prentice-Hall of Canada, Ltd., *Toronto*
Prentice-Hall of India (Private) Ltd., *New Delhi*
Prentice-Hall of Japan, Inc., *Tokyo*

Current printing (last digit):
10 9 8 7 6 5 4 3 2
C

Library of Congress Catalog Card No.: 67-10115
Printed in the United States of America

Foreword to the Series

The presentation of Russian history and civilization in this country has been shaped to a significant extent by the absence of adequate original source materials. Linguistic competence in Russian remains today indispensable for advanced training and research. It is regrettable, however, that the majority of students interested in Russia but not in command of the language should be denied opportunities for delving into the raw materials of Russian history.

Our purpose is thus relatively simple: to make widely available important Russian sources and to help remove Russian studies from the realm of the arcane and the exotic. Each volume in the series is designed to present source material on a significant problem of a given period—medieval, Imperial, or Soviet. Each volume, moreover, involves a careful translation and basic annotation so as to be intelligible to the undergraduate or the general reader and of scholarly use to the graduate student, to teachers, and to non-Russian specialists.

The series, spanning both the Tsarist and Soviet eras, concentrates on hitherto untranslated sources. In the main, too, it presents them in full text and without abridgment so as to expose both flavor and meaning in a document, memoir, or treatise. In this the series deliberately differs from the documentary collections usually found in one-volume compendia covering long periods and many themes.

The introductory essay in each volume places the issues and sources in their larger context. The essays are designed to provide guidance to the reader and generate new approaches to the understanding of the distant and recent Russian past.

Michael Cherniavsky
Ivo J. Lederer

Author's Note

My thanks go to Professors Leopold H. Haimson of Columbia University and Sidney Monas of the University of Rochester for patiently serving as walking encyclopedias of twentieth-century Russian history; to Mr. Andrew Somers of the Russian Institute, Columbia University, for checking all the legal references; and to Miss Marian McClintock of the University of Rochester for the rapid and efficient execution of the typescript.

Michael Cherniavsky

Contents

Introduction

———◆———

I

The title of this volume—Prologue to Revolution—can be mis-
leading, and hence dangerous, virtually by definition. But its
very inclusiveness is advantageous; the background of any event is
always broader than the event itself, and the background of a cata-
clysm such as the Russian Revolution of 1917 is virtually infinite in
scope. The methodological problems inherent in the analysis of the
causality of revolution have been examined, most recently and most
brilliantly, by Leopold H. Haimson.[1] The historiographic spectrum
has been limited, on the one hand, by the conception of the Russian
revolution as the result of all of Russian history—an inevitable result of all causes which can be identified in Russian history—and,
on the other hand, by the claim that the revolution was, in effect,
an accident—the consequence of a mismanaged and unsuccessful
war. Haimson has eliminated, once and for all, I hope, the second
extreme, and places the first within a proper historical framework,

———

[1] "The Problem of Social Stability in Urban Russia: 1905-1917," *Slavic Review*, XXIII, No. 4 (1964); XXIV, No. 1 (1965).

excluding the overarching teleology. He shows, conclusively, that a revolutionary situation existed, at least in the great urban centers of the Russian empire, just before the beginning of the war in July, 1914, (Russian calendar) and that, if anything, the war postponed the outbreak for some two and one-half years.

The causes, or rather the pre-conditions of revolution are many, of course. In the most general terms, one can argue that a revolution follows when a government, which represents a particular social and economic order, is unable to solve fundamental problems to the satisfaction of the great majority of the population. This inability evokes many reactions, which were long ago analyzed by Karl Marx: general discontent, the rise of revolutionary ideologies and of revolutionary parties and leaders, and the growing degeneration of the government and the whole ruling class. None of this is very new by now, and the revolutionary strands in the fabric of pre-revolutionary Russia have been examined many times. Sometimes they have been traced back to the revolution of 1905, sometimes to the period following the emancipation of the serfs in 1861, and sometimes to the Mongol conquest in the thirteenth century and thus to the origins of Russian society. One aspect of the pre-conditions of revolution, however, has received less attention: namely, the growing awareness of catastrophe; the spread of this awareness, conscious and sometimes unconscious, throughout the government, the educated, and the social elite as a whole; and the resulting paralysis, the inability to decide and to act, which overtakes the government.

It is this last aspect that the present volume is designed to illustrate. We do not intend to take too broad a view, however. It is easy, after the event, to find vague anticipations of catastrophe—be it in the feeling of the prominent nineteenth-century Russian statesman, Count P. A. Valuev, that everything in Russia is built on sand, or in the forebodings of Alexander Blok, Russia's greatest twentieth-century poet for whom personal and social doom were inextricably connected. Even though such subjective anticipations are significant, interesting, and, as it turned out, absolutely correct, our focus will be on the years immediately preceding the revolution itself. For it was in the years 1914-17 that the awareness of proximate catastrophe became not only a feature of the intellectual climate, but of the political climate as well. The growing paralysis of the government was based on very real and material circumstances, of course. But the increasingly difficult conditions evoked a feeling of hopelessness and doom which reinforced the paralysis of will and action.

One more qualification of our theme. Many Russians, of course, were anticipating a revolution in the years preceding it. But our concern will not be with those who both anticipated it and welcomed it—the revolutionaries—those who, for one reason or another, totally rejected the existing order. That their anticipation was not a foreboding, that they welcomed and worked for the liberation makes the evidence offered here the more striking. Our volume illustrates the psychological pre-condition of revolution in *the government,* in *the ruling class*—in those who feared and hated revolution, who wished to prevent it in any way possible, and yet did nothing but wait for it.

II

The text that is translated here is straightforward, simple, and dramatic, the minutes of the meetings of the Russian Council of Ministers in July, August, and early September of 1915. It was originally published in the *Arkhiv Russkoi Revolutsii (Archive of the Russian Revolution),* ed. I. V. Gessen, XVIII (Berlin, 1926), 15-136, by A. N. Iakhontov, the assistant to the Chief of Chancellery of the Council of Ministers from May, 1914, to October, 1916. According to him, the meetings of the Council were in two parts, "official, and secret." The first, or official, part of the meeting followed a printed agenda and took place in the presence of various officials and secretaries of the Chancellery. The second and secret part was devoted to the discussion of confidential questions, basic issues of policy and so forth. Of the members of the Chancellery, only Iakhontov and his chief were present at the secret part of the regular meetings, and it was Iakhontov's duty to keep notes in order to prepare and present the rationale of the reports, decisions, and summations which were required. He does not claim stenographic accuracy; indeed, he frequently summarizes a long discussion in one sentence. Much of the time, however, he was apparently able to note the precise wording and specific intonations of the individual speakers. Iakhontov informs his readers that his notes for the summer of

1915 were more complete than those for any other period during his service, and that he selected them for publication for that reason. He asserts that the entire text was put on paper during or immediately following the occasion; and his frequent asides, scattered throughout the text, reveal the kind of traditional, conservative bureaucrat who, if anything, would tend to underemphasize the tension, anxiety, and despair of the ministers. For reasons of space it is not possible to offer the complete text here. The first meeting (that of July 16th) has been omitted. But the first sentence uttered at that meeting can serve to introduce the historical setting of our document. The Minister of War, General A. A. Polivanov,[2] began his report with the following words: "I consider it my official and my civic duty to declare to the Council of Ministers that *the fatherland is in danger*."

This historical setting was not very simple, but it was surely dramatic. After nine months of bloody and difficult warfare, the Germans mounted a major offensive on the Russian front in May, 1915. By July they had conquered all of Russian Poland and were entering the Baltic and western Russian provinces. The continuous Russian retreat (often turning into a rout) was largely due to a lack of munitions, chiefly artillery shells. In the years before the war, all the belligerents had underestimated the rate of consumption of munitions, but the effect of this error was catastrophically greater in Russia; her industrial base was quite insufficient and her military administration was not efficient in placing orders and mobilizing whatever industry existed. The military defeats, and the reasons for them, created ever-increasing dissatisfaction within the Russian legislative institutions and Russian society. The government was judged unable and unwilling to organize the country for victory. By the summer of 1915, the Russian government faced the combined opposition of the legislature and of society; hence, it had to deal with an internal crisis as well as an external one.

The composition of the legislative bodies is of interest. The

---

[2] General Aleksei Andreevich Polivanov (1855-1920): Chief of General Staff, 1905-06; Vice-Minister of War, 1906-12; dismissed by his chief, Sukhomlinov, and appointed to the State Council; Minister of War (1915-16). After October, 1917, served the Bolshevik government in an advisory capacity.

upper chamber, the State Council, was in part appointed by the Emperor and in part elected. But the electoral base was very narrow and artificial, consisting of assemblies of gentry, top merchant guilds, and universities, so that the State Council was, in effect, an assembly of the top bureaucrats, the biggest landowners, the richest merchants, and a few professors. The extremely conservative bureaucrats and gentry had an overwhelming majority. The lower chamber, the Duma, established by the Constitution of 1905, also was hardly representative of the country as a whole.[3] It was an assembly which represented the gentry, the middle class, and the professionals. Except for a minuscule left and socialist group (24 deputies out of 442), its political spectrum ranged from the liberal, "lawyer" Constitutional Democrats (the Cadets) to the most extreme factions of the right. The legislative chambers, in fact, represented "society," and it is necessary to dwell, if only briefly, on the semantics of "society" in its Russian context.

Society (*obshchestvo*) and "public opinion" (*obshchestvennoe mnenie*) had various meanings. Basically, the ambiguity of meaning derived from two aspects of "society." In a crude and material sense, "society" simply meant the upper class—the bureaucracy, the gentry, the industrialists, and the intelligentsia of the professions. In a more abstract sense, "society" meant that part of the Russian population which articulated its views and opinions, and which was conscious of its own existence as a corporate entity distinct from the government. The problem, as for all societies, was that the articulate population was virtually identical with the upper class (except for some groups of skilled and well-organized workers). At the same time, it could be speaking for the great silent masses, for the country as a whole. Hence, the "public opinion" of the upper class could be, in its own view and in the government's, the opinion of all Russia.

Therefore, depending on one's political view of Russia and

---

[3] The Duma, the lower chamber of the legislature, was established by the Constitution of 1905, but the suffrage laws were changed in June, 1907, to both restrict and distort the electorate in favor of the propertied groups. For a recent summary of this *coup d'état*, see A. Levin, "June 3, 1907: Action and Reaction," in *Essays in Russian History*, eds. A. D. Ferguson and A. Levin (Hamden, Conn., 1964), pp. 231-75.

its interests, the legislative chambers might be representing the position of the whole population, of the articulate upper classes, or of themselves only.

In general, the articulate opposition to the government was based on the claim that the defeats at the front were a consequence of government mismanagement and stupidity. The opposition demanded a greater role in the war effort and, hence, in government. There were three important opposition groups: The Duma was demanding a government which would be responsive to the suggestions of the Duma majority, one composed of ministers who possessed the Duma's confidence, and strong and decisive enough to carry out effective measures for the defense of the country. The industrialists gained the grudging consent of the government to form, together with representatives of the Ministry of War, a Military-Industrial Committee whose function was to allocate contracts and mobilize and allocate resources. Finally, there was the *Zemgor,* the combined organization of the Union of the *Zemstvos* and the Union of the Towns.[4] Starting out as symbols of public initiative to help care for the wounded, these two organizations took over, or became involved in, broader and broader functions—the

---

[4] The *zemstvo* was the local self-government organization created as part of the "Great" Reforms by Alexander II in 1864, following the emancipation of the serfs in 1861. Since suffrage was based on property, the *zemstvo* was completely dominated by the gentry; however, it often represented the public-spirited, liberal gentry. It had the right to raise taxes for local improvements—roads, medical care, schools. Much of its autonomy was abolished in the years of reaction, in the 1890's. The basic unit was the county (*uezd*); the county *zemstvos* sent delegates to the provincial *zemstvo* assembly. The All-Russian Union of the *zemstvos* first emerged during the Russo-Japanese War, in 1904-05, with the purpose of helping in the care of the wounded and sending gifts to the soldiers. The War, in 1914, gave new life to the Union, which was headed by Prince G. E. L'vov (1861-1925), a prominent *zemstvo* public figure since 1904. After the Revolution, in February 1917, he headed the Russian Provisional Government until July 1917.

In 1870, again as part of Alexander II's reforms, towns received the right of local self-government, by electing representatives to a town or city council. Again, these rights were cut back in the 1890's. The suffrage base was extraordinarily narrow (in Moscow, which had a population of some 1,500,000, only 9,500 inhabitants had the right to vote for representatives to the city council). The Union of Towns, also created in 1904, was headed during the war by M. V. Chelnokov, a member of a wealthy industrial family, a Duma deputy since 1906 and Mayor of Moscow from 1914.

care of millions of refugees, and the mobilization and allocation of agricultural resources, small-scale industrial production, and so forth.

The reaction of the government to the crises it faced and to the opposition of society is revealed by our text. But it can be better understood if we examine the make-up of this government. It was headed by I. L. Goremykin, Chairman of the Council of Ministers. Seventy-five years of age, a conservative, and a life-long bureaucrat, he was, in his own words, "pulled like a winter coat out of mothballs," in January, 1914, to lead the government, and he could as easily have been put back into the trunk.[5] He chaired a Council of the Navy Minister, Admiral I. L. Grigorovich;[6] the State Comptroller, P. A. Kharitonov;[7] the Minister of Communications, S. V. Rukhlov;[8] the Minister of Agriculture, A. V. Krivoshein;[9] the Minister of Foreign Affairs, S. D. Sazonov;[10] the Minister of Finance, P. L. Bark;[11] the Minister of Public Education, Count P. N. Ignat'ev;[12] the Minister of Trade and Industry, Prince V. N. Shakhov-

---

[5] Ivan Longinovich Goremykin (1839-1917): member of the State Council; senator; attained the highest bureaucratic rank; old gentry family; Minister of Internal Affairs in 1895; Chairman of the Council of Ministers in 1906, and again from January, 1914, until January, 1916.

[6] Admiral Ivan Konstantinovich Grigorovich: born 1853; Vice-Minister of the Navy in 1909; member of the State Council; Navy Minister from 1911 until the revolution.

[7] Petr Alekseevich Kharitonov (1852-1916): jurist; member of the State Council; senator; State Comptroller, 1907-16.

[8] Sergei Vasilevich Rukhlov (1853-1918): right-wing member of the State Council; one of the founders of the All-Russian National Union, an extreme, right-wing, anti-Semitic organization. Minister of Communications, 1909-15.

[9] Alexander Vasilevich Krivoshein (1858-1923): worked in the agricultural administration; member of the State Council from 1906; Vice-Minister of Finance, 1906-08; Acting (*ispolniaiushchii dolzhnost'*) Minister of Agriculture 1908-15. Head of the White government in the Crimea during the Civil War, 1919-20.

[10] Sergei Dimitrovich Sazonov: born 1861; ambassador to Washington in 1907; Vice-Minister of Foreign Affairs in 1909; Minister of Foreign Affairs, 1910-16; member of the State Council.

[11] Petr L'vovich Bark: born 1869; served in the Ministry of Finances and in private banking; member of the State Council; Minister of Finance from January, 1914, to December, 1915.

[12] Count Pavel Nikolaevich Ignat'ev (1870-1926): large landowner; son of the famous Slavophile general, Count N. P. Ignat'ev; Russian Ambassador to Constantinople. Served in the *zemstvo* and in agricultural administration. Minister of Public Education, January, 1915 to December, 1916.

skoy;[13] and the Minister of the Imperial Court and of Crown Properties, Count V. B. Fredericks, who felt that his was a nonpolitical post and so never attended the meetings of the Council. The ministers listed above could be characterized in a number of ways: Kharitonov and Krivoshein were, and were considered to be, the most intelligent; Goremykin was, at least in the eyes of society, senile. Bark, the Minister of Finance, was reputed to be both incompetent and disreputable. Sazonov, Grigorovich, Ignat'ev, and Krivoshein made up the liberal wing of the Council, and Rukhlov was a rabid reactionary. All had one thing in common—they were professional bureaucrats.

This list of the ministers, however, is not complete. In June, 1915, before Iakhontov's published record opens, Emperor Nicholas II had dismissed four of the most unpopular ministers in consequence of the military disasters and the discontent they provoked. These were N. A. Maklakov,[14] the violent and ruthless Minister of Internal Affairs (a key post, for the Minister of Internal Affairs was in charge of all the police); I. G. Shcheglovitov,[15] the Minister of Justice who made a travesty of justice; V. K. Sabler,[16] the lay administrator of the Orthodox Church, i.e., Supreme Procurator of the Holy Synod and a protégé of Rasputin;[17] and General V. A. Sukhomlinov, Min-

---

[13] Prince Vsevolod Nikolaevich Shakhovskoy: born 1868; in government service from 1910; Minister of Trade and Industry from February, 1915, until the revolution.

[14] Nikolai Alekseevich Maklakov (1871-1918): in government service from 1894 on; member of the right-wing group of the State Council; Minister of Internal Affairs, 1912-July, 1915; notorious for reactionary policy and illegal methods of administration.

[15] Ivan Grigorevich Shcheglovitov (1861-1918): rich landowner; jurist; leader of the right wing of the State Council; Minister of Justice from 1906 to July, 1915; notorious for undermining the great judicial reforms of 1864, and for placing the administration of justice at the service of the political aims of the government.

[16] Vladimir Karlovich Sabler (Desiatovsky): born 1845; right-wing member of the State Council; senator; lawyer by profession and bureaucrat from 1873 on; Supreme Procurator of the Holy Synod, 1911-15; connected with Rasputin.

[17] Grigory Efimovich Rasputin (Novykh): Siberian peasant, hypnotist, healer, professional holy fool; introduced to the Imperial family by Grand Duke Nicholas, *ca.* 1907. Because of his ability to help Alexis, the hemophiliac heir to the throne, Rasputin gained increasing influence over Nicholas II, and particularly over the Empress Alexandra Feodorovna. During World

ister of War, who was held responsible for the defeats by most of society and charged with treason as well as with incompetence.[18] In the place of these four, Nicholas II appointed General A. A. Polivanov, popular in Duma circles and in society at large, as Minister of War; A. A. Khvostov, of an old gentry family, a right-wing group member of the State Council with twenty-five years of service in the Ministry of Justice, as head of that ministry;[19] Prince N. B. Shcherbatov, leader of the nobility of Poltava province, in charge of the state stud farms (1913-1915), as Minister of Internal Affairs;[20] and A. D. Samarin, of old Moscow gentry, son of the famous Slavophile and a highly respected conservative public figure among the gentry, as Supreme Procurator of the Holy Synod.[21] This was the extent of the concessions made by the government in the summer of 1915. But one could argue, at least in theory, that the homogeneity of the Council of Ministers was destroyed—Samarin and Prince Shcherbatov were not professional bureaucrats. Though they had served the State previously, they had done so as leaders of their class, the gentry, and they derived their status from their birth and from the opinion held of them by their peers rather than from State service.

War I, he had virtually complete control of the chief government appointments; he was, of course, surrounded by numerous obscure and prominent adventurers who took advantage of his influence. He was murdered, in December, 1916, by a group which included Grand Duke Dimitry Pavlovich, first cousin of the Emperor; Prince Felix Iusupov, husband of the Imperial princess Irina Alexandrovna; and V. M. Purishkevich [cf. note 47], who were attempting to forestall the revolution.

[18] Vladimir Alexandrovich Sukhomlinov (1848-1926): Chief of the General Staff in 1908; Minister of War, 1909-15; accused of treason by a specially appointed investigating committee in 1916; brought to trial in April, 1917, after the revolution and condemned to a life sentence of hard labor; released after the October revolution.

[19] Alexander Alekseevich Khvostov: born 1857; right-wing member of the State Council; senator; old gentry family; lawyer by profession; Minister of Justice, 1915-16; Minister of Internal Affairs, 1916.

[20] Prince Nikolai Borisovich Shcherbatov: born 1868; elected leader of Poltava Province gentry in 1907; head of the State Stud Farms, 1913-15; Minister of Internal Affairs, June-September, 1915.

[21] Alexander Dimitrevich Samarin: born 1869; son of the famous Slavophile writer, D. S. Samarin; right-wing member of the State Council; leader of the Moscow Province gentry, 1908-15; Supreme Procurator of the Holy Synod, July-September, 1915.

The problems which this partly renewed Cabinet faced in the summer of 1915, and which are revealed in our text, were serious. We need list, in summary, only the chief ones. There was the issue of divided authority. According to Russian wartime regulations, the military authorities held absolute power over everything and everyone within the theatre of operations; consequently as the Russians retreated, the theatre of operations embraced more and more of Russia. This division of authority complicated enormously all the problems caused by the retreat: the Polish question, for the conquering Germans were trying to lure the Poles to their side with the promise of postwar independence; the Jewish question, for the military authorities had declared all Jews to be German spies and had ordered their evacuation from the military zone, which necessarily meant the breakdown of the century-old legal constraints on the right of residence in the interior of Russia;[22] and, finally, the refugee problem as a whole, for Headquarters had embarked on a scorched earth policy and millions of refugees were pouring into the central provinces where no provision had been made for them. The government was also faced with social discontent: the Duma's complete distrust of the government and its measures; labor unrest over worsening economic conditions; the enmity of the press; and the encroachment of the public organizations which, in their desire to organize the defense effort, necessarily infringed on government authority. The Cabinet had to cope, moreover, with problems arising from the exercise of Imperial authority: Nicholas II was being approached privately and irresponsibly on behalf of candidates for office who the Cabinet knew would be highly unpopular or considered highly undesirable. And, while these were minor consequences of the autocracy, a major aspect of this problem confronted the Cabinet on August 6, 1915, when, in response to the military situation, Nicholas II (or those who influenced him) decided to dismiss the Supreme Commander, Grand Duke Nicholas,[23] and to

---

[22] The Jews were confined, by law, to certain areas of west and southwest Russia, i.e., the Zone of Settlement. Jews were also allowed to live in some of the cities if they were merchants of the top guilds or had a university education.

[23] Grand Duke Nikolai Nikolaevich: born 1856; grandson of Emperor Nicholas I; cavalry general; Supreme Commander of all Russian armed forces, July, 1914-August, 1915; 1915 until the revolution, Viceroy and Com-

assume Supreme Command himself. Then the Cabinet, which considered this action to be extremely dangerous, by reason of the Emperor's unpopularity, found itself engaged in a prolonged effort to induce the Emperor to change his mind.

III

To some degree, these same problems—influence, stupidity, unpreparedness, even social discontent—were encountered by the governments of all the belligerent powers. Our concern is with something else: What was the particular mood of the government, the kind of spirit in which it handled the issues facing it? The text should provide the answers to these questions. But insofar as the government, that is, the Cabinet itself, was (consciously or unconsciously) a part of society, our understanding of this mood of hopelessness and helplessness, of paralysis and alienation, will be greater if we can identify such a mood in society at large—that is, in the nonrevolutionary majority of the upper classes.

Here, our difficulty is the plethora of evidence. So many shared the feeling of despair and perdition that it is easy to delineate this mood, briefly and impressionistically, confining ourselves to a few individuals who represented the various levels of the social elite. We have, for example, the letters written by Count V. V. Musin-Pushkin, a member of the highest social circle, to his father-in-law. Count Musin-Pushkin was a very rich landowner, held the court rank of *jägermeister* (master of the hunt) and, as a deputy to the Duma, was a prominent member of the center group. His father-in-law was the seventy-seven-year-old count I. I. Vorontsov-Dashkov, Viceroy of the Caucasus, a former minister of the Imperial court, a personal friend of three Russian emperors, and one of the wealthiest and noblest seigneurs in Russia. It is interesting to note, by the way, that Musin-Pushkin, describing the political atmosphere in St. Petersburg, did not care to send his letters by post, but used personal mes-

---

mander-in-Chief in the Caucasus. Was very close to the Emperor and introduced Rasputin to him. Later, he turned against Rasputin, and his relations with Nicholas II steadily worsened until he was dismissed from the Supreme Command in 1915.

sengers. Writing in February, 1914, he dated the beginning of a pre-revolutionary mood back to the previous summer:

Even last summer, sitting alone in Pokrovskoe [his estate] I felt, from my reading of the newspapers, that something had happened in the country, that the tension was rising. . . . Upon my arrival here [St. Petersburg], my impressions were confirmed chiefly by government circles. Many of my acquaintances, in talking with one or another minister, were amazed by their pessimism and by their dissatisfaction with themselves [as a government]. . . .[24]

In a letter of April 19, he tried to characterize the political situation:

It is horrible. Goremykin, deliberately or out of senile egotism, is preaching the Kuropatkin system of patience,[25] and is trying, secretly, to knock down [N. A.] Maklakov [the Minister of Internal Affairs] who, so far, is all-powerful and, together with Meshchersky[26] and Rasputin, does whatever he pleases. No one wants a revolution and everyone (even the Cadets) fears it, but all are coming to the conclusion that it is inevitable and are only trying to guess when it will come and what will set it off. Some think that a change of the cabinet could forestall the explosion, while others, for example Guchkov and V. Maklakov,[27] think that the discontent is too great and that it is too late. The most bourgeois circles are becoming revolutionary, and it is worse in the provinces than in the

---

[24] *Krasnyi Arkhiv*, 61 (1933), p. 131. The background of the letters is described in an Introduction, pp. 129-131.

[25] General Kuropatkin commanded the Russian field army in the Far East in the Russo-Japanese War of 1904-05. He held some commands during World War I, as well. His famous slogan in response to all the defeats suffered by his army in 1905 was "Patience, patience, patience."

[26] Prince Vladimir Petrovich Meshchersky (1838-1914): publicist; editor of the weekly *Grazhdanin* (*Citizen*); extremely reactionary; very close to Alexander III and to Nicholas II, who read his paper assiduously.

[27] Alexander Ivanovich Guchkov: born 1862; President of the 3rd Duma; founder and leader of the Octobrist Party; member of a rich Moscow merchant family; chairman of the Military-Industrial Committee during the war. Great enemy of General Sukhomlinov and supporter of General Polivanov; involved in plotting a palace revolution before 1917. Minister of War and Navy in the Provisional Government in March and April, 1917.

Vasilii Alekseevich Maklakov: born 1870; younger brother of N. A. Maklakov, the reactionary Minister of Internal Affairs until 1915; deputy to the 2nd, 3rd, and 4th Duma; member of the Cadet (*liberal*) party and on its central committee; prominent lawyer in political cases.

capitals. Absolutely everyone is discontented. What is most stupid and annoying is that there are no basic reasons for discontent. The country is becoming more prosperous . . . but there is such hatred for the government that society is no longer guided by reason . . .

Musin-Pushkin may have been wrong about the well-being of the Russians, but his conclusion was prophetic; commenting on the growing armament race and on the competence of the government, he wrote: "Such nonentities as Maklakov, Sabler, Kasso [the Minister of Education], Sukhomlinov, and Company could ruin everything. There will not even be a grandiose catastrophe—just the loathsomeness and stink of corruption!" He concluded:

Unfortunately there is nothing pleasant or joyous in my letter, but I thought that you would be interested to know what the new policy has led to. In any event, I assure you that I exaggerate nothing and have tried to be only an echo of the general opinion and mood, rather than of my own.

The memoirs of I. V. Gessen reveal a different mood. Gessen, a prominent lawyer, a leader of the Cadet Party and for many years the editor of its newspaper *Rech,* was virtually a symbol of the professional, liberal, upper intelligentsia. His pages on the war years are dominated by one feeling—fear: "Formerly one used to say that, for war, one needed money, money, and more money. Now it has become clear that more important are nerves, nerves, and more nerves . . ." [28] And, listening to the optimistic plans of the Cadet chief, Professor P. N. Miliukov,[29] (about Russia getting the Dardanelles after the war) Gessen and his most intimate friends said nothing: ". . . what was there to say if we were doomed?" [30] In his despair, Gessen sought the reasons for his gloom in the demonic and the personal. Russia, in 1915, was ruled by two men: N. N.

[28] I. V. Gessen, *V Dvukh Vekakh: zhiznennyi otchet (In Two Centuries: An Accounting of a Life),* published in the *Arkhiv Russkoi Revolutsii,* ed. I. V. Gessen, XXII (Berlin, 1937), p. 329.

[29] Pavel Nikolaevich Miliukov: famous Russian historian; founder and leader of the Cadet Party. After the February Revolution he was Minister of Foreign Affairs until May, 1917; obsessed with the Russian war aim of winning the Dardanelles, and hence with the need to continue the war until victory.

[30] Gessen, p. 329.

Ianushkevich,[31] chief of staff to the Supreme Commander, Grand Duke Nicholas; and Rasputin, who ruled in the interior. Both, Gessen felt, were irresponsible, mad, and evil.[32] And the general and total chaos was reflected in the poisonous growth of decadent art, literature, and social customs.[33] Above all, he feared revolution; when it came, his fear gave him the insight to observe: "The government had gone on strike. Long ago, while it was officially all-powerful, it had ceased to doubt that the crash will come, sooner or later . . ." [34]

But Gessen was a representative of the rational, middle-class Cadet intelligentsia, and his sensitivity was limited. As usual, the greatest sensitivity, even in political matters, was to be found among the artists and literati. A most striking example is the diary of the poetess Zinaida Gippius, wife of the famous novelist Dimitri Merezhkovsky. By birth, education, and position Zinaida Gippius was a member of the liberal, nonrevolutionary intelligentsia; she did not understand much of what was going on, but she felt deeply that something dreadful was happening. On August 1, 1914, she wrote:

I was amazed by the disorders which occurred in Petersburg in the last days [before the war]. . . . I understood absolutely nothing and I could feel that those who told me about it also understood nothing. And it was even clear that the rioting workers themselves understand nothing, even though they smash streetcars, stop traffic, there is shooting, Cossacks are galloping. . . . And the intelligentsia [stood there] with its mouth hanging open—for them, all of this was like a snowfall in July.[35]

On April 1, 1915, she commented on the split within the intelligentsia, into those who "accepted" the war and were willing

---

[31] General Nikolai Nikolaevich Ianushkevich (1868-1918): professor of the Nicholas Academy of the General Staff; March, 1914, Chief of the General Staff; with the outbreak of the war, Chief of Staff to the Supreme Commander, Grand Duke Nicholas; after August, 1915, Assistant to the Viceroy and Commander in the Caucasus.

[32] Gessen, p. 337.

[33] *Ibid.*, p. 346.

[34] *Ibid.*, p. 355.

[35] Zinaida Gippius, *Siniia Kniga: Peterburgskii Dnevnik, 1914-1918* (*The Blue Book: St. Petersburg Diary, 1914-1918*) (Belgrade, 1929), pp. 7, 8.

to work with the government, and those who did not believe it possible to cooperate:

And how shall one act? The "accepting" are frantically trying to act, to help "even the devil himself, let alone the government" and . . . they try in vain, for the government, most decidedly, refuses to allow anyone anything, and "politely requests" everyone not to poke their noses into its business; no public assistance is necessary, if you please. And, if you are so loyal, sit quietly and obey dumbly, that is the way you can help.[36]

On May 15, 1915, she commented on the slogan "Everything for the War," offered by the liberals in the Duma:

What words-words-words! Terrible, how sincere they are and how fatally childish! We cannot make a move, we cannot reach out for each other without having our hands slapped; and then, to "consider" that "we" are fighting the war ("the people!") and accept help from the Tsar only condescendingly. Whom do they cheat? Themselves, themselves! The people are not fighting any war; they understand absolutely nothing. And there is absolutely nothing that we can say to them. . . . Well, why try to guess ahead; here are the facts. We—the whole, thin, conscious layer of Russia—are voiceless and motionless, no matter how much we wriggle. Perhaps we are already atrophied. The ignorant mass goes to war on orders from above, by the inertia of blind obedience. But such obedience is terrifying. . . . Let us wait.[37]

And, on July 23, she wrote about the new session of the Duma:

The Duma opened on the nineteenth; the government gave way on this [convening the Duma]—but why? Yet it [the government] acts secretively, quietly, all the time. It changed some ministers around, [exchanged] some crows for other crows and . . . it either wants nothing else or can do nothing else. At the past two sittings—countless patriotic words. The left [deputies] were sharp without purpose.[38] They are trained so that they can only complain and, withal, rather abstractly. The "Statesman" Miliukov uttered beautiful words, but did *not* ask for a responsible government [i.e., responsible before the Duma]. . . . I know that with the present government Russia cannot properly get the better of the Germans.

---

[36] *Ibid.*, p. 17.

[37] *Ibid.*, pp. 22, 23.

[38] By "Left," Zinaida Gippius means the nonradical Left, mainly the Cadets.

This is already confirmed by past events. This is definite and final. But *how* to get the better of the government, I do not know. . . . I don't understand (I say so, honestly, to myself) and I'm afraid that everyone is lost, everyone understands nothing.[39]

And finally, writing in August and September of 1915, Zinaida Gippius characterized the whole political spectrum as she saw it: "The Right—does not understand, and is not going anywhere, and will not let anyone do anything. The Center—they understand, but are going noplace, standing, waiting (for what?). The Left—understands nothing, but is going somewhere—not knowing where or why, blindly." [40]

Zinaida Gippius's prescience allowed her to see the helplessness of both government and society, and the threatening dark "mass" beyond. Certainly she saw far more clearly and further than political personages saw or admitted to seeing. Perhaps it was to be expected that these men, in their public utterances, could not admit to despair. Yet, from them, too, there came a mounting chorus of a particular discontent which spread from the Cadets to the right. The theme was always the same—the incompetence of the government, the conflict with society, the lack of a program. Miliukov, leader of the Cadets, opened the attack on July 19, 1915, the day on which the Duma started its new session:

Gentlemen, the real cause of the [government's] mistakes is the abnormal relationship between the government and the public. . . . "Distrust of the people, limited only by fear"—this Gladstonian definition of conservatism—has remained as the guiding principle of our internal policy. . . . We have heard, today, benevolent speeches [by the ministers at the opening of the Duma], we value them, but we have not heard of a definite and determined political program. . . . Men whom the country knows and respects, whom it trusts in advance—such men are not part of the [new] cabinet . . .[41]

He was echoed by Rodichev,[42] a fellow Cadet, on August 18:

[39] *Ibid.*, pp. 29-30.
[40] *Ibid.*, p. 32.
[41] *Gosudarstvennaia Duma: Stenograficheskii Otchet (The State Duma: Stenographic Account)*, 1st Sitting, July 19, 1915 (Petrograd, 1915), pp. 94-104.
[42] Fedor Izmailovich Rodichev: born 1856; deputy to the 1st, 2nd, 3rd, and

They [the government] have not understood that they had to have a program, that they had to know what they are doing, that they had to come here with the absolution of [their] political crimes . . . which is required by Russia . . . They are doomed to moral impotence. Until such time [that they understand] they will not have and cannot have any prestige in the country, in Europe, in the world.[43]

A week later, on August 25th, the attack was mounted by Godnev,[44] a member of the centrist Octobrist Party.[45] Commenting on the constant use of extraordinary and extralegal measures by the government, Godnev declared:

. . . this shows clearly that, within the Council of Ministers, there is no person capable of governing the country under normal conditions and by normal laws. . . . All this [illegality] is taking place, I believe, because there is, up to the present time, on the part of the government, no confidence of the kind that the government should manifest towards the Russian people. And therefore I must say to you that, if there is lack of confidence towards the people on the part of the government, then, to speak sincerely, one must say that there is no particular confidence towards the government on the part of the Russian people.[46]

By 1916 this distrust of the stability and competence of the government was manifested, by the extreme right of the Duma, and was voiced by the reactionary monarchist Purishkevich.[47] Of

4th Dumas; one of the founders and leaders of the Cadet Party; a dedicated fighter for constitutional rights.

[43] *Duma,* 11th Sitting, August 18, 1915, pp. 880-81.

[44] Ivan Vasilevich Godnev: Octobrist deputy to the 3rd and 4th Dumas; State Comptroller of the Provisional Government, March to July, 1917.

[45] The Octobrist Party, founded by Guchkov, had as its program the guarantees of the constitution of 1905. After the change in the electoral law in 1907 the Octobrists were a party of the center, largely composed of industrialists, big merchants, and big landowners. In 1913 the Octobrist Party (the Party of October 17th, as it was formally called) split into three sub-groups: a right wing; a center, called Zemtsy Octobrist; and the left, known as the Left Octobrists.

[46] *Duma,* 14th Sitting, August 25, 1915, pp. 1053-54.

[47] Vladimir Mitrofanovich Purishkevich (1870-1920): extreme right-wing deputy to the 2nd, 3rd, and 4th Dumas. One of the founders of the Union of the Russian people. During the war, Purishkevich abandoned most of his political activities and worked at the front as representative of the Red Cross.

course, he blamed Russia's misfortunes on the influence of Rasputin and other irresponsible adventurers. But the political conclusions he drew on February 12th were applauded by virtually the whole Duma:

Is it normal, gentlemen, this quickened ministerial leapfrog, due, I would say, also to a whole series of outside influences, and of which we are witnesses? (*Laughter.*) What are the reasons for this sad and threatening situation . . . ? It is my profound conviction that the reason is only in the following: We have, at the present, ministers, but we have no Cabinet; a Cabinet united by a single will, a single spirit—the spirit of support of a government which would assign itself a program agreeable to us or not, but one [which would mean] that all are for one and one is for all. . . . And what about the question of the refugees? (I simply pick, *au hazard*, one question out of a whole series which cannot but give anxiety to us, the representatives of the people, gentlemen, as they give anxiety to the whole Russian people.) Is this refugee question, and the complete *non possumus* of the government to manage it . . . is this refugee question a normal situation? [48]

And, as Purishkevich's witticism about the rapid change of ministers became the talk of all "society," Savenko,[49] who had started out as an extreme right-wing deputy in the Duma, spoke to the questions posed by Purishkevich:

What a terrible thing it is for the country that, during the time of the greatest trials experienced by our Fatherland, the country does not trust the government; no one trusts the government, even the Right does not trust the government—in fact, the government does not trust itself and is not sure about tomorrow.[50]

An identical development took place in that most conservative chamber, the State Council. It would be redundant to pick and

---

[48] *Duma*, 20th Sitting, February 12, 1916, pp. 1502-4.
[49] Anatoly Ivanovich Savenko: Duma deputy of the Nationalist faction.

The Nationalists came mainly from the southwest of Russia, where they "defended" Russian "interests" against Jewish, Ukrainian, and Polish aspirations. They constituted the right-wing faction of the Duma. A left splinter group of the Nationalist Party, the Progressive Nationalists, emerged in 1915.
[50] *Duma*, 28th Sitting, February 29, 1916, pp. 2427-28. See also the speech of the rightist deputy, Dimitry Nikolaevich Chikhachev, leader of the Nationalists, *ibid.*, pp. 2440 ff.

quote all the available speeches, but Professor D. D. Grimm of the academic group, in July 1915,[51] Baron V. V. Meller-Zakomel'sky of the center group, in February of 1916,[52] and V. I. Karpov, of the right, in November, 1916,[53] all echoed the several notes—on the part of the liberal and center elements, distrust of the government; on the right wing a plea for a firm policy and firm authority.[54] And, as a final piece of evidence that awareness of reality had penetrated those furthest removed from reality, one can offer the letter of Grand Duke Alexander Mikhailovich, grandson of Emperor Nicholas I, third cousin of the Emperor. This letter to the Emperor was written in stages, from December 25, 1916, to February 4, 1917 —the eve of the revolution:

That which the people and society want is quite little—a reasonable government (I am not using commonplaces, meaningless words; strong and firm government, of course, for weak government is not government) which meets popular needs and allows the possibility of living freely and allowing others to live freely. . . .

The main requirement is that the program (of policy) once established, is not to be changed under any conditions, and that the government must be sure that no outside influences will be able to sway You, and that You will support the government with all Your unlimited power. Now one sees exactly the reverse—no single minister can be responsible for the day to come, all are disunited. Men are appointed as ministers who do not possess a shred of confidence [of the country] and are, probably, themselves surprised that they became ministers. . . .

---

[51] Davyd Davydovich Grimm: born 1864; professor of Roman Law; rector of St. Petersburg University until 1911; elected by the Academic and University electorate to the State Council in 1907. Cf. *Gosudarstvennyi Sovet:Stenograficheskie Otchety (State Council: Stenographic Accounts)*, 11th Session, Meetings 1-10 (Petrograd, 1915), pp. 50-51.

[52] Baron Vladimir Vladimirovich Meller-Zakomel'sky: born in 1863; elected to the State Council in 1912 by the gentry of St. Petersburg Province. Cf. *Sovet,* 12th Session, meetings 1-33, pp. 40 ff.

[53] Viktor Ivanovich Karpov: born 1859; elected to the State Council by the gentry in 1907; member of the group of the Right; member of the permanent committee of the United Gentry.

[54] See Alexander Blok, *Poslednie dni starogo rezhima (The Last Days of the Old Régime)* in *Arkhiv Russkoi Revolutsii,* ed. I. V. Gessen, IV (Berlin, 1922), 8-9. See also the letters sent by extreme right-wing members of the State Council, united in two groups around A. A. Rimsky-Korsakov and M. Ia. Govorukho-Otrok. In these letters (*Ibid.,* V, 337-338) they plead with the Emperor to stop imitating "the walk of a drunk—staggering from wall to wall."

No matter how much I thought about it, I still cannot understand what You and Your advisers are fighting for, trying to achieve . . . Such a situation cannot go on.[55]

None of these exhortations, pleas, and demands achieved anything, as we well know. But as one reads the text that follows, these opinions, selective though they necessarily are, and limited to the liberal and conservative sections of the educated class, should provide the context of the mood of defeat and hopelessness which, it is argued here, is one of the pre-conditions of revolution.

---

[55] *Ibid.,* V, 333-35.

I

The Meeting of
24 July 1915

————◆————

During the week, there were none of the ordinary meetings. There were conferences in the ministerial pavilion at the Duma and there were meetings of particular ministers with the Chairman of the Council. I was not well during this time. I. L. Goremykin and I. N. Lodyzhensky[1] told me what had happened. Unfortunately, I did not write down immediately their information. Hence, maintaining my rule to set forth only what I have in my notes, I pass directly to the meeting of the 24th of July.

The general situation at the front continues to be pretty hopeless. The Germans are attacking, and are meeting hardly any resistance. The public is becoming anxious. In some places there have been disturbances among the mobilized soldiers and in local garrisons. It is becoming clear that the Duma is in an irreconcilable mood. The government cannot expect any help from it. The population, whipped up by the press, sees the Duma as the magic healer

---

[1] Ivan Nikolaevich Lodyzhensky: born 1872; Senator; from May, 1914, Chief of Chancellery of the Council of Ministers.

of all ills and misfortunes. From the *Stavka*[2] come pleas for replacements and ammunition. The generals are beginning to occupy themselves more and more with internal politics, trying to divert attention from themselves and to shift responsibility onto other shoulders.

The atmosphere in the Council of Ministers is a depressed one. One feels some kind of confusion. The relations between the individual members and their relationship to the Chairman are acquiring a very nervous character.

The conversations began with the announcement by A. V. KRIVOSHEIN that the *Stavka* had presented him with a firm demand for the immediate publication of a formal Imperial decree announcing the endowment with land of those soldiers who had suffered most or had distinguished themselves most. The allotment should be not less than six to nine *desiatins*.[3] The allotments can be made from government land and the land of the Peasant Bank, but should primarily be from the confiscated estates of German colonists and enemy subjects. "Concerning this," continued A. V. KRIVOSHEIN, "I received yesterday a letter of absolutely incredible content from General Ianushkevich [Chief of Staff]. He writes that 'Fairy-tale heroes, idealistic soldiers, altruists, are encountered very rarely'; that 'such are no more than one per cent, and all the others are men of the 20th [*i.e.*, payday].' The Chief of Staff of the Supreme Commander insists that of course 'it is beautiful to fight for Russia, but the masses do not understand it.' That 'a Tambovets is ready to stand to the death for Tambov province, but the war in Poland seems strange and unnecessary to him.' That 'therefore, the soldiers surrender in huge numbers.' And so forth. (Unfortunately, all these statements were read with such speed that I had time to write down only separate sentences.) From this, General Ianushkevich concludes that 'the Russian soldier must be made materially interested in resisting the enemy, and that it is necessary to lure him on with land allotments and threat of confiscation of the land of those who surrender.' And so forth, in the same flattering tone, about soldiers who are being led by Headquarters. 'Heroes must be

---

[2] *Stavka* ("Headquarters of the Supreme Commander of the Russian armies"). Henceforth referred to as "Headquarters."

[3] A *desiatina* is 2.4 acres.

bought,' is the opinion of the closest collaborator of the Grand Duke."

Having concluded the transmission of all these considerations, A. V. KRIVOSHEIN exclaimed: The incredible naïveté or, more correctly, the stupidity of the letter from the Supreme Commander's Chief of Staff makes me shudder. One can get to feel utterly desperate. At the front everything is collapsing, the enemy is approaching the heart of Russia, and Mr. Ianushkevich is worrying about how to exonerate himself of the responsibility for all that is happening. In the letter which I have read there is particularly clearly manifested his perpetual desire to establish his own alibi. With the first defeats, Headquarters began to shout all over the place about the lack of ammunition, shells, and about the inactivity of the rear. The defeats continued—Headquarters began to shout that the rear is sending up only old men incapable of battle, instead of real replacements. Now catastrophe has come—they begin to libel the whole Russian people. Everyone is inactive; everyone is guilty of the fact that the Germans keep on beating us. Only Headquarters is sinless, only it is at work. General Ianushkevich himself is pure self-satisfaction, a genius persecuted by fate and human injustice. In order to elevate himself, he is ready to libel anyone and everyone; even those who, under his brilliant leadership, die without a murmur during the endless retreats and incomprehensible defeats. But after all, if a shortage of shells developed, Headquarters could not have failed to know about it. Why then, being able to anticipate the coming disaster, did the Chief of Staff not bother to report to his Commander-in-Chief on the necessity of changing the plan of operations? Why did he not bother to consult with other staff members, instead of climbing the Carpathian mountains? [4] Why now, when everything is topsy-turvy, are the plans not being modified, why are means to resist the enemy not being sought? The French have mobilized much older age groups, and their old men are doing beautifully in the trenches. Why can't our men be utilized instead of this shouting about the purchase of heroes? How can General Ianushkevich have the courage to continue to direct military operations when he no longer believes in the army, in the love for the

---

[4] The reference is to the continued Russian attempts to pursue an offensive in the south, against the Austrians.

fatherland, in the Russian people? What utter horror! Gentlemen, just think, in whose hands the fate of Russia, the monarchy, and the whole world is placed! Something quite mad is taking place. Why is poor Russia fated to live through such a tragedy? I cannot remain silent any longer, no matter what the consequences may be for me. I do not have the right to shout in the crossroads and in the streets, but to you and to the Tsar I must say this. I reserve for myself the right to report tomorrow, to His Majesty, General Ianushkevich's letter and to express to him everything that I think about this outrageous letter."

All this was said by A. V. Krivoshein with extreme passion, with a feeling which carried everyone away. One could see how deeply he was shaken by the revelations of the Chief of Staff. After this statement I have in my notes: "General outrage." I had to leave the room for a few minutes; I was called to the phone. When I returned, I heard the following.

P. A. KHARITONOV: If Ianushkevich thinks to buy heroes, and only by this method to guarantee the defense of the motherland, there is no place in Headquarters for him. Let him seek to utilize his talents in some other place, less harmful for Russia. One must liberate the Grand Duke from such a collaborator. We may end up with the fable of the anchorite and the bear. We must warn the Sovereign.

P. L. BARK: Complete demoralization! What we are heading for, with such commanders, is horrible to contemplate. Even without all this, there is anxiety in financial circles. Abroad, our situation is being evaluated as getting worse all the time. And now the closest and most influential subordinate of the Commander-in-Chief displays such hysteria.

PRINCE N. B. SHCHERBATOV: In reply to General Ianushkevich's letter, one should send him a bucket of valerian drops. Clearly, his nerves have gone to pieces and he needs sedatives. And in addition, one must explain to him (apparently, such aspects of the human soul are not understandable to him) that no one has ever been able to buy heroes, that self-sacrifice and love for the motherland are not commodities. How could such a thought even enter his head? The soldiers are fleeing, driven to despair, and Headquarters will begin to persuade them: "Don't run, you'll get a little land." What shame, and what moral degradation! And in general, does this Ianushkevich understand what he is suggesting, not only from the moral, but also from the practical point of view? One cannot promise the unattainable. In fact, it is impossible to make land allotments to an army of many millions, for after all, nearly all of it has suffered or distinguished itself. In any event, one cannot buy everyone—what about the townspeople, the workers, and others? The army led by the Supreme Headquarters is not composed of peasants alone. How does the Chief of Staff plan to purchase the heroism of nonlandowners?

s. D. SAZONOV: I am not surprised by this shameful letter. From Mr. Ianushkevich one can expect anything. The horrible thing is that the Grand Duke is a prisoner of such gentlemen. It is not a secret from anyone that he is hypnotized by Ianushkevich and [General G. N.] Danilov;[5] he is in their pockets. They jealously guard the Commander-in-Chief from contact with the outside world. Headquarters has created an intermediary wall. Nothing reaches the Grand Duke. His trust [in people] is used for career purposes. It's ridiculous, but General Ruzsky, called upon to command a whole Front[6] and to defend the capital of the empire, was not admitted to the Supreme Commander to get his instructions directly and discuss the tasks assigned to him. He was summoned to Headquarters and forced to wait nearly an hour in the waiting room. Then General Ianushkevich emerged from the Grand Duke's study and dryly announced the order to concentrate all efforts on the defense of Petrograd[7] and to depart immediately for his new post. The devil knows what sort of a thing this is! Thanks to such narcissistic nincompoops, we have already lost the campaign which had begun so exceptionally well for us, and have disgraced ourselves before the whole world. Well, now we have to reconcile ourselves to a lost war and submissively stick our head into the German yoke. From the letter conveyed to us by Alexander Vasilevich

---

[5] General Georgy Nikiforovich Danilov (known as the "Black Danilov"), Chief of Operations (*general-kvartirmeister*) at Headquarters under Grand Duke Nicholas.

[6] *Front.* The Russian term for an army group.

[7] Petrograd—St. Petersburg was Russified into Petrograd at the beginning of World War I. This name remained until 1924, when the city was renamed Leningrad.

[Krivoshein], it is clearly the opinion of the controller of fate at Headquarters that our soldiers cannot resist, that one must start to form a new army by bribing and luring future heroes. Poor Russia! She has nothing left. Even her army, the thunder of whose victories once resounded through the world and which amazed everyone by its self-sacrifice, even it, apparently, consists only of cowards and deserters. Will we really always remain silent? Will the Council of Ministers really lack the courage to open the eyes of those whose eyes should be opened? Under certain conditions, overcautiousness becomes a crime.

The discussion concluded with a decision to request General Ruzsky, in his function as commander of the Front defending Petrograd, to come to the next meeting of the Council of Ministers for a private exchange of opinions about the situation in the theater of operations and about the safety of the capital. This meeting should not be given, in any sense, an official character, so that Ruzsky can speak quite frankly and thus provide the government with information for future actions. Ruzsky is quite beyond the influence of Ianushkevich; he behaves quite independently and his answers may reflect the true picture, not influenced by the interested staffs, and which may suggest the essence of what is taking place in the theater of operations. After this, properly informed, the Council of Ministers must request the calling of a meeting under the Monarch's chairmanship, and must try to reveal to the Tsar the truth of the present and the dangers of the future.

I. L. GOREMYKIN: I do not oppose such a formulation, but I consider it my duty to repeat once again, before the Council of Ministers, my insistent advice to speak with extreme caution before the Sovereign on any matters and questions touching Headquarters and the Grand Duke. The irritation against him in Tsarskoe Selo[8] is assuming a character which could have dangerous results. I am fearful lest our pronunciamentos act as a cause for great difficulties."

This decision obviated the need for immediate discussion of the relations between the government and the military authorities in the theater of operations (which had been submitted for discussion by the Chief of Chancellery).

---

[8] *Tsarskoe Selo* ("the Tsar's Village"). The Imperial palace outside of St. Petersburg, which became the chief residence of Nicholas II after 1905.

Even though the general question was postponed, it arose again in the course of further conversations during the meeting.

PRINCE N. B. SHCHERBATOV: I beg the help of the Council of Ministers. As I had foreseen, my position in the Duma is becoming most ticklish. I am being asked a whole raft of questions about local affairs in the frontal zone. This is, undoubtedly, a tactical maneuver on the part of the deputies, as they know perfectly well that the Ministry of Internal Affairs has no voice or power there and that everything is managed by the military authorities, who are armored by the terrifying words—"military necessity." To all questions I return generalities but, from day to day, my situation is becoming more uncomfortable.

I. L. GOREMYKIN: The Supreme Commander has agreed to appoint a special representative to explain questions [arising] in the Duma and for the maintenance of contact with the government when the government has to speak [in the Duma] about affairs of the frontal zone. (*Note:* I cannot remember that such a representative was ever appointed.) Hence, I beg of you to suffer a few more days and everything will be arranged.

A. V. KRIVOSHEIN: It seems that our Chairman does not wish us to touch upon the unique character of internal politics at Headquarters. Allow me to announce one curious fact. Appointed as military Governor-General in Arkhangelsk, General Valuev,[9] who himself hardly fits a position which is so important these days, took as his Chief of Chancellery the *Kameriunker* Verigin.[10] You all know, of course, how much this gentleman is compromised in the sad affair of the murder of P. A. Stolypin.[11] After that episode, he suffered various social and professional unpleasantnesses. And now, right now, by order of military authorities who are independent of everyone and anyone, Verigin pops up as the closest col-

---

[9] General Valuev cannot be identified.

[10] Mitrofan Nikolaevich Verigin (1878-1920): served in the Police Department of the Ministry of Internal Affairs; after the murder of Prime Minister P. A. Stolypin (*q.v.*) was charged, with others, with not guarding the minister properly; dismissed from the service and deprived of his court rank of *kameriunker* ("junior chamberlain").

[11] Petr Arkadevich Stolypin (1862-1911): Chairman of the Council of Ministers, 1907-11; instituted the *coup d'état* of 1907; murdered in Kiev in 1911 by Dimitry Bogrov, who was, at the time, an agent of the secret police. Stolypin controlled the right–center majority of the Duma.

laborator (in fact, as the instructor) of the supervisor of our only window to Europe. Of course, we dare not discuss subjects determined by military necessity, but still it may not be useless to direct the attention of Headquarters to the desirability of more careful selection of people who are serving this very military necessity. One must take account of public opinion and not vex it needlessly with names which are too well-known. I do not think that Verigin is the only man in the world for the job.

P. A. KHARITONOV: In general, if one takes a look, what a nice little company they're getting together—Kurlov,[12] Reinbot,[13] Kotten,[14] Verigin, and other statesmen the names of whom only you know, oh Lord.

S. D. SAZONOV: The Grand Duke probably doesn't even know the reputation of all these gentlemen. One should open his eyes to it. It is not like His Highness to disregard public opinion. On the contrary, he tries to attract it to his side in every way.

PRINCE N. B. SHCHERBATOV: The continuation of Kurlov in a position of authority has been making a very bad impression on the Duma. I, and probably other members of the Council, have had to listen to pretty frank hints on this score. One may expect a parliamentary question which would be rather difficult to answer.

---

[12] Pavel Grigorevich Kurlov (1869-1923): dismissed from service in 1906 for illegal acts while Governor of Minsk province; investigation stopped by the Senate; appointed to the Police Department of the Ministry of Internal Affairs, 1907; Vice-Minister and Chief of the Corps of Gendarmes, 1909. After the murder of Stolypin (*q.v.*), dismissed from service; investigation of his involvement in the murder was stopped by a personal Imperial order. Appointed to Riga in 1914, with the rights of a Governor-General in the Baltic provinces. In 1916, there was another attempt to bring him back as Vice-Minister of Internal Affairs, but public pressure forced his dismissal. Kurlov was involved with the Rasputin circle and with all the shady operations of the secret police.

[13] Anatoly Anatolevich Reinbot (1868-1918): Major-General in the Suite of His Majesty; in 1907, dismissed as Head of the Moscow administration after an investigation of his activities, and dismissed from the Suite; tried by the Senate and condemned to one year's imprisonment, in 1911, for exceeding his authority and for embezzlement of State funds; pardoned by the Emperor; taken back into the military service as a Major-General in 1914.

[14] Mikhail Fridrikhovich von Kotten (1870-1917): Major-General in the Corps of Gendarmes.

I. L. GOREMYKIN: It seems to me that the problem of Kurlov, from the viewpoint of the relations of the Duma to the Supreme Command, is so serious that one should let His Majesty know, so that he can have him [Kurlov] removed.

P. A. KHARITONOV: There is a quite sufficient reason for doing this. Nearly the whole Baltic district is being evacuated. Hence, there is no longer a need for a governor-generalship and it can be abolished. Quite naturally, General Kurlov is also abolished. However, considering the mood reigning in Headquarters, one cannot be sure that they will not find some other honorable post for him.

A. V. KRIVOSHEIN: I join wholeheartedly in the suggestion of our Chairman to request Headquarters to dismiss Kurlov in the interest of preserving good relations with the Duma. We will do good service to our cause and to the Grand Duke himself. The presence of such subordinates has an adverse effect on the popularity of the Supreme Commander.

I. L. GOREMYKIN: If there are no objections, I would suggest that the negotiation of this matter be the responsibility of the Minister of Internal Affairs, whose competence this question touches most closely. Addressing the Grand Duke, one must refer, of course, to the unanimous opinion of the Council of Ministers.

I. L. GOREMYKIN: All of you gentlemen are aware of the formula adopted by the Duma—its expectation of an investigation and trial of those guilty of insufficient provisioning of the army. I offer for your discussion the question: How should the government react to this request? It seems to me that if it is left unanswered, one must expect anger and provocative speeches. A solution can be found in the appointment of a special investigatory committee similar to that which was appointed after *Khodynka*.[15] That investigation was assigned to Count Palen,[16] with the participation of the high officials of the interested departments. In this particular case, one

---

[15] *Khodynka*. The place in Moscow where public festivities were held to celebrate the coronation of Nicholas II in 1896 and where, as a result of police inefficiency, hundreds of people were crushed and trampled to death.

[16] Count Konstantin Konstantinovich von der Palen: born 1862; large landowner; jurist; senator; son of the Minister of Justice, Count K. I. von der Palen; regarded as a man of great probity and frequently assigned to investigate official misbehavior.

could widen the composition of the investigating commission by including members of the State Council and the Duma, and also persons appointed by the Supreme Commander.

P. A. KHARITONOV: For tactical reasons, one should avoid the word "investigatory" in the title of the commission. I would think one could limit oneself to such a title as "Commission for Inquiry into the Slowdown in the Provisioning of the Army." [17]

S. D. SAZONOV: But then the Grand Duke Sergei Mikhailovich[18] will end up on the bench of those being investigated.

P. A. KHARITONOV: Well, so what? We can't worry about that.

A. V. KRIVOSHEIN: I warmly support Ivan Longinovich's [Goremykin's] idea. We must respond to the Duma's formula. It reflects the feelings which are permeating broad circles of society. We will show that the government is not afraid of light and that we are ready to consider legitimate and reasonable demands of the Duma. Such a course of action is the best, also because it will force the Duma to take account of our legitimate and reasonable demands. Dissatisfaction with the former Minister of War [Sukhomlinov] is not revolution. Even the right-wing group of the State Council has recognized the permissibility of making a demonstration against Sukhomlinov by refusing to admit him into its ranks. It is advantageous for the government to shed light on this whole affair which has undoubtedly been exaggerated. The insufficiency of supplies is, in large measure, the consequence not only of our, but everybody's, mistaken notion that the war cannot last long. For this notion our Allies are also paying. In any event, it is too early to assign guilt. First, let the commission sort everything out; if there is enough evidence for a trial, we will not be afraid to put the question that way.

A. A. KHVOSTOV: Quite right. The commission must be of a preliminary nature. Its title must in no way provide justification for transforming it into some kind of tribunal. There is no one guilty as yet. The task of the commission will be to find out whether there are any guilty persons and what the nature of the crime was.

---

[17] This argument is based on the distinction between *sledstvennaia* which connotes a formal, prosecuting investigation (*sledovatel'* means an examining magistrate) and *razsledovanie*—inquiry, getting information, which has less formal and more neutral implications.

[18] Uncle of the Emperor. Head of the Artillery Administration of the army.

A. V. KRIVOSHEIN: As the Duma and broad segments of the public assign great importance to the shedding of light on this matter, the commission should be given a particularly official and ceremonious character.

I. L. GOREMYKIN: Stage-settings are a useful thing. For the crowd, they are always more important than the substance.

A. V. KRIVOSHEIN: At the head of the commission one must place someone very high up, someone known for his independence and impartiality and possessing a spotless reputation. It would be desirable to get such a person from the military. I would suggest the member of the State Council, General Petrov.[19] He gained wide sympathy with his work on the railroad questionnaire. Also, the Vice-Chairman of the State Council, Golubev,[20] the Vice-Chairman of the State Duma, Protopopov[21] (he is the senior one), senators, and representatives of the army appointed by the Supreme Commander should be in the commission. With such a membership, even the most shameless people would be embarrassed to speak about government pressure and artificial selection. Those appointed would be people known to all, and above suspicion.

P. A. KHARITONOV: It would be more cautious to simply say "Vice-Chairman of the Duma," without naming Protopopov. He is not at all popular amongst the deputies. No matter how hard he tried, he could not get himself elected chairman of the Military-Naval Committee. He is regarded as a supplier of cloth for the War Ministry and as a friend of Sukhomlinov.

---

[19] Nikolai Pavlovich Petrov: born 1836; general of the army engineers; member of the State Council; in 1915, appointed as Chairman of The Supreme Commission for the Complete Investigation of the Circumstances which Caused the Late and Insufficient Supplies of Munitions. As a result of that investigation, criminal charges were preferred against General Sukhomlinov, the former Minister of War.

[20] Ivan Iakovlevich Golubev (1841-1918): Vice-President of the State Council, 1906-17; jurist; suspected of liberalism and sympathy for the Progressive Bloc (q.v.) in 1916-17.

[21] Alexander Dimitrovich Protopopov (1866-1918): very rich gentry landowner; Left-Octobrist deputy to the 3rd and 4th Dumas; Vice-President of the 4th Duma; member of the Progressive Bloc; in September, 1916, made Minister of Internal Affairs through the influence of Rasputin, whom he sought out; supposedly suffering from progressive and rapid mental degeneration.

I. L. GOREMYKIN: Shouldn't one also include in the commission elected representatives of the State Council and the Duma?

PRINCE N. B. SHCHERBATOV: This would be very desirable, tactically. And substantively, not at all useless. The Duma shouts so much about the outrages taking place in the whole supply problem—let it disclose to the commission the evidence on which it bases its accusations.

After clearing up further details about the internal organization and the tasks of the commission, I. L. GOREMYKIN raised the question of whether the decision [to establish the commission] should be announced immediately after it is confirmed by the Emperor or after the end of the Duma session.

A. D. SAMARIN: It is my conviction that we have nothing to hide here, and that the decree should be published at once. The Duma has expressed a wish that is quite acceptable to the government; hence, it is transformed into a corresponding decree. What is there to be silent about and to postpone? This measure, designed to make a good impression, would lose its effect and the Duma would end its session unsatisfied. One must say out loud that the government, in agreement with the Duma, is taking all measures in order to clear up the question which is worrying public opinion.

This point of view of the Supreme Procurator of the Holy Synod was accepted by all.

PRINCE N. B. SHCHERBATOV: It is absolutely necessary, somehow or other, to solve the Moscow problem. If this uncertainty continues, a scandal is inevitable and new disturbances will take place. Prince Iusupov[22] is continuing his strike until his demands will be met, and has no intention of departing in peace. I have reported the existing situation to His Majesty and His Majesty has ordered me to think about appointing Iusupov as Governor-General of Moscow. In His Majesty's opinion, such an appointment would legalize his [Iusupov's] position and bring his activity within the framework of nor-

---

[22] Prince Felix Felixovich Iusupov (Count Sumarokov-El'ston): General-Adjutant of the Emperor; Governor-General of Moscow; one of the richest noblemen in Russia; related to the Imperial family through his son (see note on Rasputin); violent opponent of Rasputin and of all Germans.

mal law. For his part, Iusupov is willing to return when the following of his demands are fulfilled: (1) the Moscow garrison is to pass
into his hands and be removed from military authority; in addition
to which, the units must be immediately supplied with machine
guns (the Prince is willing to accept those captured from the Austrians); (2) Iusupov is to have complete authority to declare martial
law in Moscow whenever he feels it necessary; (3) he is to be given
complete authority to requisition and to sequester; (4) the chief of
chancellery of the governor-generalship is to be immediately removed from Moscow; (5) he [Iusupov] is to have the authority to
dismiss members of the police, including the Chief of Police; and (6)
he is to be given sufficient funds for the distribution of allotments.
That is the ultimatum. I request your instructions. What should I
report about all this to the Emperor? In any event, some solution
cannot be postponed. I declare categorically to the Council of Ministers that, in the existing situation, I cannot be responsible for
order in Moscow. There is no real power and authority there now,
and there is no one to oppose disturbances. The police alone cannot
manage, and there is no accord between civil and military authorities. Beside all this, the chief of the city, Klimovich,[23] and Prince
Iusupov, neither one of whom fit their roles, do not agree with each
other and there is constant friction between them. If Iusupov is
given the rights he demands, then Moscow, in effect, slips out of the
hands of the Ministry of Internal Affairs and becomes an independent satrapy. Can one reconcile oneself to this? The great influence which Moscow is again beginning to gain is being felt not only
in the rear but at the front, too. With Iusupov there and his demands granted, the government will hardly be able to influence the
Moscow administration and to put through the measures which circumstances may require.

A. V. KRIVOSHEIN: What is important are not the demands of
Iusupov, from whom one can expect anything, but the question:
Is he desirable as the despot of Moscow? This question the Minister
of Internal Affairs answers negatively. Hence, one should take ad-

---

[23] *Gradonachal'nik.* Head of a city administration. Lieutenant-General Evgeny
Konstantinovich Klimovich was born in 1871; served for many years as a
Corps of Gendarmes officer; in 1916, Director of the Department of Police,
and senator.

vantage of the favorable situation in order to remove Iusupov, along with his Austrian machine guns and his idiosyncratic policies. Even in peacetime such satraps, with such fantasies, are dangerous, but in wartime they may be fatal.

A. D. SAMARIN: I must point out to the Council of Ministers that Iusupov has been able to gain quite a wide popularity among the Moscow masses. He is regarded as an irreconcilable enemy of the Germans and as the destroyer of German treason in the state. Considering the present mood, no matter how one looks at this fact, one must take it into account. Knowing Moscow, I am convinced that Iusupov's forced removal would have dire consequences. Everything now serves the cause of agitation. There will be howls that the government is playing along with the Germans by removing an unshakable foe of German spies. I agree with Prince Nikolai Borisovich [Shcherbatov] that the good of the cause requires Iusupov's dismissal but I believe it is necessary to arrange an honorable way out for him, in the shape of some higher post.

P. A. KHARITONOV: Yes, but what can one think up for the prince? One cannot tempt him with honors. The man is disgustingly rich. He has virtually the status of a Highness and needs no one and nothing.

PRINCE N. B. SHCHERBATOV: I fully understand the points of view of Alexander Dimitrovich [Samarin] and of Petr Alekseevich [Kharitonov]. But what's to be done? Is the controversy so unique that one must reconcile oneself with the surrender of Moscow into the full power of Iusupov until such time when he himself finds it possible to give up the burden of governing?

I. L. GOREMYKIN: The Emperor was pleased to appoint him Governor-General in Moscow. Iusupov insists that he must be given a real opportunity to govern and to possess the necessary authority and force. His demands are contained in the points before us. It is our duty to examine them and to report our conclusions to His Majesty. I do not consider it possible to do that so quickly. I think that they should be discussed in detail by the interested ministers (the War Minister and the Minister of Internal Affairs, I believe), and that they should convey to us, at our next meeting, their conclusions—which we then will submit to the Emperor.

At the end of the meeting, Admiral Grigorovich cheered everyone by announcing that the Commander of Naval Forces considers our position on the Black Sea so much stronger that he has permitted the resumption of commercial traffic between some ports. At the moment, the procedures for restoring requisitioned steamships to their owners are being drawn up.

II

The Meeting of
30 July 1915

───────◆───────

I n the theater of war, darkness. The retreat continues.

A. A. POLIVANOV says that he is unable to give any picture of
the front which would correspond to the reality. The whole army
is constantly retreating into the depths of the country, and the front
line changes virtually every hour. Demoralization, surrender, and
desertion are acquiring grandiose proportions. Headquarters has
apparently lost its head, and its directives are acquiring an hysterical
character. Accusations about the guilt of the rear are incessant, becoming even louder and acting like water on the mill of anti-government agitation.

Meanwhile, an advance is developing in the Caucasus. The
army is pushing a wedge into enemy territory.

P. A. KHARITONOV: Where are we going in the Caucasus? I hope
it won't all end in catastrophe. I am not a judge of strategic and
tactical nuances; nevertheless, I cannot help seeing that naked political considerations are triumphing over purely military ones. Everyone knows the extraordinary sympathy of the Viceroy [Count
Vorontsov-Dashkov] for the Armenians. Isn't he being carried away
by these sympathies? Even a superficial look at the map shows that

the army is being directed mainly toward Armenian territories. As it is, the situation is difficult enough everywhere, and here we are about to take risks for the sake of restoring Armenia. By the way, the Caucasian deputies are very much upset by the course of events in the Caucasus. Chkheidze[1] screams unceasingly about the danger, and accuses the local authorities of an exaggerated partiality for Armenian demands which are so influential in the vice-regal palace. All this should be brought to the attention of the Emperor.

A. A. POLIVANOV: Even though the State Comptroller is not a strategist, he has analyzed the situation in the Caucasus correctly. I, too, view the situation there with anxiety. I hope no catastrophe occurs. I hear rumors that General Iudenich[2] is outraged by the orders from Tiflis,[3] and has little hope for the future.

The other members of the Council of Ministers expressed themselves in the same spirit, feeling that even if one leaves aside the purely military aspects of things, it would be undesirable, in the context of general policy, to bring up the Armenian question too soon. Even without all this, it is being presented in certain circles abroad as one of the goals of the war.

I. L. GOREMYKIN: The creation of an Armenia will only be a burden for us, and will become a future source of various complications in the east.

S. D. SAZONOV: I hesitate to formulate this question so categorically. I agree that it should not be blown up and that one should not take risks over it. But it would be unpolitic to say this too loudly. Abroad, among our Allies, particularly in England, there is an old tradition of great sympathy for the Armenians.

A. V. KRIVOSHEIN: Yes, of course, we should not shout about it, and we weren't about to do so. But we cannot, out of fear of the English, who have themselves not lifted a finger to relieve the situa-

---

[1] Nikolai Semenovich Chkheidze (1864-1926): deputy from Tiflis to the 3rd and 4th Dumas; journalist; one of the leaders of the Social-Democrats (*Mensheviks*); after the February revolution, presided over the Council (*Sovet*) of Soldiers' and Workers' Deputies, which emerged as the real government of revolutionary Russia.

[2] General Iudenich commanded the Russian field army in the Caucasus; was prominent during the Civil War, when he led the White armies in the northwest and tried to take Petrograd.

[3] Tiflis [Tbilisi] was the capital of Georgia, where the Viceroy had his residence.

tion of Armenians, we cannot remain silent when we see that the authorities in the Caucasus are prepared to sacrifice Russian interests for the sake of Armenian ones. In our opinion a crime is taking place in the Caucasus, and it is our duty to turn our attention to this and to point out the approaching danger in time.

Finally, the Minister of War was assigned the responsibility of reporting to the Emperor about the development of events in the Caucasus.

[After a brief mention of rumors concerning Bulgarian volunteers in the Turkish army, the discussion turned to the problem of converting public buildings—schools, monasteries, palaces—to hospitals to provide for the enormous influx of wounded. The Council of Ministers was concerned again with the lack of organization and provision by the military authorities and with the possible political consequences of idleness caused by closing down schools.—*Ed.*]

I. L. GOREMYKIN: The problem is so complicated that it should be discussed by specialists. The best thing would be to call a special committee, under the chairmanship of Prince Vasil'chikov with the participation of senior members from all the departments. They will work out a plan for satisfying the need for beds, and submit it to us for confirmation. As for school buildings, this particular question can be assigned to governors, supported by the injunctions conveyed in the journal of the Council of Ministers.

A. A. POLIVANOV: Ivan Longinovich speaks justly. The problem is complicated, even most complicated, for we do not know how much of Russia we will have to clear out of, and how soon the evacuation-refugee period of military actions will come to an end.

After this bitterly ironic statement by the Minister of War, the conversation passed to the problem of refugees, which has frequently been the subject of discussion. In my notes I have only the general substance of this conversation, with notations as to who said what: Headquarters has completely lost its head. It does not realize what it is doing, into what kind of an abyss it is dragging Russia. One cannot refer to the example of 1812 and transform the territory left to the enemy into a desert. The present conditions, the situation, the very scope of actions have nothing in common with those of

1812. In 1812, separate armies were maneuvering about, and the area of their actions was comparatively limited. Now there is a solid front from the Baltic almost to the Black Sea, embracing gigantic areas hundreds of kilometers deep. To depopulate tens of provinces and to chase their populations out into the middle of the country—this is equivalent to condemning all of Russia to horrible disasters. But logic, and the requirements of the State, are not thought of highly by Headquarters. Civilian reasoning must be silent before "military necessity," no matter what horrors it hides. Finally, the external defeat of Russia is being complemented by an internal one.

In the flood of refugees one can distinguish three currents. First of all, the Jews, who are being chased out of the frontal zone with whips and accused—all, without discrimination—of espionage, signaling, and other methods of helping the enemy, despite the frequent objections of the Council of Ministers. Of course, this whole Jewish mass is extremely irritated and arrives in the new regions it will inhabit in a revolutionary mood; the situation is complicated by the fact that the local inhabitants, suffering more and more heavily the burden of military disasters, receive the hungry and homeless Jews in by-no-means a friendly manner. Secondly, there are the service personnel of the civilian and the rear military organizations, with dozens of carloads of goods. While tens of thousands of people are trudging alongside the train rails, they are passed by speeding trains loaded down with couches from officer clubs and carrying various junk, including the bird cages of bird-loving quartermasters. Thirdly, there are the voluntary refugees, driven, in most cases, by rumors of the incredible bestiality of the Germans. Finally, and fourthly, there are refugees who are being forcibly driven out on the orders of military authorities, for the purpose of depopulating territory being given up to the enemy. This group is the most numerous and the most irritated. People are torn from their birthplaces, given a few hours to collect their things, and driven toward an unknown goal. Before their very eyes, their remaining supplies, and frequently their very houses, are set afire. It is easy to understand the psychology of these forced refugees. It is doubtful that they are accumulating good will toward the authority which permits actions which are incomprehensible, and not only to simple people. And this whole bewildered, irritated, tired-out crowd rolls like a continuous flood along all the roads, getting in the way of military transport and bringing complete chaos into the life of the rear. Along with it come wandering cattle and carts filled with homely junk. To feed, to water, to warm this multitude is, of course, impossible. Men die by the hundreds from cold, hunger, and disease. Infant mortality has reached horrifying proportions. Unburied corpses lie along the roads. Everywhere there is carrion and unbearable stench. This human mass is pouring over Russia in a wide wave, everywhere increasing the burdens of wartime, creating supply crises, increasing the cost of living, and exciting already heightened tempers in various places. Only very recently, after this evil had time to become elemental, has Headquarters begun to understand that this cannot be allowed to continue, and it has tried to cooperate with the government's demands that civilian authorities be involved in the regulation of the refugee movement. The members of the State Council, Zubchaninov and Urusov, who were selected by the Council of Ministers as plenipotentiaries for refugee affairs on both fronts [Western and Caucasian] have been well received at Headquarters and have been promised full support. Nevertheless, it is difficult to hope for the quick success of their mission. Everything is so mixed up that it will take years to work out the existing chaos and to train the military commanders to take civilian interests into account. Beside all this, Headquarters does not seem inclined to give up its Kutuzov-like luring on, in the hope of defeating the German offensive by a devastated space.[4] Under such conditions no plenipotentiaries can help, and this new migration of peoples will continue, with all the catastrophic consequences which attend such an event.

The conversation ended on this pessimistic note. I added to my notes: They recognize their helplessness. The same damn question about the interrelations of the military and civil authorities. And truly, what can the government do when the Supreme Commander considers it necessary, for victory, to give one or another order? In ordinary wars, ordinary rules obtain—"When a forest is cut down, splinters fly." [5] But what can one do when things are on such an

---

[4] Field Marshal M. I. Kutuzov commanded the Russian army in 1812 in its retreat before Napoleon, and later, in its pursuit of the French. The popular conception was that the retreat was deliberate, designed to lure the French on until they were cut off from their bases and found themselves in the midst of a devastated wilderness.

[5] Russian proverb.

incredible scale? And yet these "splinters" threaten to set fire to all of Russia. It is tragic.

The discussion concluded with a decision to wait for new reports from the plenipotentiaries and then to report to the Emperor on the general question of convening a united Military Council, under the chairmanship of His Majesty, to reexamine the plans for the war.

[The Council of Ministers next spent some time discussing the desirability of buying up the Bulgarian and Rumanian grain crops in order to keep them out of German hands and the difficulty of financing this operation without the help of Allies.—*Ed.*]

Finally, the purchase of the crop in Bulgaria was approved, on condition that a balance of Russian and Allied interests be maintained, and the decision on Rumanian grain was postponed until the Minister of Foreign Affairs could give additional information and explanations.

PRINCE N. B. SHCHERBATOV: As long as we are dealing with financial questions, may I call your attention to what is happening to Russian currency in Finland? Our ruble is falling there with incredible speed. It is a fantastic absurdity. Within the bounds of a single empire, one district is speculating at the expense of the rest of the country. The situation evokes the justifiable anger of the population. In the Duma it is commented on with a shrug. One should put a limit to the Finns, who have lost all measure.

P. L. BARK explained that the Ministry of Finance had taken extraordinary and immediate measures for the support of our currency in Finland, and that the question of involving this periphery in the expenses of the war was under discussion.

P. A. KHARITONOV: A blessed country. A whole empire is exhausted by military burdens, and the Finns enjoy themselves and get rich at our expense. They are free even of the main civic responsibility of defending the country from the enemy. We should long ago have imposed on them at least a financial duty, instead of a natural duty (if the latter is not desired by them). And now, to top it off, they even dare to play tricks with our ruble. It would be useful to speak about this with the Governor-General of Finland. What are his plans, and does he have any plans at all?

s. d. SAZONOV: For God's sake, do not arouse the zeal of General Zein;[6] leave the Finns alone. This matter is being very carefully and jealously watched by the Swedes, and it is better to forget about it completely.

I. L. GOREMYKIN: I am in full agreement with the Minister of Foreign Affairs. The sheepskin is not worth the labor.[7] The utility of this bunch of *chukhontsy*[8] would be small, and one would have enormous troubles. Everything is becoming too complicated as it is, without bothering with the Finns. The devil with all of them! The Minister of Finance will take measures to safeguard the ruble, and general decrees will be prepared and discussed in the Finnish Committee. Let's wait and see what happens, but for the moment I ask that we not touch the Finnish question. As it is, we are up to our necks in all kinds of questions.

As noted in the minutes of the preceding meeting, in response to the Duma's request for the identification of the guilty parties responsible for the inadequacies in army supplies, the Council of Ministers decided to assign this task to a special High Commission. The Minister of War informed the Duma of this decision. Dissatisfaction arose in the Duma concerning the vagueness of this Commission's aims and powers. In this connection, the Council of Ministers again raised the issue whether one should not, in order to avoid further rumors, call the Commission "investigatory."

A. V. KRIVOSHEIN: I am most definitely against this word. I've always felt, and in these times, particularly, I feel sharply the burden and sorrow of the responsibility of being a member of the government. But I do not wish to be guilty without guilt;[9] I do not wish to acknowledge it [the guilt] and to place my head on the block before all of Russia. Really! What kind of impression will we make on public opinion if we immediately appoint an investigatory commission? It will be said, and with logic, that the government slept for a whole year, doing nothing, interested in nothing, and then

---

[6] Lieutenant-General Franz-Albert Alexandrovich Zein (1862-1918): from 1909, Governor-General of Finland; greatly disliked by the Finns.

[7] A Russian proverb.

[8] A contemptuous Russian colloquial name for the Finns.

[9] A Russian expression; *bez viny vinovat*.

came the saviour—the Duma. It shouted, and now this same government tries to show its zeal, even to the extent of admitting the criminality of its own organs. Undoubtedly, one should by all means try to maintain good relations with the legislative institutions. But there are limits even to such an objective. We have no right to brand whole ministries with a careless word and to demolish finally the already badly shaken prestige of government institutions.

I. L. GOREMYKIN: I share Alexander Vasilevich's [Krivoshein's] opinions fully. First one has to find out if there is any reason for speaking of guilt. If such reasons exist, then one can petition His Majesty the Emperor, to direct the affair according to the criminal code.

S. D. RUKHLOV: I also am in full agreement with Alexander Vasilevich's [Krivoshein's] point of view. This whole affair is being extraordinarily exaggerated. Some want to use it to exonerate themselves from the responsibility for military defeats; others are just trying to bury an extra mine under the existing order and build an extra step for themselves toward a portfolio and a future cabinet possessing public confidence, as it is now fashionable to say. It is unnecessary for us to play along with all these attempts and intrigues. It will be sufficient for the government to establish a commission of inquiry. As for investigation and trial, it is too early to worry about that.

A. A. POLIVANOV: After all, at our last meeting we agreed to create precisely a Supreme Commission of Inquiry. I used precisely that term in the Duma, and I did not mention an investigation. The dissatisfaction of a few deputies is not cause for reexamining a decision of the Council of Ministers which has already been arrived at, and which has been approved by His Majesty in principle. In substance, Alexander Vasilevich [Krivoshein] is quite correct. Even though it is not my affair, and though grateful countrymen and scared commanders have not accused me, so far, of aiding the enemy, I must say that one cannot expose men and whole institutions to disgrace without firm knowledge of the existence of necessary causes for this.

III

The Meeting of
4 August 1915

---∙◆∙---

For the first time since the days of Count Witte,[1] a person of "free profession," unconnected with government service, was present during the official part of the meeting. He was Alexander Ivanovich Guchkov, who had been invited to the meeting at the insistence of General Polivanov, to participate in the examination of the decree concerning the Military-Industrial Committee. Everyone felt tense and uneasy. Guchkov looked as if he had found himself at the headquarters of a band of robbers, under the pressure of threats of dreadful punishment. More accurately, he reminded one of a shy man appearing in strange society with the preconceived notion of becoming angry at the first excuse and thus showing his independence. Guchkov replied to all the remarks made about the various paragraphs of the projected decree with a sharpness which was not called for by the substance of the objections, and he demanded either

---

[1] Count Sergei Iulevich Witte (Vitte) (1849-1915): Russian statesman; Minister of Finance under Alexander III and Nicholas II; Chairman of the Council of Ministers during the revolution of 1905; drafted the constitution of 1905; Russian plenipotentiary at Portsmouth, where he very successfully ended the Russo-Japanese War.

complete approval for the project about the Committee or else the denial of sanction for this institution, stressing the fact that this project had been worked out by representatives of public organizations who selflessly wanted to serve the cause of supplying the army. The result was that the discussion was cut short, everyone appearing to be in a hurry to end this not very pleasant encounter.

By established custom, the secret part of the meeting opened with the report by the Minister of War on the situation at the front. Still nothing hopeful, nothing bracing! A total picture of defeat and confusion. "I rely," said A. A. Polivanov, "on impassable spaces, on impenetrable mud, and on the mercy of St. Nicholas, the patron of Holy Russia."

P. A. KHARITONOV: And meanwhile, in the Caucasus, the march forward is continuing. Chkheidze is virtually having hysterics, and is predicting irremediable disasters. In my presence, during the intermission at the Duma, he was shouting that the army of the Caucasus is commanded not by the Supreme Commander, and not by the Viceroy, but by Countess Vorontsova-Dashkova, who is entangled in Armenian nets. And in fact, where the hell are we shoving, pardon the expression?

A. A. POLIVANOV: Well, we know where—toward the creation of a Great Armenia. I had an opportunity yesterday to speak with His Majesty about the advance in the Caucasus, and about its possible sad consequences. But I also remarked that the gathering of the Armenian lands is apparently the main desire of Count Vorontsov-Dashkov. At these words His Majesty the Emperor, smiling, kindly deigned to correct me: "Not of the Count, but of the Countess."

A. V. KRIVOSHEIN: Gentlemen, do pay attention to this extraordinary historical coincidence: The importance of Countess Vorontsova to our Caucasian strategy is noted by His Majesty, and also by the leader of the Social Democratic faction in the Duma, Mr. Chkheidze.

In connection with the question of extraordinary credits for the needs of refugees, the conversation again touched upon the refugee movement and its threatening spread. The elements have risen. Where they will stop, how they will settle down, what events will accompany them—all this is an equation with many unknowns. Neither governmental, public, nor charitable organizations have the forces to bring the elements into their proper course. And to top it off, the retreat and the evacuations are continuing, dragging from their places more and newer crowds of desperate people.

A. V. KRIVOSHEIN: Of all the burdensome consequences of the war, this one is the most unexpected and the most terrifying and the most irremediable. What is most terrible—it is not caused by real necessity or by popular enthusiasm, but has been thought up by wise strategists, to scare the enemy. A nice method of fighting! Curses, sickness, misery, and poverty are spreading over all Russia. The naked and the hungry spread panic everywhere, dampening the last remnants of the enthusiasm which existed in the first months of the war. They come in a solid phalanx, trampling down the crops, ruining the meadows, the forests. Behind them is left a virtual desert, as if the locusts or the army of Tamerlane had come through. The railroads are jammed; the transportation even of military loads or the bringing up of food will soon become impossible. I do not know what has happened in the areas that were left to the enemy, but I do know that not only the immediate, but also the deep rear area behind our army is devastated, ruined, stripped of its very last stockpiles. I think that the Germans are watching, not without pleasure, the results of this repetition of 1812. Even though they are being deprived of certain local supplies, they are simultaneously being freed of the burden of caring for the population and they have full freedom of action in the depopulated districts. Well, these details are not within my competence. Obviously, they must have been weighed beforehand by Headquarters and at that time have been recognized as inconsequential. But it is within my competence as a member of the Council of Ministers, to declare that the second [2] great migration of peoples arranged by Headquarters is dragging Russia into the abyss, into revolution, and into destruction.

Other ministers also adduced various facts from refugee life which portrayed all the horrors of this phenomenon in its political, economic, organizational, and daily aspects. No decisions were arrived at, in view of the agreement reached at the previous meeting

---

[2] Krivoshein is alluding to the great migrations of late antiquity, which he calls "the first migrations."

to submit the refugee question to general discussion in the presence of the Emperor.

An exchange of views about the situation in the Duma: It is becoming more strident. Its aggressive intentions are becoming clearer and clearer. Not just "an attack," but a "charge" against the government is beginning. There is no desire to carry on the work of examining the legislative proposals submitted by the government, even though they are called forth by the needs of defense; on the contrary, there is a desire for, and a tendency toward, emotional speeches and parliamentary questions. All Russians have good reason to be anxious and excited—but why fall into exaggerated pathos, why abandon oneself to excited rhetoric which is then strongly reflected in the mood of the country?

I. L. GOREMYKIN: Well, is the Duma planning to fulfill its promise to speed up the resolution of the legislative project on soldiers of the second class? [3] When will this question be decided?

A. A. POLIVANOV: I have constantly reminded them of it, but so far without success. By the way, the committee [dealing with the government project] demands from me, insistently, explanations about the situation at the front and about supplies. I dodge the first question—saying that one must direct such inquiries to Headquarters; and I say that the second question cannot be discussed publicly in wartime even before the legislative bodies. But I think that without satisfying this demand we will not get the law on the soldiers.

P. A. KHARITONOV: Can't you turn the question around? Let the Duma examine this law immediately, and in return we will communicate military information insofar as the need for military secrecy allows.

PRINCE N. B. SHCHERBATOV: In any event, it is most important to get the law about second-class soldiers through the Duma. I must

---

[3] *Ratniki vtorogo razriada* (Soldiers of the second class). Men, forty-three years of age and older, capable of bearing arms, who were neither in the army nor in the reserve. Soldiers of the first class (*ratniki pervogo razriada*) included men who were able to serve but who had not been called up for military service, and all reservists under forty-three. The term "first class" applied to men whose physical condition allowed them to be combat soldiers; the second class was made up of the rest.

point out that our mobilizations are less and less successful each time. The police are unable to manage the mass of draft-dodgers. Men are hiding in the woods and in the grain fields. If it becomes known that the mobilization of second-class soldiers is taking place without the sanction of the Duma, I am afraid that, with the present mood, we will not get a single man. Agitation is being conducted full blast, disposing as it does of gigantic resources which are coming from somewhere.

I. K. GRIGOROVICH: Well, we know the sources. German ones.

N. B. SHCHERBATOV: The agitators, of course, will not pass up such an issue, and will create, on this basis, unrest and disturbances. I cannot fail to indicate to the Council of Ministers that the character of the agitation is becoming more and more anti-militaristic or, more simply, openly defeatist. Its direct influence can be seen in mass surrenders.

A. D. SAMARIN: However sad Prince Nikolai Borisovich's [Shcherbatov's] words, they are based on our grim joyless reality. Nevertheless, I consider it incorrect to place ourselves in this question, completely at the mercy of the Duma's decision. It would be better to manage, somehow, without the soldiers of the second class. Wandering in the rear is a whole mass of greycoats.[4] Can't we find more useful jobs for them at the front?

A. V. KRIVOSHEIN: Alexander Dimitrovich [Samarin] has formulated the situation marvelously well, both substantively and from the viewpoint of relations with the Duma. If it wants to put pressure on us with the law about the soldiers, we should not grab the lure. I cannot judge the technical aspects of the matter, but the number of soldiers wandering around the cities, villages, railroads and, in general, across the whole Russian land, astonishes my non-expert eye. Without thinking about it, one has to raise the question: Why take from the population the last working force, when one only has to corral, and place in the trenches, the whole mob of strollers who are only demoralizing the rear even more by their presence? However, this is a military matter, an area forbidden to the Council of Ministers. Returning to the Duma, I recall that when the question of its extraordinary session was being decided, we had in mind a

---

[4] Men in uniform.

short session, until about the beginning of August. This date is approaching, but it seems to me that it probably should be extended. One should not create tensions for the sake of two or three days. One should give the Duma a chance to express itself on the mobilization. What do you think, Ivan Longinovich, about the date of adjournment?

I. L. GOREMYKIN: In the Duma they are talking, not of adjournment but of an interruption of the session by their own decision in the middle of August. I find it necessary to limit it to a short term on the condition of legislating the mobilization act and, if this legislation is not worked out, to adjourn it nevertheless.

A. V. KRIVOSHEIN: The middle of August is an unacceptable date, because the military situation requires emergency legislation. When legislative bodies are meeting, such emergency measures are, in fact, not likely, but we have no right to invoke Article 87.[5] Apparently, the members of the Duma do not understand or do not want to understand this [need for speed]. One should talk it over with Rodzianko[6] and other well-disposed deputies, and explain to them the impossibility of managing in wartime with normal legislative procedures. If all these negotiations and conversations do not help, and if the law concerning the soldiers is deliberately postponed, then I agree with our Chairman about taking decisive action. Let everyone know then that the adjournment of the Duma was caused by its unwillingness to solve a question which is connected with the need for replacements for the army and that this question does not allow of further postponement. Reasonable men will not condemn us for such a solution of the problem, and no concession we make will stop the evil-minded agitation which is supported by German funds. One must fight that in other ways. And finally, such a way of dealing with the Duma would give us

---

[5] The constitutional provision which allowed the government to legislate, temporarily, when the Duma was not in session; however, the government was required to submit the appropriate law to the legislative chambers when they convened.

[6] Mikhail Vladimirovich Rodzianko (1859-1924): rich landowner; held the court rank of *kamerger* ("chamberlain"); deputy to the 3rd and 4th Dumas; Octobrist; President of the 3rd and 4th Dumas from March 11, 1911, until the revolution.

the right to petition for the mobilization of the soldiers of the second class through an Imperial Manifesto which would refer to the extraordinary circumstances of the motherland.

The Ministers of War and of Internal Affairs were charged with discussing the matter with M. V. Rodzianko, with the chairman of the committee examining the proposed legislation, and with the leaders of the parties (such leaders, of course, added A. V. KRIVO-SHEIN, who are capable of conversing at all with representatives of the hated bureaucracy).

Again, discussion of Prince Iusupov's ultimatum and his obstinate unwillingness to go to Moscow [as Governor-General] without the power he has demanded.

A. A. POLIVANOV: As instructed by the Council of Ministers, the Minister of Internal Affairs and I have discussed the points submitted by Prince Iusupov, and I reported our conclusions to His Majesty the Emperor. As for handing over the whole of the Moscow garrison [to Iusupov] I said that such a measure is impermissible, for it would break down the internal arrangements of the War Ministry and could create general disorganization. Everywhere garrisons are subordinated to the chiefs of the military districts, to whom the civil authorities address themselves when they need the help of troops, and such a district chief is available in Moscow. Concerning the arming of the militia with Austrian machine guns, which the Prince wishes to do, I pointed out that all weapons outside the theater of war are concentrated in the hands of the War Ministry, which distributes them according to the needs of particular districts and available reserves; this distribution is carried out according to a prepared plan which cannot be disregarded without injury to general interests. Finally, concerning his pretensions to the independent operation of martial law in Moscow, I explained that, by presently established laws, such a measure can only be initiated by a direct Imperial decree to the Governing Senate,[7] announced through the Ministry of War, and that there appeared

---

[7] *Pravitel'stvuishchii Senat* (*The Governing Senate*) The supreme judicial and administrative body in the Russian Empire, established by Peter the Great. It supervised, controlled and certified all acts, decrees, and laws of the government. The senators were appointed by the Emperor, usually upon retirement from active bureaucratic or military service.

to be, on the face of it, no extraordinary circumstances requiring the changing of the law for the sake of a particular person. Having listened attentively to my considerations, His Majesty was thoughtful, and asked me: "Advise me how I should manage this with Iusupov, for he refuses to make any concessions." Then, without waiting for an answer, the Emperor said: "Try to reason with him, to convince him, write to him, and in general show him more attention. This should sway him." But as far as the substance of my report is concerned, I received no Imperial suggestions or orders. I request the Council of Ministers to take some steps toward the solution of this question. With the approach of the front line, Moscow is becoming more and more important to the organization of the rear, and to continue such a vague and ambiguous situation and such a confused hierarchy will endanger the whole organization of supplies.

I. L. GOREMYKIN: His Majesty the Emperor finds it necessary to appoint a Governor-General for Moscow and has chosen a particular person for this [post]. Our objections to this candidate, which I have, for my part, reported to the Emperor, His Majesty finds unconvincing. He pointed out to me that Iusupov's hesitation is based on the small numbers, poor equipment, and insufficient organization of the Moscow police. These circumstances call for placing the local garrison at the disposition of the Governor-General, as Moscow is far from serene and one can expect outbursts at any moment.

PRINCE N. B. SHCHERBATOV: If the Governor-Generalship has been decided on, then one must immediately decide to get rid of the city chief. A Governor-General and a city chief cannot exist simultaneously. Considering Iusupov's despotic inclinations, it is all the more impossible.

A. D. SAMARIN: Iusupov wants to be the unlimited boss of Moscow and to have his own troops for this purpose. It seems to me that prestige and authority are achieved by other means. In any event, it is difficult to conquer Moscow with the clenched fist.

I. L. GOREMYKIN: The fact is that he does not wish to go to Moscow with bare hands. I, too, believe that it would be inconvenient to subordinate the garrison to him and break all the existing regulations. Couldn't one solve the problem by immediately strengthening the cadres of the Moscow police?

PRINCE N. B. SHCHERBATOV: This task takes time; besides, it is difficult to get good people these days. The Governor-General, or any other civil authority, has a right, at any moment, to demand the cooperation of the military authorities, who in turn have no right to refuse and who are guided by rules prescribed by law. If one is to accept the declared pretensions, then there will be, simultaneously, military units of a dual type in Moscow: a city garrison subordinate to the Governor-General, and the troops of the district subordinate to the commander of the military district. One can easily predict what kind of a mess would result. Isn't Prince Iusupov capable of understanding that troops under different authorities in one place will lead not to the strengthening, but on the contrary, to the weakening, of government authority? If he does not understand it, one must think of a way to enlighten him.

I. L. GOREMYKIN: He believes that calling out troops in the ordinary way always involves a loss of time and inevitably entails friction. He finds that the internal situation, at this moment, does not allow for any delay in the making of decisions. He also finds that the commander of the Moscow military district (General Ol'khovsky) is not fit for his job at all, and that any discussions with him are useless, particularly if the moment for action comes.

A. D. SAMARIN: I do not quite understand the formulation of the problem: Moscow for the sake of Iusupov, or the Governor-General for the sake of Moscow? In the first instance, all substantive discussions are quite irrelevant. In the second instance, the Council of Ministers is apparently not opposed to the utility of concentrating supreme authority in Moscow in one pair of hands, but the majority of its members finds that Prince Iusupov is not fit for this role. At our last meeting, the gentlemen members of the Council agreed with my opinion that simply to remove or dismiss Iusupov from Moscow would be politically undesirable. Hence, it follows that we have to think up, and submit for consideration by His Majesty the Emperor, some honorable solution which would satisfy Iusupov and eliminate the possibility of unfavorable rumors.

PRINCE N. B. SHCHERBATOV: I would offer a petition for a ceremonious appointment (even in the form of an Imperial Rescript) of Prince Iusupov as Assigned to the Person of His Imperial Majesty. It seems to me that even Iusupov, with all his exaggerated inclination

to independence, would not dare argue about such an appointment.

A. V. KRIVOSHEIN: A splendid solution. Even Iusupov would not
dare answer such an appointment with ultimatums.

I. L. GOREMYKIN: Gentlemen, I repeat that His Majesty finds
it necessary to restore the Governor-Generalship in Moscow and
that he has decided to appoint Iusupov to that post. We must help
the Emperor and find a way out of the difficulty.

A. V. KRIVOSHEIN: I find it and feel it my duty to say, openly,
that Iusupov has demonstrated his complete unfitness, not only for
a Governor-Generalship but in general, for any responsible post.
He undoubtedly suffers from delusions of grandeur, and in a rather
dangerous form. Without yet being the ruler of Moscow, he is
already negotiating with the government as if with a foreign power.
What kind of acts can be expected from him in the future? It is my
conviction that to let him go to Moscow is to move toward a scandal.
To plead with him, and to make concessions to him, is useless. He
only works himself up still more, and begins to be silly. The most
politic thing to do would be to postpone the question about Iusupov,
in every way, to defer his departure for Moscow, and to use this
time to figure out a way out. I agree with A. D. Samarin that it is
dangerous, considering Moscow's mood, to dismiss this gentleman
in a demonstrative fashion. One can always think of a way out and
to sugar-coat the pill. If he were appointed to the Person of the
Emperor, no one could call it a disgrace.

A. D. SAMARIN: As far as a Governor-Generalship for Moscow
is concerned, it is necessary, but only on condition that one has
the really right person for it. Prince Iusupov does not meet this
condition. In that case, why the whole discussion and mess? Let
Iusupov stay in his present position, not show up in Moscow, and
be gradually forgotten.

PRINCE V. N. SHAKHOVSKOY: I would also argue that one should
do everything in order not to let Prince Iusupov go to Moscow, and
solve the question of his position later. I am very frightened by his
discussions and experiments with the workers. This is dangerous
demagoguery from above, which usually has negative consequences.

PRINCE N. B. SHCHERBATOV: His discussions please the crowd
greatly and stir up the simple people, exciting them against German

treason, which Iusupov sees everywhere, virtually in the Council of Ministers itself.

A. V. KRIVOSHEIN: In general, he has some kind of a mess in his brains. He is always jumping from one extreme to another. Either he sees Germans everywhere, or revolutionary plots, or he throws himself into the arms of Astrov[8] and considers him his chief counselor. While he was still in Moscow, he was visited, on business, by Count V. N. Kokovtsev.[9] The Prince did not receive him, sending word that he was occupied on serious business with Astrov.

P. A. KHARITONOV: All considerations bear out the fact that Prince Iusupov is not only undesirable but absolutely impossible in Moscow. What more can we say about it? By now, the Council of Ministers has been forced, virtually for the tenth time, to waste time by examining and trying to reconcile princely pretensions with common sense. We must simply report to His Majesty that in the opinion of the Council of Ministers, or at least in the opinion of the majority of the Council, the calm of Moscow is more important than the mood of Prince Iusupov. And that's that. What orders follow is not up to us.

I. L. GOREMYKIN: I will speak to the Emperor again and try to persuade him to postpone his decision on this issue. We will see later what will happen.

The Minister of Public Education proposed the necessity of granting deferments to students in the coming mobilization of August 7.

COUNT P. N. IGNAT'EV: Since everyone was convinced that they would get them, the refusal of deferments will make a very bad impression. And the mood of the student youth now is so tense that one should try to avoid creating an extra cause for dissatisfaction.

A. A. POLIVANOV: Deferments for students in higher educational

---

[8] Nikolai Ivanovich Astrov: prominent public figure and an influential deputy in the Moscow City Council and the Moscow provincial *zemstvo* assembly.

[9] Vladimir Nikolaevich Kokovtsev: born 1853; old gentry family; Vice-Minister of Finance in 1896; Minister of Finance, 1906-14; Chairman of the Council of Ministers 1911-14; senator; member of the State Council; dismissed, in 1914, in favor of Goremykin, and made a count.

institutions are impossible, for the students provide the material for the accelerated training of officers, the lack of which is more and more strongly apparent at the front. I don't care about students of middle and lower schools.

s. v. RUKHLOV: I absolutely insist on draft exemptions for railroad schools. Every technician is precious, and we cannot afford to give up a single man. This is necessary not only for civilian, but for military purposes as well. One cannot fight without railroads, and the railroads cannot do without technicians. That is clear to everyone.

COUNT P. N. IGNAT'EV: It would hardly be correct to associate the question of deferments with the rank and type of scholarly institutions. It seems to me that we would create a greater burst of dissatisfaction by such a measure than by a complete abolition of exemptions.

A. V. KRIVOSHEIN: And that would actually be the correct solution—to abolish all exemptions from mobilization. Now is not the time to study, but to fight the enemy. Such a formulation would be undoubtedly understood by the youth, by the parents, and by the whole Russian people. When the motherland is virtually threatened by the German yoke, the interests of education and, in general, all the interests of daily life should recede before the main, the chief task of Russia—not to allow herself to be enslaved. All other considerations are harmful sentimentality.

I. L. GOREMYKIN: I am in complete agreement with Alexander Vasilevich [Krivoshein]. What kind of cramming can penetrate a brain now, anyway? Only nonsense can come out of these studies. But if the Ministers of Public Education and Communications insist, then I find it necessary to hand the question over to an interministerial commission at the Ministry of Internal Affairs, for detailed consideration.

PRINCE N. B. SHCHERBATOV: I must warn you, in advance, that the establishment of exemptions and postponements is hardly practical at the present time. Everything is ready, and any last-minute change will create complete confusion. Even without this, the mobilization is extremely difficult and one should not complicate it further. Otherwise, general interests may suffer because of particular interests.

* * *

From the moment that our retreat had started, the Council of Ministers constantly encountered the problem of the Jews.[10] Headquarters became convinced that the Jewish population in the theater of war was a focus of espionage and help to the enemy. On this basis, it developed the idea of the necessity for clearing the frontal zone of all Jews. The application of this measure began in Galicia. The authorities in the rear began to send out, into the inner Russian provinces, thousands and tens of thousands of Austrian Jews. All this took place, of course, not voluntarily, but by force. The Jews were driven out *en masse*, without regard for sex or age. The common mass included the sick, the infirm, and even pregnant women.

News of this action, and of the coercion which accompanied it, immediately spread throughout Russia and abroad. Influential Jewry raised the alarm. The Allied governments began to protest such a policy, and to point out its dangerous consequences. The Ministry of Finance began to encounter various difficulties in the conduct of financial operations. The Council of Ministers, in written form and also in oral communications of its chairman and of particular ministers, frequently called the attention of the Supreme Commander and General Ianushkevich to the necessity of stopping the persecution of the whole Jewish mass and ceasing the blanket accusations of treason, explaining that this was required both by internal and international considerations.

Nevertheless, Headquarters remained deaf to all arguments and evidence. On the contrary, our retreat led to the evacuation of purely Russian provinces; then, first of all in Courland, and then in other localities, the enforced Jewish migration was carried out on a mass scale by especially appointed military units. What went on is indescribable. Even the most irreconcilable anti-Semites came to see the members of the government with protests and complaints against the outrageous treatment of the Jews at the front. And ultimately it became impossible to survive in the provinces within the zone of settlement into which the involuntary refugees, driven by the military authorities, were moved—not only for the ruined newcomers, but for the native population as well. All kinds of

---

[10] Most probably the explanation of the Jewish question which follows was added by Iakhontov at a later date.

crises occurred: in supplies, in housing, and so forth. Epidemics began. In various localities the atmosphere became more and more dangerous; the Jews were angry at everyone and everything, while the local inhabitants were angry at the uninvited guests who, moreover, were being denounced as traitors and were angered by conditions under which it became impossible to survive in one's own home.

The Jewish intelligentsia, and the circles of the Russian public which are united with them, are utterly outraged. The press, the factions in the Duma, various organizations, and prominent individual representatives of Russian Jewry demand that the government take decisive steps to stop the mass persecutions. In the Allied countries, and particularly in America, one hears heated appeals for aid to the suffering Jews in Russia. There are protest meetings about the policy of racial persecution, and so forth. The consequences of this movement: growing difficulty in obtaining credits, both in internal and external markets. The repercussions were greatest in our financial dealings with the United States, who, by that time, were becoming more and more influential as the banker of warring Europe.

In this grave atmosphere, the Minister of Internal Affairs appeared before the Council of Ministers with a declaration in favor of urgent exploration of ways to ameliorate the situation.

PRINCE N. B. SHCHERBATOV: Our attempts to reason with Headquarters have been in vain. All the means of struggle available to us against preconceived tendencies have been used. All together, and separately, we have spoken and written and pleaded and complained frequently. But the all-powerful Ianushkevich thinks that national considerations and interests are not binding on him. It is his plan to maintain the army's prejudice against all the Jews, and to represent them as responsible for the defeats at the front. Such a policy is bearing fruit, and a disposition toward pogroms is growing in the army. One does not like to say this, but we are among ourselves here and I will not disguise my suspicion that, for Ianushkevich, the Jews are probably one of those alibis about which A. V. Krivoshein spoke the last time. Be that as it may, we are apparently deprived of the possibility of killing the evil at its root, and there remains for us to search for ways of diminishing its baleful influence on State interests and on the internal policy of the government. Moreover, even if Headquarters were to give the order to stop the outrages against the Jews, the evil has already spread so deeply that one could not manage without pretty strong medicine. At the moment, the situation is as follows: Hundreds of thousands of Jews of all sexes, ages, and condition have been moved, and continue to move, eastward from the war theater. The distribution of this mass within the zone of settlement is not only difficult, but simply impossible. The local governors report that every place is filled to the brim, and that if further immigration is not stopped at once, they cannot be responsible for the safety of the new inhabitants, because the people are worked up and there is agitation for pogroms, particularly on the part of soldiers coming back from the front. Not only the problems of daily living, but economic and sanitary conditions require a thinning out of the population. All this points to the necessity of permitting, at least temporarily, the establishment of forcibly evacuated Jews in areas beyond the zone of settlement. I must say that even now the prohibited line is frequently being transgressed. Students from middle and higher institutions and schools evacuated from regions occupied by the enemy, Jewish soldiers who received the St. George Cross or who were wounded, and other similar elements are spreading everywhere. There are also inevitable police oversights, caused by bribes. But in many cases the transgression of the law is being deliberately allowed by the Ministry itself, for the law was written for peacetime and we are living through a catastrophe and must adjust to the unexpected demands of the time. Nevertheless, individual exemptions cannot alleviate the problem or noticeably modify the crisis. The fact remains a fact. The leaders of Russian Jewry are firmly demanding general measures and a legal basis for ameliorating the situation of their compatriots. In the heat of discussion I was bluntly told that a revolutionary mood is growing irrepressibly in the Jewish masses, that people are being driven to the last limit of despair, that every day it is becoming more and more difficult to struggle against the desire for active defense, that major unrest and disturbances are possible, and so forth and so on. It was pointed out to me that abroad, too, patience is wearing thin and that the day may come when Russia will not be able to borrow a penny. In other words, the protests are virtually acquiring the form of an ultimatum: If you want to have money to conduct the war, then—. What is desired, essentially, is the issuance of a decree which, by

improving the situation of Jewish refugees, would serve to rehabili-
tate the Jewish mass which has been branded by the rumors of
treason. I do not doubt that my suggestion will have the full support of the Minister of Finance—announce, without delay, a government decision to abrogate temporarily the rules concerning the
zone of settlement; namely, to make official what is, in fact, being
frequently done anyway. Deciding on such a step, we should utilize
it in a political sense, too: We must call together the Jewish leaders
and present our demands to them—we are willing to meet you halfway, but you will be kind enough to use your influence to quiet
down the masses, and then one can speak with you about the future
too. But we must hurry, lest we remain behind events. Otherwise,
the significance of such a gesture will be lost and we will not be able
to profit much from it. From the practical point of view, there is
only one problem: That is, how far should one go in this measure?
Should one allow the settlement of Jews, outside the zone of settlement, only in the towns or also in rural areas? I, myself, am in favor
of the first alternative. The police are, in general, so weak now that,
may God help us manage in the towns; no control is actually possible in the villages.

PRINCE V. N. SHAKHOVSKOY: I should like to support, most decisively and firmly, the suggestion of the Minister of Internal Affairs.
I do not want to touch on the principle of the matter. At the present time, unfortunately, one has to forego principles. The political
aspect has been fully and conclusively described to us by Prince
N. B. Shcherbatov. I will allow myself to state to the Council of
Ministers that some solution of the Jewish question appears to be
extraordinarily important from the point of view of trade and
industry. You know that a great number of industrial, commercial,
artisan, and other establishments have been evacuated from the
districts being abandoned by our troops. All this is now concentrated
in a small area; their problems are complicated by the already serious problem of working hands, they suffer from the lack of materials
and raw goods, and are gradually being ruined and destined to fail.
The loss for national wealth will be irreparable. I should like to
call your attention to the fact that allowing Jews only into towns
will not solve the problem, because factories must often seek locations in rural districts. And, as the majority of the evacuated institutions are Jewish, serious difficulties, which would greatly weaken

the economic significance of the measure under discussion, can arise.

A. V. KRIVOSHEIN: The Minister of Finance, who is, at this moment, being torn apart in the Duma, and who will probably not arrive in time for our meeting, asked me to inform you of his thoughts, which are quite similar to those of the Minister of Internal Affairs, concerning the absolute necessity of taking decisive steps about the Jewish question and concerning the desirability of such an act, which should have a demonstrative significance not only in Russia, but also abroad. Kamenka, Baron Ginsburg, and Varshavsky[11] came to see P. L. Bark a few days ago, with statements concerning the increasing difficulty of placing and selling government papers, the failure of the internal loan, and the negative opinion of Russia held in foreign financial circles, the universal outrage over the treatment of the Jews, and so forth and so on. Moreover, they did not disguise the fact that the improvement of our financial transactions would, in large measure, depend on a change in our policy on the Jewish question: They do not blame the government for what takes place at the front, but they expect, from the government, measures suggested by humanitarian considerations, and other things in the same spirit. Briefly, the conversation can be summed up in the words: Give, and we will give. Well, one must say, what a dignified situation has the government been placed in by the mischievous Ianushkevich! The causes have had the consequences which we foresaw. Now the knife is at the throat and there is nothing to be done. Just as the Minister of Internal Affairs has arrived at this by way of internal considerations, so the Minister of Finance, by financial considerations, has been led to the same conclusion: It is necessary to issue a demonstrative government decree on the Jewish question immediately. And the sooner, the better. If we do not do it now, then, perhaps in a short time, it will be necessary for us to give the same, or even more, for concessions far less profitable for us. We should not drag behind the events, but foretell them, and take the wheel into our hands. So far we are still being asked politely, and we can name our own conditions. Speaking in my own name and that of P. L. Bark in favor of the measure suggested by Prince N. B. Shcherbatov, I

---

[11] Prominent Jewish financiers.

consider it necessary to use this occasion to get the most profit out of our concessions. In answer to the hints of the Jewish leaders, we must present them an ultimatum no less blunt: We grant you the change in the rules governing the zone of settlements, a very substantial change, and you will grant us financial help on the Russian and foreign markets and will exert influence on that press which is dependent on Jewish capital (and this is nearly all the press), in the sense of changing its revolutionary tone. If such an ultimatum is not accepted (which I do not believe), we will have to adopt heroic measures to increase the size of financial foreign markets and will have to demand more decisive help from the Allies.

S. D. SAZONOV: The Allies also depend on Jewish capital, and will answer us with the suggestion that we reconcile ourselves, first of all, with the Jews.[12]

PRINCE N. B. SHCHERBATOV: We are caught in a charmed circle. Right now we are helpless, for the money is in Jewish hands, and without the money we cannot borrow a penny, and without money one cannot conduct a war.

I. L. GOREMYKIN: One must admit that concessions are inevitable. The question is one of their magnitude. I personally agree with the Minister of Internal Affairs that the right of free residence can be granted to the Jews only in the towns, irrespective of the zone of settlement. It is our duty to protect the rural districts from Jewish invasion.

PRINCE N. B. SHCHERBATOV: For this we have a rather convincing reason. As I have already said, a disposition toward pogroms is growing in the villages. We are not in a position to protect the Jews, for we have practically no rural police now.

A. V. KRIVOSHEIN: The Jews themselves understand this perfectly, and they are not yearning for the villages. All their interests are connected with town life.

PRINCE V. N. SHAKHOVSKOY: I should like to insist that the concession apply to factory regions also.[13]

---

[12] Even the liberal ministers did not question, for a moment, the standard anti-Semitic myth that the Jews control world capital. In general, as these pages show, anti-Semitism was an integral part of the official ideology of Imperial Russia.

[13] Many of the factories were in rural or suburban localities.

A. V. KRIVOSHEIN: This is a detail. The overwhelming majority of the industrial regions coincide with the towns. It is not worthwhile to clutter up with details an act that is designed to impress. Addenda and footnotes only cool the reader down. The decree must be brief and definite. In the event of misunderstandings and omissions, one can always add the explanations later.

P. A. KHARITONOV: I feel that the decree should be given a definitive and comprehensive character. If we try to foresee the possibility of various interpretations and explanations, the significance of the act will be practically nil. Right now, the main difficulty in the situation of the Jews comes from the ambiguity and confusion of the laws, which the police utilize for despotic actions and extortions. If, in our new rules, we do not give well-formulated and clear decisions, but leave loopholes, then we know well that little police crooks are far more skillful than any senatorial high secretary in interpreting the law. They will work it out in such a way that the new will be worse than the old.

S. V. RUKHLOV: All Russia is suffering from the war, but the Jews are the first to receive relief. My feelings, somehow, cannot accept this. The saying that money buys everything is confirmed. And such confirmation is provided by a government act. Undoubtedly, everyone will discover its origin and motivations. What kind of an impression will this make—not on the Jewish bankers, but on the army, and on the whole Russian people, who do not take a favorable view of the role of the Jews in present events? It is possible that the consequence of the proposed concession will be an explosion of outrage, and bloody catastrophe for these same Jews. In any event, this formulation of the issue at today's meeting is a surprise to me, and I find it difficult, in all conscience, to give an answer now. I must think about it and prepare myself for a final and definite answer.

I. L. GOREMYKIN: In view of Sergei Vasilevich's [Rukhlov's] statement, we will not formulate a final decision today, and we will request the Chief of Chancellery to prepare, for our next meeting, a draft of a decree in accordance with today's discussion. But, in order to lighten the task for Ivan Nikolaevich Lodyzhensky, I would like to ask all the members to express themselves on the substance of the issue.

A. D. SAMARIN: I fully understand the feeling of protest which rises in the heart of Sergei Vasilevich. It is painful for me, too, to give my consent to an act the consequences of which are enormous and with which the Russian people will have to live in the future. But there come about, in the life of governments, such concatenations of events that one must sacrifice much for the sake of the interests of the moment. I see the presence of such extraordinary circumstances in the contemporary situation and, hence, I find myself obliged to express my consent to the projected measure, but only with the proviso that it should apply to the towns alone and that it be effective for the duration of the war only.

COUNT P. N. IGNAT'EV: Everything that I have heard here convinces me of the necessity of the projected act.

A. A. POLIVANOV: In my capacity as minister in charge of Cossack districts, I am forced to declare to the Council of Ministers that the right of free residence is hardly applicable to these districts, even as far as towns alone are concerned. It seems to me that Cossack townships must be exempted from the general rule in the interests of the Jews themselves. Cossacks and Jews have, historically, never gotten along with each other. Their encounters have always ended badly. One should not lose track of the contemporary fact that the Cossack units are the chief executors of General Ianushkevich's orders to save the Russian army from Jewish treason.

PRINCE N. B. SHCHERBATOV: The Minister of War is absolutely correct. The Jews cannot be allowed into the Cossack lands. The Cossacks will never reconcile themselves to such compatriotship and we could get a wave of pogroms out of it.

I. L. GOREMYKIN: Apparently, except for the Minister of Communications, no one is opposed to the measure suggested by the Minister of Internal Affairs. As far as the details are concerned, we will reconcile them in the journal. And now that everyone else has expressed himself, I will allow myself to recount the opinion of Count Sergei Iulevich Witte, who occupied himself much with the Jewish question and who tried to reform it basically during his years in power. He told me, definitely, that the granting of free residence in the towns to the Jews of our whole Empire would be tantamount to solving the Jewish question.

P. A. KHARITONOV: Ah, but gentlemen, are you not afraid of complications with the police? After all, they are losing a nice living. For all we know, the police officers will start a strike to protest the violence used by the government against them, or will start a few little pogroms to prove the incongruity of our decision with the desires of genuinely Russian people.

With this kind of joke, which the late State Comptroller was always inclined to make, the meeting ended.

IV

The Meeting of
6 August 1915

———◆———

D espite custom, the secret part of the meeting did not begin with the Minister of War's report on the situation at the front, but with the Jewish question, in connection with the journal on this question submitted by the Chief of Chancellery.

The Chairman of the Council of Ministers [Goremykin] declared that he had had an opportunity to report to the Emperor on the discussions at the last meeting about the change of regulations on the zone of Jewish settlement. His Majesty, having heard out in detail the various expressed considerations and agreeing with the reasoning, gave his approval, in principle, to the proposed decree [to allow Jews to live in towns].

A. V. KRIVOSHEIN: I am convinced that, formulated exactly this way, this concession to the Jews will be useful not only politically, but also economically. The interests of national economy, particularly of our declining center, have long required an influx of active entrepreneurship. The transfer of Jewish businesses from the western periphery will give impetus to the development of industry, and will ensure a rise in the local economy. Up to now, our policy in this area has been like that of the stingy man who sleeps on his gold, deriving no income out of it himself and not allowing others to do so. One cannot build our entire economic future only on agriculture. We will not get far with it, particularly when the time comes to liquidate the economic and financial consequences of the war. The Jews will wake up the sleepy tsardom[1] and stir up the Russian merchant guild, which has become lazy under government protectionism. They will quickly create competition where, up to now, a few firms have had complete control, and they will force them to change the ancient ways of doing business to better ones. As for the purely national point of view, one must confess that our cities have long been a mixture of innumerable tribes and languages. Everywhere, even in the most Russian of cities, there are quite a few Jews, usually rich ones, who have found one or another loophole. It would be most profitable to set off against them the Jewish masses, and to weaken them by the competition of their co-religionists. As for the village, that's another matter. About that there can be no doubts. Not only must one not allow any Jews there, but one must fight illegal penetration in every way.

PRINCE V. N. SHAKHOVSKOY: There is nothing to add to what Alexander Vasilevich [Krivoshein] has said. I will allow myself only to repeat what I said last time. A whole group of businesses, for various reasons, need large amounts of space and cannot be established within the city line. Hence, to derive full economic profit from the projected measure, one should also extend the concession to industrial organizations which are being set up outside of the towns.

PRINCE N. B. SHCHERBATOV: I am against such an extension. We will only create an excuse for abuses, for it will be impossible to supervise everything. In my opinion, one must limit oneself to towns, exempting Cossack districts and Imperial residences.

P. A. KHARITONOV: It would be preferable, in order to avoid emphasis, to express it thus—except for towns subordinated to the Ministry of the Imperial Court and to the Ministry of War.

I. L. GOREMYKIN: I am also against the suggestion of the Minister of Trade [Shakhovskoy]. Exceptions will only confuse the text of the regulations. If, in practice, there is found to be a need for particular transgressions or exemptions, then the relevant min-

---

[1] A fairy-tale image, like the Sleeping Beauty, etc.

istry can always come to the Council of Ministers with a petition to obtain the Imperial Grace in accordance with the particularities of each case.

s. v. RUKHLOV: I confess openly that the doubts expressed by me at the last meeting have not only not diminished, but my feelings of protest are even stronger. I do not feel the right to expose discord [amongst us] and to transfer the burden of the solution of such a cardinal question to the Russian Tsar. But I cannot be silent, either. In substance, the admission of Jews to free residence beyond the line of settlement, even though only in the cities, is a basic and irrevocable change in legislation which has evolved historically and which had, as its purpose, the guarding of Russian prosperity from Jewish grabbing and of the Russian people from the putrefying influence of Jewish neighborhoods. With one stroke of the pen, a question which even the first Duma did not dare approach is solved. In two or three days, one of the bases of national policy, carried out by the government over many years, is destroyed. You limit it by claiming that the concession is only for the duration of the war. Pardon me, but such a limitation is nothing but a figleaf, a tranquilizing illusion. Do you, really, seriously think that after the war it will be possible to drive the Jews back to the zone of settlement? It is evident on the face of it that this is unthinkable: There will not be a government which could handle that kind of a thing. No, one must frankly recognize that, by its decision, the Council of Ministers is in favor of solving the whole further direction of the Jewish question in Russia, and that this decision inevitably will create, in the near future, the necessity for new concessions on the road to equality. And all this is taking place under the pressure of the Jewish purse! It is not that the government considers this necessary; it is being forced to it by the critical circumstances experienced by the motherland. Russians are dying in the trenches, and the Jews who settle down in the heart of Russia will benefit from the public disaster and general ruination. How will the army and the whole Russian people view this? Is there some guarantee that there will not be bloody consequences? After all, rumors of Jewish treason are not, all of them, merely libel. It is not a secret, to anyone, that the majority of spies belong to the Chosen People. Two more words. We well know how badly Poland, as part of the zone of settlement, suffered from

Jewish control. Now we want to transfer this burden to native Russian lands. Believe me, the Jews will never return to Poland, for they will be afraid of the Poles, who, upon becoming masters of their own local life after autonomy, will not allow these locusts back. I repeat, I do not have the right to create discord, but I openly state before the Council of Ministers that my soul does not accept this. Now I will be silent.

P. L. BARK: Unfortunately, we must be guided not by feelings, but by the demands of an extraordinarily critical moment. It is not we who created this moment, but those whom we have long and vainly begged to refrain from whipping up the Jewish question with Cossack whips. But it is we who have to pay for these whips, as the money for the war is being demanded from the government. And we cannot obtain the money, for it is in the hands of that tribe which General Ianushkevich has visited with violence and injuries unthinkable in any civilized state. I must inform the Council of Ministers that, of our last military loan of one billion [rubles], 480 million have actually not been placed—virtually half, which has to be covered by various bookkeeping combinations. I must also state that the financial market abroad is closed to us now, and we cannot obtain a penny there. How do you suggest, under such conditions, that we cover the ever-growing expenses caused by the war? It is being openly hinted to me that we will not be able to extricate ourselves from our financial difficulties until some demonstrative steps are taken on the Jewish question. In a word, the dilemma is the following: Either we make concessions to the Jews and reestablish our credit so that we can obtain the means to continue the war or—. The third way out, I, as Minister of Finance, cannot see. The days of Minin and Pozharsky[2] apparently do not repeat themselves. At least it is difficult right now to see any indication of it.

I. L. GOREMYKIN: The question has been quite exhausted, substantively. Sergei Vasilevich [Rukhlov] has determined not to emphasize any discord, and we can now turn to working out the final formula.

* * *

---

[2] Kozma Minin and Prince Dimitry Pozharsky. Leaders in the national struggle to drive out the invading Poles and restore internal order at the end of the Time of Troubles, in 1611-13.

In the debate that followed, the ways of effectuating the projected measure were discussed. Legislative channels were rejected, as requiring considerable time; besides this, at the present time, any excitement created in the Duma by debates on the Jewish question would be impermissible, for these debates could assume dangerous forms and serve to sharpen national antagonisms; finally, there is no assurance that the law would pass, and the possibility of a conflict between the Duma and the State Council is not to be discounted; and, again, the lengthy legislative process deprives the measure of the necessary demonstrativeness and of its character of an act of grace. Basically, the same considerations dictate that Article 87 not be employed. Finally, they [the Ministers] ended up with the idea of having the Ministry of Internal Affairs publish a circular.

A. H. KHVOSTOV: A circular can neither change nor cancel a law. We have had the example of the late P. A. Stolypin's famous circular on the Jewish question, and the possibility that the local authorities might refuse to act on the circular is not to be excluded. The local authorities, of course, will not sympathize with the concessions. The Governing Senate, of course, would be forced to recognize such a refusal as legal.

P. A. KHARITONOV: I suggest that we use the wise regulation which exists in [the law governing] the Establishment of the Ministries. I have in mind Article 158, which charges the minister, in extraordinary cases, to take all measures which should become necessary, and to so inform the Senate.

A. A. KHVOSTOV: The existence of this article in the Establishment of the Ministries, after the promulgation of the new Fundamental Laws [of 1905], is some kind of a misunderstanding. In any event, to base a change of so basic a law (as the zone of Jewish settlement) on it would be stretching things pretty far.

P. A. KHARITONOV: I am afraid we have to do this. I do not see any other way. The existence of an irresistible force is clear—the transport, by the military authorities, of hundreds of thousands of Jews into the interior of Russia, whom the Minister of Internal Affairs is obliged to take care of, and for whom there is not enough room within the zone of settlement. Believe me, no one will squawk about illegality and no one will protest. Not only the Cadets and the more leftist groups, but even the Octobrists will feel it a duty to welcome this act of humanity and the reestablishment of justice for the undeservedly persecuted little sheep. What kind of parliamentary questions and protests can one anticipate about this? As far as the rightist parties are concerned, one can manage to talk it over with them and convince them not to create a scandal.

PRINCE N. B. SHCHERBATOV: I am ready to assume the responsibility of publishing the circular, because I realize that there is no other way out and that we should not wait another minute. Only one purely practical doubt. A circular will have only temporary force. How will that affect factories? With only a temporary right of residence, there will be insecurity about industrial activity. No one will risk the expenditure of the huge sums entailed in moving enterprises and establishing them in a new place. What kind of a guarantee will the industrialist have that he will not be chased behind the line again after the war?

I. L. GOREMYKIN: Moral guarantee and fact. I assure you, the Jews will understand this perfectly.

P. A. KHARITONOV: They know, on the basis of their own experience, that in Russia a circular has irresistible validity and endless life—especially one supported by such a meaningful gesture.

A. V. KRIVOSHEIN: If we are going to try to foresee all the details and special cases, we will never finish discussing this. The situation demands quick and demonstrative action. The remarks of the Minister of Finance [Bark] lead one to tragic thoughts. Let us hurry. One cannot conduct a war with Germany and with the Jews. Even though General Ianushkevich differs, I allow myself to insist that these wars must be separated. If the right of residence alone is not enough, one will have to amend the circular with instructions to the effect that the setting up of businesses in towns beyond the line will be resolved by the appropriate ministry, which is being supplied with the necessary authority.

PRINCE V. N. SHAKHOVSKOY: The whole question amounts to the acquisition of immovable property for the needs of business.

I. N. LODYZHENSKY: The Jews are not legally forbidden to acquire immovable property in towns in which they have the right of residence. The limitation touches only rural areas.

P. A. KHARITONOV: I am not quite in agreement with Alexander Vasilevich [Krivoshein] concerning details. The circular must be thoroughly clear, so that local authorities can find categorical prescriptions in it. Otherwise, we will never have an end to petti-ness, discussions and, to speak frankly, police extortion.

PRINCE N. B. SHCHERBATOV: I cannot conceal from the Council of Ministers that our decision will call forth a storm of outrage in rightist circles. I have had occasion to discuss the Jewish question with the member of the Duma, Makogon,[3] who had apparently heard some rumors about our discussions. He put it bluntly—if there is equality, then clubs and stakes are inevitable. Undoubtedly, the measure we have decided on will be interpreted as the first step toward equality and will create agitation.

P. A. KHARITONOV: This is exactly what one has to point out to the Jewish representatives, so that they understand the full significance of the measure being undertaken by the government.

PRINCE N. B. SHCHERBATOV: And explain to them that we are not allowing Jews into the villages and into the Cossack districts because there we are in fact unable to guard them from the clubs.

A. V. KRIVOSHEIN: And, I would add, we do not wish to guard them there, for this would contradict the national and economic interests of the Russian people.

I. L. GOREMYKIN: We can consider the question closed. There-fore, the Council of Ministers authorizes the Minister of Internal Affairs [Shcherbatov] to immediately issue, on the basis of Article 158, a circular which permits the Jews, for the duration of the war, free residence in towns with the exception of the capitals and the regions subordinated to the Ministries of the Court and of War. There are no objections.

S. D. SAZONOV: Not only no objections, but I, as Minister of Foreign Affairs, welcome the decision arrived at. It will make discussions with the Allies much easier for me; they have been very embarrassed, lately, by the turn the Jewish question has taken in Russia, and have seen in it a serious threat to common interests. I know, from a reliable source, that the all-powerful Leopold Roth-schild didn't want more than towns. He understands fully that it is unsafe for his co-religionists to appear in the Russian village now, and that they would encounter the clubs at which the member of the Duma, Mr. Makogon, hints.

---

[3] Makogon: right-wing deputy to the Duma from the Russian southwest.

P. L. BARK: I can add that the French Rothschilds, too, are far from demanding full equality. They need, from us, an act sufficiently effective to quiet, at least for a short time, the most agitated of the foreign Jewry, and to provide an opportunity for conducting the credit operations we need. I must point out that the Rothschilds are actually very sincere about wanting to help the Allies win over Germany. Everyone knows that their house did not take advantage of the moratorium in France, and that this resulted in enormous sacrifice for them. It is characteristic that [Field Marshal] Kitchener has repeated constantly that one of the most important conditions for the success of the war is the amelioration of the lot of the Jews in Russia. I am convinced that our decision today will have a very favorable effect on our finances, and make easier the task of feeding the war with money.

In conclusion the discussion touched on the conditions one should demand from influential Jewish circles in connection with the measure undertaken by the government. Politically, the conditions should amount to the demands that the Jewish masses be influenced, in the sense of quieting them down, to the cessation of revolutionary agitation, and also to a change in the policy of the press, which is dependent upon Jewish capital. The financial aspects involve the working out of technical details, which should be handled by the Minister of Finance [Bark] with the participation of the State Comptroller [Kharitonov]. The final redaction of the conditions to be submitted and the negotiations themselves were turned over to a group headed by the Chairman of the Council of Ministers [Goremykin] and including the Minister of Internal Affairs [Shcherbatov] and the Minister of Finance [Bark].

PRINCE N. B. SHCHERBATOV remarked on this point: I imagine that the official discussion should be preceded by a private conversation which would pave the way. Such a conversation could be most conveniently assigned to the Minister of Internal Affairs, as the Jews consider that the Minister of Finance is subject to their pressure by his very function.

I. L. GOREMYKIN: We will clear this up in our discussion. To resume, the Chief of Chancellery will reconcile the projected journal with today's conversation, then we will sign this journal, and then we shall see what will happen. I, at least, do not have any exaggerated hopes.

* * *

The Chairman of the Council of Ministers announced that His Majesty had proposed to Prince Iusupov that he negotiate his demands concerning the authority of the Governor-General with the Minister of War [Polivanov].

A. A. POLIVANOV: A task which is not at all easy for the Minister of War, who is loaded down with numerous pressing matters.

A. V. KRIVOSHEIN: One can be quite sure that the Minister of War, for the good of the fatherland, will invest into these discussions all the diplomatic slowness and confusion to allow him to continue them endlessly.

P. A. KHARITONOV: My word of honor! One is nauseated by all this mess caused by egotistical demands.

THE NAVY MINISTER [Grigorovich] reported that the workers of the Kolomensky factory are restless, and are accusing the government of unwillingness to bring the plant up to its full productive potential and of catering to German interests. The unrest is acquiring a dangerous character and could result in the coercion of [technical] personnel.

THE MINISTER OF WAR [Polivanov] explained that the situation at the Kolomensky factory had been investigated by the Chief Quartermaster [Shuvaev[4]], who traveled there and discovered the absurdity of the workers' accusations. General Shuvaev's opinion, based on his conversations with the workers, is that the whole conflict is nothing more than the fruit of deliberate incitement. Among other things, he was told during these conversations that the issue will be pursued in any event, and that for that purpose the workers are preparing to send a delegation to the Grand Duke at Headquarters, and to the Duma.

P. A. KHARITONOV: And to the government? Or is this considered unnecessary? Well, one must say, what a great prestige the government has! The Mogilev and the Tauride demagoguery is having results.[5]

A. V. KRIVOSHEIN: The question is a very serious one. As long

---

[4] General Dimitry Savelovich Shuvaev: born 1854; 1909-16, head of the Quartermaster and Supply Department; Minister of War, March 17, 1916, to January, 1917.

[5] Mogilev, in western Russia, was the location of Supreme Headquarters. The Tauride Palace in St. Petersburg was the seat of the Duma.

as the government exists, it cannot allow such things. Since the Minister of Internal Affairs is denied any authority in the capital of the Empire,[6] one must categorically demand, of the appropriate generals, that they take all measures to prevent any kind of workers' deputations and protests about questions of internal order from being brought to the legislative chambers. Such questions have nothing to do with the competence of the Duma. Otherwise, things can go so far that there will be no way back. It seems to me that one should warn Rodzianko, and point out to him the impropriety and impossibility of receiving deputations.

I. L. GOREMYKIN: The President of the Duma is in such an excited state that it is useless to speak with him. It is necessary that the Minister of Internal Affairs and the War Minister immediately take all measures required to stop such outrages. In a case like this, one should stop at nothing; and one should make an example. We know what peaceful deputations can lead to. I am surprised. What is the factory inspectorate doing about it?

PRINCE V. N. SHAKHOVSKOY: The factory inspectorate is in a very difficult situation, since the military authorities pay no attention to it and do not wish to listen to its advice. The arrival of inspectors at a factory is viewed virtually as interference with someone else's sphere of competence. All this diminishes the prestige of the inspectorate in the eyes of the workers and deprives these officials of the possibility of doing any fruitful work. I must remark that the general mood is as tense in the factories as it can get. The workers suspect treason, betrayal, and pro-German sabotage everywhere and are carried away by the search for, and identification of, those responsible for our military misfortunes. In this respect, the policy of the military authorities, their attitude towards the inspectorate and towards factory managements, is not conducive to a pacification of spirits. This matter should be taken seriously.

N. V. SHCHERBATOV: Revolutionary agitators are taking advantage of this mood of the workers; they try to fan the patriotic indignation of the masses and push them into demanding the exposure of those responsible for the shortage of ammunition. This

---

[6] St. Petersburg, or Petrograd, was under military jurisdiction during the war, both for political reasons and because it was the rear area of the Northern Front.

is now the most fashionable issue in the Duma, in various public organizations, and in the press. It is a convenient basis for riots and workers' demonstrations: Go ahead, try to disperse forcibly a crowd which is marching along, carrying the Tsar's portraits and national flags, and demanding the extermination of German [-inspired] treason! We had to live through such a moment in Moscow, and we know how that ended.[7] Both the revolutionary and the more-and-more active defeatist organizations are perfectly aware of all this, and fan [popular] distrust and suspicion. It is important to them, no matter how, to get the mob out on the streets. Then the herd can be steered any which way. We must act decisively, or it will be too late. The various, accidental, military administrators unconsciously throw coals on the fire and all of Russia will pay the bill for it. I consider that it would be most useful to restore to the factory inspectorate its former authority. It has both the knowledge and the experience which the rear-echelon ensigns are far from possessing.

I. L. GOREMYKIN: The issue is so serious that, without delay, the Minister of Internal Affairs [Shcherbatov] should coordinate this with the Minister of Trade [Shakhovskoy] and take all necessary measures. If the military authorities start to interfere, then I will ask the Emperor to stop them. What is going on here is completely outrageous!

GENERAL POLIVANOV had participated little in the exchange of opinions during the meeting, and had sat silently most of the time. It was clear that something was bothering him. The usual tic of his head and shoulder was particularly pronounced. When all the other matters were finished with, the Chairman asked him to inform the Council of Ministers about the situation at the front. A. A. Polivanov, with barely concealed excitement, in short, abrupt sentences, painted a picture of military defeat and disorganization sadder than anything that had existed earlier.

[A. A. POLIVANOV:] The military circumstances have both worsened and grown more complicated. Considering the present situa-

---

[7] Shcherbatov is referring to the Moscow riots and pogroms against supposedly German-owned business in May, 1915, after the beginning of the German offensive.

tion both at the front and in the rear of the armies, one can expect an irreparable catastrophe momentarily. The army is no longer retreating—it is simply running away. Its faith in its own forces is completely undermined. The tiniest rumor about the enemy, the appearance of a small German patrol, evokes panic and results in the flight of whole regiments. So far, we are being saved from total disaster only by our artillery, which is really superb and which works with total selflessness. But its ranks are thinning, there are virtually no shells, and the guns are worn out. Headquarters has completely lost its head: Contradictory orders, rushing from solution to solution, feverish rotation of commanders, and universal disorder—all this bewilders even the most steadfast people. The psychology of retreat has eaten its way so deeply into the organism of Headquarters that, outside of the notorious scheme of luring the enemy into our great spaces, no solution, no struggle is being recognized or sought. This confusion at the top is no longer a secret in the army, and it demoralizes the troops still more. A characteristic example of the influence of this kind of psychology: The commander of the Kovno fortress, General Grigoriev, frightened by the thunder of heavy German artillery, abandoned his post so rapidly and moved so far under the protection of our spaces that, for the past few days he cannot be found anywhere; now the gendarmes are searching for him in the rear, in order to deliver him to a court-martial especially ordered by the Grand Duke [Nicholas] to try this sad hero. In general, gentlemen, one would like to be optimistic, but the future looks most gloomy. But, no matter how terrible things are at the front, there is a far more horrible event which threatens Russia. I am deliberately violating the secrecy [imposed by] my post and my word to remain silent for a time. I feel obliged to inform the government that this morning, during my report, His Majesty told me of his decision to remove the Grand Duke and to personally assume the supreme command of the army.

These revelations of the Minister of War evoked the greatest excitement in the Council. Everyone spoke at once, and there was such a cross fire of conversation that it was impossible to catch individual statements. One could see to what a degree the majority [of the Council] were shaken by the news they had heard—the latest, stunning blow in the midst of the military misfortunes and internal complications which were being suffered.

A. A. POLIVANOV: Knowing the Emperor's suspiciousness and his stubbornness about all decisions of a personal nature, I tried, with the greatest caution, to dissuade him, to beg him at least to postpone acting on this decision. I allowed myself to emphasize how dangerous it was for the Head of the State to assume command at a time when the army was demoralized and depressed in consequence of continuous misfortune and a long-lasting retreat. I explained that, right now, materiel and equipment are in a desperate state and that the measures undertaken to supplement them can only bear fruit after some time has elapsed. I did not feel it right to remain silent about the possible consequences for the internal life of the country if the personal leadership of the troops by the Tsar were not to improve the situation at the front and stop the advance of the enemy into the country; with all this, I reported that, considering our forces, there is no hope to gain even local successes at present, and that it is less than likely that the victorious march of the Germans can be halted. It is horrible to think what impression would be made on the country if His Majesty the Emperor were to give the order for the evacuation of Petrograd, or, God help us, Moscow, in his own name. His Majesty listened to me attentively and replied that he had weighed everything, and was conscious of the difficulties of the moment and that, nevertheless, his decision was final.

PRINCE N. B. SHCHERBATOV: I have recently heard rumors about intrigues in Tsarskoe Selo against the Grand Duke, and I suspected that it might end with the assumption of the supreme command by the Emperor. But I never thought that this blow would come right now, at the most unfavorable moment for such a decision. In my reports I constantly brought to the attention of His Majesty the growth of revolutionary feelings, and presented letters obtained through military censorship, from people of various social classes, including some closest to the Court. In these letters one can vividly see the dissatisfaction with the government, with the regulations, with the confusion in the rear, with the military defeats, and so on. Moreover, the Emperor himself is held responsible for much of

this. In such circumstances, His Majesty's taking over direct command of the troops will make a very bad impression and can greatly
complicate the internal situation. Besides, Grand Duke Nicholas has
not lost his popularity despite everything that is happening at the
front; both in the army and in the broad circles of the population,
hopes for the future are connected with his name. No, everything
speaks for the fact that the execution of the Emperor's decision is
absolutely impermissible and that one must resist him with all
means. If His Majesty goes to the front, how could one guarantee
his safety there, in all the confusion? The Tsar's automobile could
not even move quickly through the mass of refugees along the
crowded roads. And how to defend the Emperor from the thousands
of deserters—hungry, angry men wandering in the forests? And the
Imperial family? I could not guarantee the safety of Tsarskoe Selo.
There are virtually no troops there. The police are insufficient. A
small band of energetic criminals could penetrate there, and the
garrison, weakened by the departure of the personal guard of the
Emperor, would find itself in a difficult situation. And the possibility
of such attempts is not to be excluded, considering the present
stirred-up feelings and the hunt for those responsible for our
disasters. Forgive me; I know I am speaking chaotically and in-
coherently, but the news conveyed to us by the War Minister
makes it easy to lose all composure.

I. L. GOREMYKIN: I must confirm the words of the Minister of
War. His Majesty warned me, a few days ago, of the decision he has
taken. When I wanted you, in our previous meetings, when we were
discussing the interrelations between military and civilian authorities, to touch very, very cautiously on the question of Headquarters
with the Emperor, I had in mind exactly the danger of hastening
such a decision.

S. D. SAZONOV: How could you, then, hide this danger from your
colleagues in the Cabinet? After all, this issue affects matters on
which the fate of Russia depends. If you had told us frankly, we
would probably have found ways of counteracting the decision of the
Emperor, which I cannot call anything but ruinous.

I. L. GOREMYKIN: I did not consider it possible to announce
that which the Emperor ordered me to keep secret. If I speak of it
now, it is only because the Minister of War [Polivanov] found it
possible to violate the injunction and reveal the secret without the

consent of His Majesty. I am a man of the old school. For me, an Imperial order is law. But once something is done, one can't undo it.[8] I must say to the Council of Ministers that all attempts to dissuade the Emperor will be, in any event, useless. His conviction was formed a long time ago. He has told me, more than once, that he will never forgive himself for not leading the army at the front during the Japanese war. According to his own words, the duty of the Tsar, his function, dictates that the Monarch to be with his troops in moments of danger, sharing both their joy and their sorrow. Many of you gentlemen probably remember the measures which were being prepared after the declaration of the present war, and how difficult it was to dissuade the Emperor then. Now, when there is virtually a catastrophe at the front, His Majesty considers it the sacred duty of the Russian Tsar to be among the troops, to fight with them against the conqueror or perish. Considering such purely mystical feelings, you will not be able to dissuade the Emperor by any reasons from the step he has contemplated. I repeat, intrigues or personal influence have played no role in this decision. It was prompted by the Tsar's consciousness of his duty to the motherland and to the exhausted army. I, too, exerted all efforts as did the Minister of War, to restrain His Majesty from making his decision final, begged him to postpone it until circumstances are more favorable. I, too, find that the assumption of command by the Emperor is a very risky step which can have grave consequences, but he, understanding this risk perfectly, nevertheless does not want to give up his conception of the Tsar's duty. There remains for us only to bow before the will of our Tsar and help him.

s. d. sazonov: Yes, but there are situations when it is the duty of a loyal subject to be insistent toward the Tsar, in the name of larger state interests. Besides all the considerations which have already been mentioned here, we must also consider the fact that the dismissal of the Grand Duke [Nicholas] will make an extremely unfavorable impression on our Allies, who have confidence in him. In addition, the unification of the Supreme Command in the person of the Monarch will complicate communication between the Allied armies and Headquarters, and make it more difficult. It is not pos-

---

[8] A Russian saying.

sible to conceal the fact that, abroad, there is little confidence in the Emperor's firmness of character and that there is apprehension about the influences which surround him. In general, all this is so terrible that my mind is in chaos. Into what an abyss is Russia being pushed!

A. V. KRIVOSHEIN: I have long suspected the possibility of a declaration by the Emperor of his wish to head the armies directly—this is in complete accord with his spiritual make-up and with his mystical conception of his Imperial calling. But, like the Minister of Internal Affairs [Shcherbatov], I was far from thinking that the question would arise precisely at this absolutely unsuitable moment and that the government, which up to now has possessed the monarch's confidence, might be faced with a predetermined decision of such great historical importance. I am absolutely in agreement with those colleagues in the Cabinet who speak of the immediate necessity of dissuading the Emperor. What is being raised is the question of the fate of Russia and of the whole world. It is necessary to protest, to plead, to insist, to beg; in other words, to do everything we can to deter His Majesty from taking such an irrevocable step. We must explain that the issue being posed is one involving the fate of the dynasty or of the throne itself, that a blow is being inflicted against the monarchic idea in which the whole force and future of Russia lies. The people have considered His Majesty the Emperor as unlucky and unfortunate for a long time, from the times of Khodynka and the Japanese campaign. On the contrary, the popularity of the Grand Duke is still great, and he serves as a symbol around which our last hopes are united. The army also, though furious at its commanders and staffs, considers Nikolai Nikolaevich [Nicholas] its real leader. And suddenly—a change in the Supreme Command! What a dreary impression this will make on the public, the great popular masses, and the troops. I now understand those who say that it is possible to lose one's emotional balance. One needs a special kind of nerves to be able to withstand everything that is happening now. Russia has lived through far more difficult times, but there was never a time when everything was done in order to complicate and confuse an already insoluble situation.

PRINCE N. B. SHCHERBATOV: There can be no doubt that the Emperor's decision will be interpreted as the result of the influence of the notorious Rasputin. Revolutionary and antigovernment agitators will not pass up such a convenient opportunity. There are rumors in the Duma about this influence, and I fear that a scandal might result from this. One must not forget that the Grand Duke [Nicholas] has the favor of the deputies because of his attitude toward public organizations and representatives.[9]

P. A. KHARITONOV: I now have doubts about how well the Grand Duke himself will react to his dismissal. He is a nervous, sensitive, painfully ambitious man. No matter how one sugar-coats the pill, the fact that his dismissal comes while the retreat is going on and continuous disasters are taking place at the front is equivalent to the recognition that the Supreme Commander is not fit for his post, is incapable of fighting the enemy. As long as many in Headquarters stand to lose everything with the departure of the Grand Duke, there is certainly a possibility that there will be attempts to induce His Highness to take some decisive steps."

A. A. POLIVANOV silently spread his arms and shrugged his shoulders.

A. V. KRIVOSHEIN: As for the Grand Duke, I am convinced that there is no danger of disobedience. He is deeply patriotic and would never agree to complicate an already critical situation.

S. D. SAZONOV: He is not only a patriot but a gentleman. The considerations of Petr Alekseevich [Kharitonov] must be completely excluded. There are already sufficient motives for a report to the Emperor about the catastrophic nature of his decision; we should not need to frighten him with nonexisting dangers and arouse his feelings against the Grand Duke; for a long time they have not been good ones.

P. L. BARK: I concur fully with Sergei Dimitrovich Sazonov's position. Such an argument can only fan the fire. It seems to me that we must also call His Majesty's attention to the fact that a change in the Supreme Command, in view of present circumstances and of the internal complications which may follow on it, will worsen our credit, which has already fallen to a point unbelievable for a great power. The Tsar enters the last battle at the head of the army—this is our last stake. But this moment has not yet come. A risk taken at the wrong time nearly always has bad consequences. It is our duty to state our opinion to the Emperor. Otherwise we will be justifi-

---

[9] Grand Duke Nicholas was regarded as a liberal because of his cooperation with the Duma and with the various public organizations—the Military-Industrial Committee, the Union of *Zemstvos,* and the Union of Towns.

ably reproached for not having taken all possible steps to forestall disaster.

PRINCE N. V. SHAKHOVSKOY: It seems to me that the Council of Ministers should request an Imperial audience and should beg His Majesty the Emperor to reconsider his decision. It is both our duty and, to put it bluntly, our right.

I. L. GOREMYKIN: I am against such a collective *démarche*. It will not only not do any good but, on the contrary, it will make matters worse. You know the Emperor's character, and what kind of impression such demonstrations make on him. Besides all this, I repeat that his decision is unshakable. Various influences have nothing to do with this. All the rumors about this are nonsense which the government need not consider. There is nothing we can do. Everything is already sufficiently difficult for him without bothering him with our protests. My conscience as Chairman of the Council of Ministers is clear—I have done everything to deter the Emperor. I call on you, gentlemen, in your awareness of the great importance of coming events, to bow before the will of His Imperial Majesty, to unite yourself around him in this difficult moment, and to dedicate all [our] strength to our monarch.

I. L. Goremykin's appeal did not make any particular impression, and it went virtually unnoticed. Heated exchanges of opinions, bearing on the necessity of dissuading the Emperor at no matter what cost, continued. As the Chairman categorically rejected a suggestion for a collective audience, the final decision was the following: First of all, to delegate the Minister of War [Polivanov], from whom they had first heard of the Imperial intention, to report to His Majesty the opinion of the Council of Ministers, and to beg him either to reconsider his decision or at least to postpone putting it into effect until circumstances became more favorable. Secondly, to try to influence the mood of the Emperor through people close to him: One such person, named first, was General V. N. Voeikov,[10]

---

[10] Vladimir Nikolaevich Voeikov: Major-General in the Suite of His Majesty; Commandant of the Imperial Palace; very close to Nicholas II; son-in-law of Count Fredericks, Minister of the Imperial Court; supposedly anti-Rasputin, but generally quite apolitical.

the palace commandant, who should be influenced mainly by the type of considerations expressed by the Minister of Internal Affairs [Shcherbatov] concerning the difficulty of safeguarding His Majesty and the Imperial family, and also concerning the terrifying consequences of the contemplated step for the future of the dynasty. The negotiations with V. N. Voeikov were delegated to Prince N. B. Shcherbatov.

A. V. KRIVOSHEIN: Lately, I have been constantly hearing complaints that it is impossible to get anything done in government agencies during the summer months. Either there is a holiday, or some festive day, or some other excuse for doing nothing, and there isn't a soul in the various departments. Those who have business have to go quite a few times in order to catch the necessary civil servant in. This is an absolutely unforgivable situation. At the front, hundreds of thousands are undergoing incredible privations, knowing peace neither day nor night, while the gentlemen bureaucrats, exempt from mobilization for the good of the cause, celebrate Anton and Onufry[11] and, to top it off, devote themselves to resting in bucolic surroundings once or even twice a week. Right now, it is everyone's duty to be at his post. The State is on the verge of a possibly irreparable catastrophe, and its employees do not have the right to do nothing. The top officials work twenty-four hours a day while the gentlemen bureau chiefs stroll around at concerts in Pavlovsk.[12] There must be an end to the incredibly great and ever-growing number of all kinds of holidays. The Council of Ministers should issue a general order to all ministries about this. Everyone will understand and approve. The fatherland is in danger, and everyone must be constantly at his post. The Russian people have enough reasons for discontent as it is, without being irritated by the sight of bureaucratic relaxation.

A. V. Krivoshein's suggestion met with general approval. It was decided to cut down the nonbusiness days in government depart-

---

[11] Obscure saints, whose feast days could nevertheless be used to justify a celebration or holiday.

[12] A small resort town and Imperial residence on the Finnish Gulf close to Petrograd.

ments to Sundays and the twelfth holidays,[13] with the proviso that even on such days there always be some officials on duty.

When the meeting ended, the members of the Council did not leave for quite a while, and stood in separate little groups conducting lively conversations about the approaching events. Finally, everybody departed in a mood of great perturbation. In my notes I have: General mood—How could the Emperor make a decision which affects the whole governmental life so deeply and threatens such countless consequences, without consulting the government? It means there is no confidence in the Council [of Ministers].

---

[13] The twelve Church feast days from Christmas to Epiphany, December 25 to January 6.

V

The Meeting of
9 August 1915

---◈---

The record is very incomplete. It is noted that I had to leave the room frequently on various errands. On paper there are only separate sentences and then a general summary.

The NAVY MINISTER [I. K. Grigorovich] gave pleasure by announcing successful action of our fleet in the Gulf of Riga, which resulted in sizable enemy losses. The Gulf has been cleared of German ships and their designs against Riga have failed.

The CHIEF OF CHANCELLERY [I. N. Lodyzhensky] has submitted, for signature, the journal on the Jewish question.

S. V. RUKHLOV: My emotions and my conscience protest against the fact that military misfortunes are reflected, first of all, in concessions to the Jews. The Russian people are bearing unbelievable privations and suffering both at the front and at the rear, while Jewish bankers buy for their compatriots the right to make use of the misfortunes of Russia for further exploitation of the bleeding Russian people. My hand cannot sign my name to such a journal. I categorically refuse to give my signature, but I submit to the decision of the Council of Ministers and do not formally declare my opposition.

These words of the Minister of Communications called forth counterarguments—that in this matter one must be guided not by emotions but by necessity; that credit is necessary for the continuation of the war and that Russia is more interested and involved in the war than in the partial extension of the zone of settlement; and so forth. s. v. RUKHLOV remarked that, though he abides by his decision not to sign the journal and not to inflict his own opinion on anyone, he nevertheless finds it necessary to note a very substantive omission in the discussion of the problem by the Council of Ministers.

[s. v. RUKHLOV:] We discussed the financial and the economic and the military and the general political considerations in favor of a gesture concerning the Jewish question, but there was no mention of the danger inherent in the spread, over all Russia, of a source of revolutionary infection, which the Jews are. It is sufficient to remember the role of this tribe in the events of 1905; as for the present, the Minister of Internal Affairs [N. B. Shcherbatov] undoubtedly knows what percentage of the people conducting revolutionary propaganda and participating in various underground activities are Hebrews.

PRINCE N. B. SHCHERBATOV: Of course, S. V. Rukhlov is profoundly correct in his remarks about the destructive influence of Jewry. But what can we do when the knife is at our throat? If the evil influence of the Jews is undebatable, the necessity for money with which to conduct the war is equally undebatable, and the money is in Jewish hands.

A. V. KRIVOSHEIN: I, too, am accustomed to identifying Russian revolution with the Jews; nevertheless, I signed the journal of our concessions to these same Jews because I recognize the inevitability of such an act. As I have already said in the Council of Ministers, it is impossible to conduct war simultaneously against the Germans and against the Jews. This is too much, even for so powerful a country as Russia.

I. L. GOREMYKIN: The question of admitting the Jews into towns has already been decided by the Council of Ministers and approved by His Majesty. Let us not return to discussions of principles. The Minister of Communications is not creating formal discord, and I do not believe we can deny him the right not to sign the journal.

It should be noted in connection with the episode just described, that S. V. Rukhlov was not present at subsequent meetings of the Council of Ministers and that his place was taken by the Vice-Minister of Communications, P. N. Dumitrashko. The reason for his absence was illness, then a trip to inspect the railroads, and finally a lengthy furlough for therapy in the Caucasus, from whence he returned at the end of September or the beginning of October, shortly before his replacement by A. F. Trepov.[1]

I. L. GOREMYKIN announced to the Council of Ministers that the report of the Minister of War [A. A. Polivanov] to His Majesty, concerning the change of the Supreme Command, had not influenced the Emperor, whose decision remains unchanged. At present, A. A. Polivanov is at Headquarters, to which he was sent by His Majesty with a personal letter to the Grand Duke [Nicholas] and with the task of arranging with His Highness the procedures for handing over the command. I. L. Goremykin also said that the Grand Duke had been offered the post of Viceroy of the Caucasus and Commander-in-Chief of the Caucasian Army, and that Count Vorontsov-Dashkov has been sent an admonition about the desirability of immediately submitting his resignation.

The Chairman's communication produced an extremely bad impression on the Council of Ministers.

This was worsened by the MINISTER OF INTERNAL AFFAIRS' [Shcherbatov's] description of his failure to gain the cooperation of the palace commandant, V. N. Voeikov, who does not share the forebodings about the possibly serious consequences of the Emperor's assumption of personal command of the troops; on the contrary, he declares himself confident that the dismissal of the Grand Duke is absolutely necessary under the circumstances, and that only the presence of the Tsar at the head of the army can raise the morale of the Russian soldier and renew his faith in victory. Suggestions that it might be difficult to guard the Emperor and the Imperial family, that there might be danger to Tsarskoe Selo, that there might be a risk to the dynasty if the misfortunes at the front were to continue, and so on were all met virtually with a smile and with the statement

---

[1] Alexander Fedorovich Trepov: born 1864; member of a prominent top bureaucratic family; senator; right-wing member of the State Council; in charge of the Ministry of Communications, 1915-16; from November 19, 1916, to December 27, 1916, Chairman of the Council of Ministers.

that the question had been thoroughly weighed, that measures were being taken, that the dangers were exaggerated, and so on. Finishing his report, in which he portrayed in even more hopeless and dark colors the internal situation of the country, the rise of general discontent, the spread of disorder, the growing work of underground organizations, and the absolute impossibility of accepting responsibility for the future, in such an atmosphere, if the Emperor takes such a "fatal step," Prince N. B. Shcherbatov exclaimed: "Under such conditions I cannot go on carrying my responsibility and being the Minister of Internal Affairs."

In discussion, some of those present stated that the government's situation is becoming extraordinarily difficult and delicate. It is not only considered unnecessary [by the Emperor] to acquaint oneself [himself] with its [the Council's] opinion on a question of such colossal importance, but after becoming acquainted with its opinion, it is completely disregarded [by the Emperor], and an act which is considered by the Council of Ministers to be ruinous in all aspects is being hastened toward its realization.

However, the CHAIRMAN [Goremykin] did not allow the discussion to develop. He announced that the fact had been accomplished, and that one must now await the return of the Minister of War and prepare oneself for all events, in order to be on guard and help His Majesty the Emperor.

The CHIEF OF CHANCELLERY [I. N. Lodyzhensky] read a letter from the Chairman of the Central Military-Industrial Committee, A. I. Guchkov, addressed to the Chairman of the Council of Ministers and containing the resolutions of the Committee concerning the situation caused by the war and the necessity for a change in the political course [of the government].

I. L. GOREMYKIN: The letter, both in substance and in tone, is so impolite that I have no intention of answering Mr. Guchkov.

A. V. KRIVOSHEIN: Of course, it is understood that the government cannot enter into correspondence with Guchkov on questions which have nothing to do with his competence. But the very fact of such a communication is not unindicative of our times and of the atmosphere in which further government work must take place.

S. D. SAZONOV: What can a government to which Messrs. Guchkov and public organizations allow themselves to speak in such a tone, do? Apparently, in their eyes, the government has absolutely no authority or prestige.

s. v. RUKHLOV: One should take notice that Guchkov is transforming his committee into some kind of second government, making it a focus of public organizations and attracting the workers. A revolutionary organ is being formed under the very nose of the government, and it doesn't even find it necessary to hide its aims. Well, one must say, we are entering a great period.

P. A. KHARITONOV: It's understandable, for the country has no confidence in the present government. The army and the population do not rely on us, but on the Duma and on the Military-Industrial Committees.

PRINCE N. B. SHCHERBATOV: There is a lack of confidence in the government also in the one [i.e., the Emperor] who is the source of government authority.

P. A. KHARITONOV: In general, the Council of Ministers should think about the situation which is shaping up for it.

I. L. GOREMYKIN: To stay on the subject of Guchkov's letter—apparently everyone is agreed that it should not be answered.

There were no objections, but the conversation continued in the same vein—complaints about the difficult conditions of work, about one's powerlessness to prevent clearly risky experiments, and so forth. One could summarize this exchange of opinions by the words of s. D. SAZONOV: "The government hangs in mid-air, having support neither from above nor from below." In particular, the conversation touched on the personality of A. I. Guchkov, his adventuristic nature, his impossible ambition, his capacity for using any means to attain his goal, his hatred for the régime and for the Emperor Nicholas II, and so on.

A. A. KHVOSTOV: It is interesting that this gentleman is supported both by the Cadets and the more leftist groups. He is considered competent to head a battalion and march on Tsarskoe Selo, if the proper occasion arose. It is very sad that this character is rising to the surface again and that he is the head of the Military-Industrial Committee, which could become a dangerous weapon in a political struggle. S. V. Rukhlov is absolutely correct when he points to this Committee as a probable organizational center for that particular portion of the public which is not within the Town or *Zemstvo* Unions.

When the meeting ended and everyone had left, I. L. GOREMYKIN said to I. N. Lodyzhensky, Chief of Chancellery, who remained for his report: "What a smell of sourness in the Council of Ministers!"

My concluding notes read: Apparently, an internal crisis is developing within the Council of Ministers. The majority are insulted by the decision about the change of command and the dispatch of the order to the Grand Duke without the participation of the Council. Ivan Longinovich [Goremykin] holds firmly to the position that now is not the time to protest, and that the Tsar needs help at this critical moment.

VI

The Meeting of
10 August 1915

A gain, fragmentary notes, and mainly in general terms rather than quotations from particular individuals.

The beginning of the meeting was calmer. At the end, the position of the government was touched upon again, and the conversation took on a sharper tone.

The Council of Ministers learned that His Majesty had the idea of remaining in Petrograd, for the moment, and setting up Headquarters here. In fact, everything would be managed by General Ruzsky, who has excellent relations with General Alekseev.[1]

---

[1] General Nikolai Vladimirovich Ruzsky (1854-1918): General-Adjutant (cf. note 10, Chap. IX) ; during World War I, commanded the Third Army, the Sixth Army, the northern Front, and the northern and northwestern Front together.
General Mikhail Vasilevich Alekseev (1857-1918) : General-Adjutant; in World War I was Chief-of-Staff of an army, then Commander-in-Chief of the Northwestern Front. When the Emperor took over the Supreme Command, Alekseev became his Chief-of-Staff, and, in effect, commanded the Russian armies until the spring of 1917; was briefly the Supreme Commander in September, 1917. Later, organized the volunteer White army to fight the Bolsheviks.

A. V. KRIVOSHEIN: Such an arrangement is more acceptable, and the question is solving itself better than one could have expected. In any event, there is a substantive advantage in the removal of General Ianushkevich and in having Headquarters near the government.

P. A. KHARITONOV: Undoubtedly, many fears would become irrelevant. The main thing is that the unity of military and civil authority is being assured.

PRINCE N. B. SHCHERBATOV: It is necessary, however, to define most closely the basis of such a union. I am afraid that this very closeness may lead to the opposite result and introduce even greater confusion.

A. V. KRIVOSHEIN: As long as a change of command has been irrevocably decided on, it is necessary to think of a way of giving it the most acceptable and mild format. It seems to me that we should ask His Majesty to declare His Imperial will in the form of a most gracious Rescript addressed to Grand Duke Nicholas. In this Rescript, one could set down those thoughts by which His Majesty the Emperor is being guided as he enters on direct command of the army. He should refer to the duty of the Tsar: At a time, not of victory but of great misfortune, the Tsar goes forth to share the danger with the troops; the Tsar is ready to perish in the struggle against the enemy, but will not renounce his duty; the Tsar is conscious of his great responsibility for the safety of the motherland; the Tsar values deeply the military achievement of the Grand Duke and entrusts the Caucasus front to him, and so on. Now, of course, I have only jotted down separate phrases. All this must be thought through, and every word must be weighed. But I think that the idea I am suggesting is clear.

I. L. GOREMYKIN: I find A. V. Krivoshein's suggestion a very happy one, and I think that a well-prepared Rescript will help soften many sharp corners.

P. A. KHARITONOV: In view of the fact before us, A. V. Krivoshein's idea is particularly valuable. In the Rescript, one could emphasize that the Grand Duke is being replaced, not because a whole year of war ended in complete misfortune but, first of all, because of the duty of the Tsar, and secondly, because of general considerations of state: The situation is now so critical that it is necessary to concentrate all the authority of the entire government apparatus. If the Rescript is skillfully written, then the Grand Duke will not be so insulted by his replacement and an undesirable sharpening of the mood will be avoided.

All the other members of the Council expressed themselves as in complete support of this idea, although they doubted that the Emperor would agree to such phrasing in view of his extreme dissatisfaction and his personal irritation with the Grand Duke.

s. d. sazonov: A. V. Krivoshein's thought pleases me so much that I am ready to take upon myself (though I do not conceal how burdensome a task it is) the duty of discussing it with His Majesty. Tomorrow morning I am going to Tsarskoe Selo to report on my ministry, and I can submit to His Majesty the Emperor the petition of the Council of Ministers concerning the Rescript for the Grand Duke.

The suggestion was accepted and the Minister of Foreign Affairs [Sazonov] was delegated the corresponding authority.

a. d. samarin: To my deep distress, I was not present at the last meetings of the Council of Ministers, as I was away in Moscow, and so I have not had the chance to express myself in principle about His Majesty's decision. I request permission to do so now. God grant that I am mistaken, but I await terrible consequences from the change in the supreme command! Everywhere in Russia the atmosphere is extremely tense. The country is a powder keg. One spark could suffice to start a fire. It is my conviction that the removal of the Grand Duke and the entrance of His Majesty the Emperor upon the command of the army is not just a spark, but a whole candle thrown into a powder magazine. The speeches in the Duma have made a tremendous impression on all levels of the population, not excluding the villages, and have deeply influenced their attitude towards the government. Revolutionary agitation is unremitting, trying in every way to undermine what is left of any faith in native Russian fundaments. And suddenly, at such a moment, there will roll over all Russia, like thunder, the news of the dismissal of the single person with whom the hope of victory is linked, the news of the entrance of the Tsar himself on the scene of war, a Tsar about whom, from the first days of his reign, the prevalent opinion among the people has been that misfortunes follow him in all his undertakings. I know many regions of Russia well, and I know Moscow particularly well, and with full awareness I can insist that the effect will be overwhelming. The news will be received as the greatest national disaster. If I had been present in the Council of Ministers during the discussion and the report of A. A. Polivanov concerning the change of command, I would have insisted, with all my strength, that the full membership of the government protest to His Majesty the Emperor against this terrible step. Now there is nothing left for me but to grieve that this was not done, and in my first meeting with His Majesty I will consider it my duty to tell him what I have just now said before the Council of Ministers.

P. A. KHARITONOV: The whole problem lay in the fact that the decision was made deliberately without the knowledge of the Council of Ministers. When the Imperial will was announced to us, we were instructed that it was immutable and that we must bow before it. There was nothing left for us to do except to beg the Minister of War, who was going to the Emperor with his report, to place the plea of the Council of Ministers at the feet of His Imperial Majesty. The answer to this was the dispatch of the letter to the Grand Duke, accompanied by a notice of his forthcoming appointment as Viceroy of the Caucasus. What do you want the government to do under such conditions?

A. D. SAMARIN: One should have exhausted all means of persuasion. One should have begged the Emperor, on one's knees, not to destroy the throne and Russia. Is it possible that the closest servants of the Tsar, endowed by him with his confidence, could not manage to be heard out?

S. D. SAZONOV: No less warmly than you, Alexander Dimitrevich, did we want to talk the Emperor out of his ruinous decision, but in Russia even responsible ministers do not have the right to speak out.

A. D. SAMARIN: If the members of the government cannot be heard, then how can they continue to carry on their task and to perform the Emperor's business?

I. L. GOREMYKIN: Our discussion can lead us so far there will be no way out. His Majesty the Emperor considered it superfluous to gather the Council of Ministers together on such a question, which he considers to be a matter of his own conscience and of his

Imperial duty. We did everything our convictions told us to do. But this was followed by the Monarch's order, and it is our duty as loyal subjects to bow before the will of our Tsar and to help him.

The MINISTER OF PUBLIC EDUCATION [IGNAT'EV] addressed himself to the Council of Ministers for instructions. Should one not begin to prepare to evacuate the Public Library? Should one not think of the fate of the Petrograd museums, considering the continuing advance of the enemy and the threat to Petrograd?

It was decided, for the time being, to avoid any general measures of this type, in order not to create panic in the capital. Nevertheless, the situation at the front is so alarming that one must foresee the possibility of all kinds of complications. Under such conditions, one should begin the shipment of the most valuable historical relics and works of art, but only at the specific orders of the chiefs of the appropriate bureaus.

P. A. KHARITONOV: Well, this is all we would need, to have to evacuate Petrograd! A lovely little moment it would be for the change of command! The capital in danger, a Duma which has jumped its leash and is biting everyone left and right, unrest and disorders everywhere, the Tsar distrusting his ministers—really, it's hard to tell what will come!

I. L. GOREMYKIN: Yes, these days, when one sees everywhere the lack of faith and spirit, it would be a thousand times more pleasant to go off to the trenches and perish there.

After the discussion of certain current questions, not of general interest, the meeting ended. My notes concerning the impressions of the day: The temperature is rising; the arguments and objections are acquiring a tone unusual for the Council of Ministers.

VII

The Meeting of
11 August 1915

———◄●►———

They sat for a long time and spoke much. They touched upon a
mass of various questions, jumping from one to the other, always turning to their complaints that the government has no support
anywhere. One feels their growing irritation with their own helplessness in the struggle against the complications which are piling up
on all sides. The exchange of opinions was so nervous that it was
difficult to follow. I could only note down the most vivid and interesting declarations. General Ruzsky does not make a charming impression. The evasiveness and cautiousness of his answers somehow
do not inspire confidence.

THE MINISTER OF FOREIGN AFFAIRS [S. D. SAZONOV] reported on
the results of the mission with which he had been charged: This
morning I was able to report to His Majesty the Emperor everything
that we had discussed at yesterday's meeting concerning A. V.
Krivoshein's suggestion. With complete frankness, I described to His
Majesty the profound sorrow of the Council of Ministers that it had
not been asked to present its conclusions concerning the question
of the Supreme Command. I said that, in our opinion, the change
could have grave consequences under the present circumstances. The

retreat is continuing; there are hardly any troops left; all one has are barely trained peasants fresh from the plow; there is a lack of weapons and ammunition; and demoralization is increasing everywhere. The internal condition of the country is extremely tense. The endless military misfortunes and the worsening of living conditions have resulted in ferment among the masses which erupts in disorders. Revolutionary agitation is going on full blast. Speeches in the Duma and denunciations in the press are diminishing the prestige of authority, and the government is beginning to feel its own weakness in the face of approaching events and of its lack of support in the country. The dismissal of Grand Duke Nicholas will compound our difficulties enormously. His reputation is very great, both among the soldiers and in broad circles of the population; in the eyes of the people he is the Russian Hero who is fighting for the Russian Land against the infidel idol, and hundreds of prayers and masses are offered for him daily, in the most distant little corners of Russia. To my declarations the Emperor answered dryly: "All this is known to me." Then I reported that the Council of Ministers would consider it most desirable, from the political point of view, to soften this change or, as I allowed myself to express it, to spread a little straw in the form of a Most Gracious Rescript,[1] in which the necessity of unifying the military and civil administrations would be outlined, which would describe the achievements of the Grand Duke, the Tsar's duty, and so forth. His Majesty was most sympathetic toward the suggestion and exclaimed: "Marvelous thought! Quickly, to work!" I added that the Council of Ministers, conscious of the importance of such an extraordinary act, petitions for permission to submit a draft for Imperial approval. The Emperor agreed, and ordered: "Only quickly." We really should make haste, to leave no time for anyone to stick some soulless bureaucratic creation in front of His Majesty.

The report of S. D. Sazonov was met with a certain feeling of satisfaction in the Council of Ministers, as participation in the redaction of the rescript opened up opportunities to round off the corners to some extent and soften the whole impression. The working out of the project was assigned to A. V. Krivoshein.

A. D. SAMARIN announced that for his part, he considered the

---

[1] The official designation of a favorable Imperial rescript.

writing of the draft superfluous, that by its participation in it the Council of Ministers would appear to be giving its sanction to the change of command, and that the only course of action would be to continue to try to dissuade His Majesty the Emperor, before it is too late, from taking over the personal command of the army.

During the meeting, the official on duty announced that the President of the Duma, M. V. Rodzianko, had just arrived and was awaiting A. V. Krivoshein, in order to discuss an extremely important matter. A. V. Krivoshein went out and, returning in a few minutes, said that M. V. Rodzianko had pounced on him with reproaches concerning the inactivity of the government in view of the forthcoming retirement of the Grand Duke and the entrance of the Emperor on the Supreme Command.

[A. V. KRIVOSHEIN]: I answered him that he should address himself, not to [myself,] the chief administrator for agriculture, but to [I. L. Goremykin,] the head of the government, about all this. And Rodzianko asked me to convey to you, Ivan Longinovich, his request that you come out to talk to him.

I. L. GOREMYKIN went to the anteroom. After about ten minutes he returned, looking very dissatisfied, and said the following: Mr. President of the Duma forgets himself completely, and takes upon himself the unfitting role of some kind of super-arbiter. He announced to me that, having found out the intention of His Majesty the Emperor to replace the Grand Duke and himself become Supreme Commander, he went to Tsarskoe Selo and told His Majesty that such a change is impermissible. To the words of the Emperor concerning the irrevocable nature of his decision, Rodzianko supposedly answered that there are no irrevocable decisions; that the question is of the future of Russia and the dynasty; that the Tsar is our last stake; that the army will lay down its arms, that a burst of outrage is inevitable in the country, and so forth. I think that His Imperial Majesty was not very kind to Rodzianko, and so he has come here now, to demand that the government take decisive action against the Imperial decision, including a threat of collective resignation. I told him that the government is doing everything that its conscience and awareness of its duty tell it to do, and that we do not require any such advice. To this Rodzianko exclaimed sharply, "I am beginning to believe those who say there is no government in Russia," and with a completely insane air rushed out without even saying good-bye. He was in such an irresponsible state that when the doorman gave him his cane, which he forgot, he shouted "To hell with the cane," and jumped into his carriage. One can see that this is an extraordinarily well-mannered man!

I. L. Goremykin's account again started a discussion about the change of command, and withal, it was emphasized that, as A. D. SAMARIN expressed it, "Well, Rodzianko is only the first swallow [of spring]." He said that we should be prepared for much more impressive and dangerous protests.

Nevertheless, THE CHAIRMAN stopped the debate, to point out that it is useless to turn to a question that does not depend on the Council of Ministers and that "it isn't worthwhile to waste time on such half-madmen as Mr. Rodzianko."

The conversation turned to the internal situation in the country, which is becoming more tense every day, and to the tendency being expressed by the Duma to grab the role—quite unsuitable for a legislative institution—of mediator between the population and the government.

A. V. KRIVOSHEIN: We are irresistibly rolling along an inclined plane, not only toward a military but an internal catastrophe as well. If certain politicians do not want to understand correctly the leniency shown by the government, and are taking advantage of it for agitational purposes, one must speak to them in another language. There is a limit to everything. These people are going too far; their activity is reaching absurdity. Either we must recognize our helplessness and abdicate our power, or we must show that the government exists and will not allow actions which threaten the safety of the State, no matter from which camp they come. You know that Count V. N. Kokovtsev usually stands aloof and does not meddle in anything. But even he could not hold out any longer and, though I certainly am not in his favor, found it necessary to phone me in order to attract my attention—as member of the government—to the visit of the Putilov factory by deputies [from the Duma] and to their conversations with the workers. Even the Convention forbade the association of the chamber with the mob.[2] While there is, as yet,

---

[2] The reference is to the French Revolution.

no revolution here, thank God. But the time may come surprisingly soon if such things will go on. One cannot sustain this indecision; one must determine to move in one direction or another.

PRINCE N. B. SHCHERBATOV: The Council of Ministers knows that, in Moscow, there were demonstrations which ended bloodily. The fights were pretty hot and quite a few were wounded by cold steel.

P. A. KHARITONOV: Not only is it known, but before the beginning of our meeting I suggested to some members of the Council that we consider having a Thanksgiving Mass for the fact that Prince Iusupov was not in Moscow at that moment. I can imagine what he would have done there, what a mess he would have made, and what the results would have been.

PRINCE N. B. SHCHERBATOV: Much more serious disorders took place in Ivanovo-Voznesensk,[3] where it was necessary to shoot. The moment was an extraordinarily tense one, as there was no confidence in the garrison. The result of the shooting—sixteen killed, more than thirty wounded. The excitement has not died down at all, and one can expect echoes in other factory districts.

PRINCE E. N. SHAKHOVSKOY: I have the most alarming reports from factory inspectors concerning the mood of the workers. Any spark is sufficient to start a fire. I am very much afraid of a parliamentary question in the Duma about Ivanovo-Voznesensk. At this moment, with heightened feelings everywhere, such a question could have fatal significance.

I. L. GOREMYKIN: A. V. Krivoshein says, correctly, that we cannot stamp around on one spot. I would very much beg the Minister of Internal Affairs [Shcherbatov] to inform us what measures he is taking to cut off the outrages going on everywhere. The securing of order and safety in the country is his chief task.

PRINCE N. B. SHCHERBATOV: The Minister of Internal Affairs is taking all those measures which his duty dictates to him, and which practical possibilities allow him. I have constantly pointed out to Your High Excellency the abnormal situation in which the Minister of Internal Affairs is placed, thanks to the subtraction from his charge of nearly half of European Russia and thanks to the universal

---

[3] The textile center of Russia.

despotism of the rear-area ensigns with despotic inclinations and very little knowledge of the things they have responsibility for. I have [already] reported that even in the capital of the empire, Petrograd, which sets the tone for all of Russia, the Minister of Internal Affairs is a mere resident who can act only insofar as he does not contradict the fantasies of the military authorities. Nevertheless, up to now, this question has not led us further than the exchange of sympathetic opinions, and the Minister of Internal Affairs, who bears responsibility for everything, remains, as formerly, with tied hands. Only yesterday I announced that, under present conditions, I cannot bear this responsibility and remain at the head of my ministry. In my next report I will say this to the Emperor. How do you expect to fight the growing revolutionary movement when I am refused the cooperation of the troops because they're supposedly unreliable and because of the supposed lack of assurance that they can be made to shoot at the crowd? One cannot pacify all of Russia with policemen alone, particularly when the ranks of the police are thinning out, not by the day but by the hour, and when the population is being wrought up every day by speeches in the Duma, lies in the newspapers, endless defeats at the front, and rumors about disorders in the rear. After all, demonstrations and disorders arise from the most unexpected causes. In Moscow, they developed out of patriotic joy over a newspaper report of the fall of the Dardanelles and the reconquest of Kovno by our troops. The overly eloquent orator was arrested, and the whole mess began. In Ivanovo-Voznesensk, the incitors of the strike were arrested, and again the mess began. Even now it is impossible to work. What will it be like when the change of command becomes known? I, too, agree that one must act. But how shall one act when there is no support from any direction and when it is not considered necessary even to hear out the responsible collaborators on such questions which can play a crucial role in the fate of the State? [4]

s. d. sazonov: It is clear to all that the reason for universal discontent in the country is that the government is hanging in mid-air and satisfying no one.

---

[4] Again a reference to the Emperor's decision to take over the Supreme Command.

PRINCE N. B. SHCHERBATOV: Only two more words. Right now I have in my briefcase a few telegrams from governors [of provinces]. They inform me that the flow of refugees, German colonists, and Jews being displaced by the military authorities is still increasing. The population is extremely worked up against these newcomers, so much so that it is beginning to beat them with clubs. There have already been a few instances of bad wounds and even killings. The governors are asking for instructions and demanding help. What can the Minister of Internal Affairs reply? The elements have been stirred and are now moving, crushing everything in their way. By what administrative measures can one withstand these elements?

I. L. GOREMYKIN: The issue is not the general phenomena created by military misfortunes. It is important not to allow outrages in the big centers, and on this the Ministry of Internal Affairs should concentrate all its forces.

A. V. KRIVOSHEIN: We must pay attention to the sensational leaflets, which have proliferated, and which feed the mob with all kinds of nonsensical news and, as in Moscow, create causes for popular disturbances. It seems to me that the government still has enough authority to stop these—not even bandits—simply hooligans of the press.

I. L. GOREMYKIN: I hope that the Minister of Internal Affairs will take decisive measures in this respect. There is no need to manage this bunch: Shut down the newspaper and put the editors and publishers into a place that should make them wiser. The military authorities will create difficulties, but I will find a check for them. One must end all this.

Long awaited, General Ruzsky finally came to the meeting. In his capacity as Commander-in-Chief of the Front guarding Petrograd, he is the defender of the capital against the enemy and the focus of all civil and military authority in Petrograd. Though his appointment is not yet official, he has begun to perform his functions.

The Chairman of the Council addressed him with a request to express his opinion concerning the situation of Petrograd, from the military point of view, and whether one should not begin to prepare for evacuation. General Ruzsky declared, categorically, that there was not as yet a danger of enemy occupation of the capital. The situation at the front right now is, in fact, very difficult. But even if one assumes that it will not improve, and that one will not succeed in stopping the German advance, then one must take into consideration the lack of roads, the approach of autumn, bad weather, the unfavorable terrain of the district, and so forth. Even if one were to assume that the Germans could move in a triumphal march, with music and banners and without meeting any resistance, one still has to realize that it would take them at least five weeks. But it is certain that we will offer battle and that these battles, even if unsuccessful, would delay their advance for a long time.

"I do not think in general," noted General Ruzsky, "that the Germans have decided to march to the conquest of Petrograd. It is true that it is tempting to grab the capital, but the task is not an easy one and they are a systematic people. They don't get carried away. They have other plans. A swing at Bologoe, in order to cut the Nikolaevskaia Railroad, is most likely.[5] Then the capital would fall of itself. In any event, if there is the slightest danger to Petrograd, the Council of Ministers will be warned in time."

Then, General Ruzsky's statement about the general situation is summarized by me in the following words: The demands of contemporary military technology are too much for us. In any event, we cannot keep pace with the Germans. Under these conditions, if the fate of this war is to be decided on our front, and if the Allies cannot help us more actively, we should be under no illusions. It is doubtful that we will be completely crushed, but we cannot crush the Germans by ourselves. I think we can hold out for a long time, if, of course, there are no irreparable internal crises.

Concerning the change of command, General Ruzsky answered very hazily and even ambiguously: "One could say much for and against it. The whole question can be reduced to the choice of a Chief of Staff for the Supreme Commander as General Ianushkevich apparently can no longer remain at this post. I consider that the most suitable choice, under present conditions, would be General Evert. Unfortunately, the atmosphere right now is such that it is

---

[5] The Nikolaevskaia Railroad ran between Petrograd and Moscow.

impossible to appoint a man with a foreign name. The choice of General Alekseev is a fortunate one. This is a man of enormous experience and an extraordinary ability to work—calm, independent, and obstinate in the achievement of goals he sets."

In answer to questions concerning the role in the conduct of military operations which rumor is assigning to General Ruzsky, he answered by [claiming] complete ignorance: "I have not as yet been confirmed in my post. The present personnel of Headquarters is not well disposed toward me. The reason for this was my refusal to continue to command the western Front when we began our advance on the Carpathians which I considered ruinous to the course of our whole campaign. My forecasts, to my deep sorrow, have been confirmed, and they have not been forgiven me."

Concerning the relations between the military and civil authorities in Petrograd, General Ruzsky declared that he is aware of the abnormality of the situation, that it is necessary to regulate the matter, and that he will concern himself with it immediately.

It is impossible not to notice a curious fact. To the suggestions of the Council of Ministers about the desirability of convoking a military council under the chairmanship of His Majesty the Emperor, with the participation of the government, General Ruzsky replied that, in his opinion, such a convocation would be untimely and could create complete panic, for such a ceremonious convocation would be viewed by both the army and the public as meaning that the whole affair is hopeless and that the very last measures for a solution are being invoked.

In conclusion, General Ruzsky touched on the situation of the workers at the Petrograd factories, pointing out that they are working extremely hard and are experiencing the whole burden of the high cost of necessities; that the factories, meanwhile, have not set up a new wage schedule, so that the workers are being forced, in order to avoid famine, to work overtime to the point of exhaustion; that one must pay the most serious attention to this question and take immediate measures, for strikes and accompanying disorders are possible. "Then the conduct of the war," noted General Ruzsky, "will be quite hopeless."

PRINCE N. B. SHCHERBATOV: Among the workers, as among the population at large, there are monstrous rumors of bribery in connection with military contracts. There is talk of speculators, of commission takers—engineers and civil servants—who are supposedly encouraged in their deals, and there is reference, moreover, to the fact that supposedly these matters are universally known and yet no one has as yet been put on trial. All these rumors are largely, of course, the fruit of ill-intentioned agitation, but it would still not be out of order to take some demonstrative action in order to calm down the crowd. To act through the courts now would take too long. Can't one catch one of these sharks and, with a lot of noise, send him to furthest hell? In Iakutsk Province,[6] even the most stubborn one will start talking and spill the truth.

Conversation on the internal situation and about the difficulties which are complicating, daily, the work of the government continued. At adjournment, no particular satisfaction with General Ruzsky was evident. A. V. KRIVOSHEIN even declared that he "expected more."

---

[6] In northeastern Siberia, boasting the coldest climate in the Russian Empire.

VIII

The Meeting of
12 August 1915

The Minister of War returned from Mogilev whence he had gone with a personal letter from His Majesty the Emperor to the Grand Duke, concerning the change in the supreme command.

A. A. POLIVANOV: I must confess that I set out for Headquarters with very uneasy feelings, not at all sure of a successful conclusion to my mission. Fortunately, my forebodings were not confirmed. The Grand Duke, I have reason to suspect because of certain signs, had already been warned about the expected change, but did not know what form it would take and apparently feared the worst. Having read the letter, His Highness was delighted and received me as a messenger of extraordinary favor. There is no possible question of any resistance or disobedience. The Grand Duke was very pleased with his appointment to the Caucasus, which he sees as a quite honorable solution for himself. But his psychosis about Ianushkevich has not been overcome even by recent events. After the first few words, His Highness said: "Leave me Ianushkevich; transmit to the Emperor my request that he be appointed assistant to the Viceroy of the Caucasus, and I hope that this request will be supported by the Council of Ministers." The Grand Duke returned to this matter a few times in the course of our conversation, and finally declared that he definitely insists that the appointment of Ianushkevich must precede his own appointment as Viceroy. He was even more satisfied and calmed by my report that His Majesty will not enter into upon his command for two-and-a-half or three weeks, and maybe even more. This His Majesty the Emperor ordered me to tell His Highness, when he gave me the letter. I must add the Grand Duke impressed me as a man whose nerves are shot and who is completely worn out. I do not refer to the moral aspect, but in the purely physical sense his departure from Headquarters will be an enormous relief to him. I have reported to His Imperial Majesty on the results of my visit to Mogilev. Gratitude was expressed to me for the successful fulfillment of the charge, and I was ordered to write the Grand Duke that the change of command is being postponed until the situation at the front clears up and that, meanwhile, everything at Headquarters will remain the same. There was Imperial consent to the appointment of General Ianushkevich as assistant to the Viceroy of the Caucasus. In general, I must say that on my last visit to Tsarskoe Selo I felt that interest in personal leadership of the armies was considerably weakened during my absence. This is, in any case, rather symptomatic unless something even more unexpected is hidden behind it.

I. L. GOREMYKIN: It is apparent, from the report of the Minister of War, that everything is arranging itself for the best and that many of the fears expressed in the Council of Ministers have become groundless. Thank God! But it is difficult, at least for me, to credit the change of moods in Tsarskoe Selo. Tomorrow, a decision quite contradictory to the one which the Minister of War has been ordered to convey to the Grand Duke can easily be made. We are certainly accustomed to this!

PRINCE N. B. SHCHERBATOV: We should take advantage of the auspicious mood in order to turn His Majesty's attention in another direction. I wanted to share with you an idea which I had from a member of the Duma, Savich.[1] Its substance is in the following: "Under the present conditions, when the focus of the struggle against the enemy is shifting from the front to the rear, namely, to the production of weapons, ammunition, and equipment, and also to

---

[1] Nikanor Vasilevich Savich, Octobrist.

human cadres to replace enormous losses in the army, the most important task of defense is the unification of the work of supply and the association of all the active forces of the country with it. This task of unification His Majesty the Emperor should take actively into his own hands." In Savich's opinion, such an action would make an excellent impression, for there is a firm conviction in the masses that the root of our misfortunes is not at the front, but in the rear. Simultaneously, His Majesty could occupy himself with the formation of a new army with which he could enter on the battlefield at a convenient moment.

P. A. KHARITONOV: This idea is not lacking a certain superficial beauty, but its substance calls forth serious doubts. I am afraid that the participation of the Emperor in such a businesslike and often detailed affair as supply would complicate the work and slow down its tempo. Besides, it is hardly proper for the Russian Tsar to assume the role of some kind of supreme quartermaster. I would prefer to limit Savich's proposal to its second part—the formation of an army for a subsequent campaign. One could summon the guards [regiments] to Petrograd to serve as cadres for new formations. In addition, the guards' presence in the capital would not be without value, considering the present [popular] mood.

A. A. KHVOSTOV: I am in full agreement with P. A. Kharitonov. It is impossible that His Majesty the Emperor should take upon himself the control of economic and business affairs, and thus become an object of criticism. The character of these affairs is such that there are always all kinds of rumors connected with them. And then what? The name of the Tsar would be directly connected with these rumors. Only think—what food for propaganda and for discrediting the monarchic principle.

PRINCE N. B. SHCHERBATOV: In one or another of its aspects, nevertheless, Savich's idea can gain us time. And right now, each day is precious. One must admit that the confidence of the masses in the Grand Duke has begun to decline noticeably. There is the effect of constant military misfortunes—mainly the flood of refugees who carry everywhere with them sorrow and constraint, and the worsening of living conditions.

A. A. POLIVANOV: The Grand Duke's popularity will have to undergo a great test when it becomes known that we have abandoned Grodno and Brest-Litovsk without giving battle.[2] This is apparently a matter not of days, but of hours.

PRINCE N. B. SHCHERBATOV: It follows, then, that with a certain postponement, a situation can develop in which the entrance of the Emperor upon the supreme command could become admissible—if His Majesty's decision really remains irrevocable.

A. D. SAMARIN: I absolutely protest such a conclusion. Whether the Grand Duke leaves or not, His Majesty the Emperor should not directly head the army under any conditions, for he is our last trump, and, in the opinion of the people, the Tsar is unlucky. I insist on the fact that such an act would be an enormous, if not a fatal, risk for the dynasty and for Russia. We should not seek postponements and delays, but go, all together, to His Majesty and exhaust all means of persuading him to abjure, once and for all, his decision to be the Supreme Commander. The supreme leader of the people cannot simultaneously be a subordinate military commander.[3]

S. D. SAZONOV: I also maintain the opinion that the Emperor should not assume command in any event. But I think that now, when A. A. Polivanov's words indicate that the temperature has fallen a little in Tsarskoe Selo, we should not raise it by arguments and petitions. It is dangerous to evoke stubbornness. We know what this has led to sometimes. It is better, for the moment, to use the tactic of silence, acting indirectly, by roundabout ways. In this way, one can reach one's goal faster.

A. V. KRIVOSHEIN: I find it impossible to prolong the present indefiniteness, if only because Mr. Ianushkevich is being prolonged with it. His presence in Headquarters is more dangerous than a German army corps, particularly if he has already been informed of the fate that threatens him. Even without this, complete confusion reigns in Headquarters. Meanwhile, at the front, critical moments, on which the existence of Russia depends, are coming. Besides, the evil has, in large measure, already been done. The Emperor's decision is no secret to anyone. It is being discussed, it is

---

[2] Two great fortresses in Russian Poland.
[3] "Subordinate" in the sense that the Supreme Commander was, in theory, subordinate to the government, which represented the supreme authority.

being spoken about, virtually in the public squares. Everyone knows that this decision is evoking objections and protests. Further delays might reflect on the prestige of the Monarch, and strip the Imperial intention of whatever was idealistic and beautiful about it. It is necessary to bring everything into concert without delay: either to find an acceptable solution, or to end the issue of the change of command. I fear this change no less than the others, but I also fear the ruinous consequences of ambiguity and indefiniteness in this situation. We should again ask the Emperor to convoke a military council, with the participation of the government, in order to reexamine the plans for the war and to work out the consequent actions to be taken in the rear and at the front. The best place for such a meeting would be Headquarters, and there the presence of the Grand Duke would be absolutely necessary. His Majesty is so extraordinarily talented in getting along with people, even those who are definitely unsympathetic to him, that he will be able to leave an impression of good relations with the Grand Duke and so put an end to the rumors of personal dislike. After this, if a change of command is still our fate, it will appear, after such a military council, as a consequence of consultation by the Emperor with his closest collaborators and responsible military commanders. Such a setting will undoubtedly soften the sharpness of the whole question for the public. And in fact, a military council is unavoidable. I do not know whether it would have significance from a strictly military point of view, but the idea of it is in the air. Many members of the State Council, and of the Duma, and simple citizens have expressed unconcealed anxiety to me over the lengthening crisis and the fact that one sees no action from above in connection with the tragic situations at the front and in the rear.

s. d. sazonov: The convocation of a military council is necessary, not only to satisfy public opinion but also to calm down our Allies. Our growing crisis is beginning to worry them seriously. The French and the British representatives have communicated their anxiety about this to me.

p. a. kharitonov: It is undoubtedly extremely important. The people would see that something is being done, sought, thought about. [Endless] conversations and arguments are only an irritant.

a. a. polivanov: I have repeatedly reported to our Chairman, and to the whole Council of Ministers, that the convocation of a council of war is urgent from every point of view. And if the change in the supreme command takes place, then I fail to understand how one can manage the future conduct of the war without consulting the leading military men.

I. L. GOREMYKIN: I do not oppose this, but I think that nothing will come of it. His Majesty the Emperor did not make the decision to head the troops in person yesterday. He has been evolving it for a long time, since the Japanese war. That which is the result of an internal, peculiarly religious consciousness and a spiritual [conception of] Imperial duty cannot be broken by persuasion. But I repeat—I will not oppose a new attempt.

Finally, the Minister of War was charged to report to His Majesty the most sincere petition of the Council of Ministers for the convocation of a military council at Headquarters, with the participation of the Grand Duke and the government.

The examination of the position of Petrograd and of the proper time to prepare for its evacuation was labeled as one of the questions to be discussed in the Imperial presence. Anxiety is mounting in the capital. The withdrawal of money from savings banks is increasing (even acquiring dangerous dimensions). It is caused by anxiety over the news from the front. There is an energetic withdrawal of savings in Moscow, also, where disorders are feared. In order to avoid riots in Moscow, it is recognized as necessary to continue delaying the governor-generalship of Prince Iusupov and not to allow him to go there in any event.

After the examination of several current questions, the meeting was adjourned. In my notes I have: "The mood is better. They spoke more calmly, without the nervousness of the last few days. I do not understand what Polivanov is after. He is egging everyone on, both against the Grand Duke and against command by the Emperor, and also against Ivan Longinovich [Goremykin]. Is it possible that his goal is to promote his dear friend, Mr. Guchkov, as savior of the fatherland?"

IX

The Meeting of
16 August 1915

———◄◉►———

A. A. POLIVANOV: I have received from His Imperial Highness, the Supreme Commander [Nicholas], a letter which is so significant and so pregnant with consequences that I cannot fail to acquaint the Council of Ministers with it. The Grand Duke begs me, with insistence, to hasten his transfer to the Caucasus. His reason is that his forthcoming dismissal has become known everywhere, his prestige among the troops has been undermined, and he does not consider himself morally justified in commanding an army which in a short time will be removed from his guidance. All this is written in an extremely nervous and chaotic manner, and one senses some external influence. Simultaneously, I have heard that disorder is daily increasing at Headquarters. No one wants to do anything and no orders are being given. In general, one gets the impression that the situation can be definitely qualified as a strike. I am being told outright that such a way of acting, and the Grand Duke's letter itself, is solely due to the influence of the insulted General Ianushkevich. In the end, considering the events at the front, all this can turn out rather tragically. It is necessary to take extraordinary measures. Thank God, Alekseev has not lost his head. He is acting without paying any attention to the wishy-washy mood at Headquarters, and in a manner as circumstances require. One must, without delay, send Ianushkevich to the Caucasus and put General Alekseev in his place. And if the Grand Duke finds it necessary to abandon the Headquarters in which considerations of a moral nature do not allow him to stay, then the whole problem will be resolved quite nicely. According to the law, in the absence of the Supreme Commander his Chief of Staff takes over. Alekseev would assume his duties and manage everything until it is decided whether the Emperor will be at Headquarters or whether this cup will pass us by.

A. V. KRIVOSHEIN: A marvelous combination! We must beg the Minister of War [A. A. Polivanov] to use all his diplomatic talents to quietly suggest this idea to the Emperor. As excuse for a conversation with His Majesty, there is the Grand Duke's letter, which makes me shudder. I did not expect such an unworthy action from His Highness. No matter how great his personal suffering, he has no right to abandon the army to its fate. It seems to me that his moral duty is to fulfill his functions without interruption, and to remain at his post till the end.

A. D. SAMARIN: Everything that is taking place, at Headquarters and elsewhere, confirms more and more my conviction that the change of command threatens the greatest and most irrevocable consequences for the whole country. I am afraid that I shall begin to bore and annoy the Council of Ministers; nevertheless, I shall not tire of repeating that our sacred duty is for all of us, together, to plead with His Majesty the Emperor to renounce his ruinous decision and to leave the Grand Duke at the head of the army. If the Council of Ministers does not agree to undertake this immediately—that is, today or tomorrow—then I will consider it my moral and loyal duty to protest personally. Under the present conditions, when each second is precious and irreplaceable, I cannot agree that delay and prolongation are correct tactics. In the face of terrifying events one should go forward with an open visor and speak the straight truth. Lately, by the way, there has been a significant increase in the rumors concerning the hidden influences that supposedly played a decisive role in the question of the [supreme] command.[1] I will ask the Emperor about this quite openly, and I have a right to do so. When His Majesty offered me the post of Supreme Procurator of the Holy Synod, I accepted it only after His Majesty the Emperor personally told me that all these stories had been thought up by enemies of the Throne. But now, these rumors are becoming so persistent that I shall remind him of our talk, and, if the situation has really changed, I will ask him for my dismissal. I am ready to serve my legitimate Tsar to the last drop of my blood, but not . . .[2]

PRINCE N. B. SHCHERBATOV: I must point out that Rasputin was summoned to Tsarskoe Selo without the knowledge of His Majesty the Emperor and that he was actually absent when this decision was made.

A. D. SAMARIN: Yes, but in any event we must take decisive measures to put an end to the spread of rumors which undermine the monarchic principle much more than do any revolutionary *démarches*. Nevertheless, at the moment the chief problem is that of the [supreme] command. I repeat—if the Council of Ministers does not consider it possible to associate itself with me, I shall go alone to the Emperor and tell him that the departure of the Grand Duke is the beginning of the end of everything.

P. A. KHARITONOV: It is too late now. Even if His Majesty made concessions, the Grand Duke would not agree to remain at Headquarters.

A. D. SAMARIN: I am convinced of the reverse. In his heart the Grand Duke is a loyal soldier, and loves the motherland above all. In her name he will remain, no matter how difficult it might be for him personally.

PRINCE N. B. SHCHERBATOV: I am not convinced of that. The Grand Duke's nerves are shattered.

A. A. POLIVANOV: Judging by the letter which I have read, one may conclude that His Highness will hardly agree.

I. L. GOREMYKIN: I have repeatedly said that the Emperor's decision is irrevocable. He did not arrive at it yesterday, and it derives from an inner conviction. Instead of exhausting the

---

[1] The words "hidden influence" refer to Rasputin.
[2] Either Samarin did not finish the sentence, or Iakhontov did not record some unprintable reference to Rasputin.

Emperor, who is already suffering under a monstrous burden, with our petitions, our duty is to rally round the Tsar and help. As far as the question of influence is concerned, it is an intrusion into a sphere not subject to us. Let everyone behave in personal matters as he wishes; but this has nothing to do with the Council of Ministers.

A. D. SAMARIN: No, this is not a personal matter, but one concerning all of Russia and the monarchy. The very person, the rumors of whose influence are so painful to all loyal subjects, has the nerve to say openly that he has removed the Grand Duke. We cannot remain indifferent to such escapades.

I. L. GOREMYKIN: At the present time, this question was not placed by me [on the agenda] for discussion by the Council of Ministers. We are discussing the letter of the Supreme Commander which has been conveyed to us by the Minister of War, and I ask that you not be diverted.

PRINCE N. B. SHCHERBATOV: Undoubtedly, the idea of immediately assuming command has lost much of its urgency, and the Emperor, as far as I hear, considers its realization a matter for the future. I know that His Majesty was sympathetic to the idea of an overall unification of supply and the formation of a new army based on the cadres of the guards. If this is so, it would mean that the Emperor would remain in Petrograd while Alekseev would be complete master at Headquarters. Practically, this is the most important thing.

PRINCE V. M. SHAKHOVSKOY: From the very beginning I was against the change of command and the assumption by His Majesty the Emperor of the personal leadership of the army. But now it seems to me to be too late to reconsider, for everyone knows of His Majesty's intention, and the renunciation of an arrived-at decision might be interpreted as a sign of fear and of a weak will. All this could reflect most unfavorably on the prestige of the Monarch. Now, as far as the role of General Alekseev is concerned, I feel that he should not have, even for a single hour, the title of "Acting Supreme Commander." It is impossible, in the present atmosphere, to replace the Grand Duke with a mere general. This could create dangerous dissatisfaction both in the army and among the people.

A. V. KRIVOSHEIN: I absolutely disagree with Prince V. N. Shakhovskoy. Quite the contrary. With the Grand Duke, apparently, everything is finished, and people are getting accustomed to [the idea of] his departure. And, as has been pointed out here, even his popularity has declined considerably—not only in the army, but also among the civilian population, which is outraged by the flood of refugees and the endless mobilizations, while hundreds of thousands of idlers in gray greatcoats stroll about all over the place. The appointment of Alekseev would be a transitional, temporary measure, while the Emperor is occupied in the rear, preparing a new army with which His Majesty would enter on the field of battle when the proper time and situation occur.

s. d. sazonov: For the information of His Majesty, one should convey the view of the Council of Ministers, or at least of the majority of its members, exactly this way. Not a refusal, but a postponement—that's the formula. Let Alekseev be the goat, now, for the mistakes of the past, and let him try to repair them. And when he has prepared everything and placed it back on the rails, then, perhaps, the moment will come for the appearance of the Russian Tsar.

p. a. kharitonov: Oh, if one could only hope for all this! Unfortunately, experience teaches us otherwise. Sometimes everything seems to be so well planned and arranged, and yet the result is the most unforeseeable one.

a. v. krivoshein: We have historical precedent to show how men close to the Throne have behaved under conditions similar to ours. When our retreat before Napoleon took on an overly hurried and hopeless character, then Arakcheev, Shishkov, and Levashev demanded the departure of Alexander I from the army, announcing: "If Barclay[3] is beaten, then Russia will merely be upset; but if the all-Russian Emperor is beaten, Russia will not be able to tolerate it." Let Alekseev play the role of Barclay; it is our duty to guard the Russian Tsar from a situation which is impossible for him.

Further on, I noted: The conversation went on for a long time in the same vein. It was decided that the Minister of War would speak with the Emperor, and would try to persuade him to allow Alekseev to perform the "grateful" task of being the scapegoat for the sins of Ianushkevich.

---

[3] Barclay de Tolly was the Commander-in-Chief of the Russian army at the beginning of the Napoleonic invasion.

A. A. POLIVANOV: His Majesty the Emperor has expressed his consent to attend the opening of the Special Conference on Defense and address a welcoming word to those present.[4] His Majesty expects the text of this address from the Council of Ministers. Concerning the important matter of dress, the Emperor warned me that he shall be wearing his decorations. Therefore we, and all officials, have to wear all the Russian, Allied, and neutral regalia that we have.

A. A. KHVOSTOV: It appears to be a little too much honor for the mixed lot of gentlemen being assembled.

P. A. KHARITONOV: One must be prepared for the fact that, as in previous instances, the deputies will come in shirts and jackets.[5] It's more liberal that way. We shall shine with our stars and they with their virtues.

A. D. SAMARIN: It seems to me that this meeting should be made a bit more intimate. Public opinion connects many hopes with the Special Conference. One cannot limit the ceremony to one Imperial entrance and welcome. The Presidents of the State Council and the Duma should also offer a welcoming address to the Tsar. This is particularly important in the event that His Majesty takes it upon himself to actively direct the preparation of defense.

I. L. GOREMYKIN: But can one guarantee that Rodzianko will not pop up with preachments which might place the Emperor in an embarrassing situation and create complications? One can expect anything from that madman.

A. D. SAMARIN: I don't think so. It is true, of course, that the President of the Duma gets carried away by his self-imagined role of the chief representative of popular representation; still, he is a well-mannered man and loyal to the Monarch.

PRINCE N. B. SHCHERBATOV: He undoubtedly suffers from delusions of grandeur.

---

[4] The Special Conference on Defense and Supply was made up of representatives of the government, industry, and all the public groups and organizations, including workers, town, and *zemstvos*; it was to suggest the measures necessary to increase war production and mobilize Russian society for this task.

[5] Kharitonov used the word *kosovorotka,* the Russian shirt worn by peasants and the urban lower classes, and *spinzhak,* the word for jacket as it was, supposedly, mispronounced by the lower classes (correctly, *pidzhak*).

A. V. KRIVOSHEIN: And, withal, in a very dangerous stage of development.

It was decided to discuss the speeches of the presidents of the legislative chambers with the Minister of the Imperial Court, and the drafting of the Imperial welcome was assigned to A. V. Krivoshein.

The CHAIRMAN OF THE COUNCIL OF MINISTERS [Goremykin] offered for discussion a Duma proposal for the creation of a permanent organization with rather vague functions; it was to be made up of the elected representatives of the legislative institutions who were members of the Special Conference.

A. V. KRIVOSHEIN: I want to speak most decisively against this. It is either some kind of a Convention or a Committee of Public Safety.[6] Under the cloak of patriotic anxiety, they want to create some kind of second government. This proposal is nothing but an insolent attack against the government, a desire to create an extra reason for discrediting the government and to be able to scream about the restriction of self-sacrificing public initiative. Enough of such games, sewn with such white threads [sic]. One must take decisive measures that such a novella[7] not see the light. First of all, one should speak with the influential deputies. If they are not convinced (which is most probable), one must speak in the State Council and we must all vote against the projected law. And if this is not enough, I consider the question sufficiently important to petition the Emperor to refuse Imperial sanction. One cannot give way all the time—there will be no end to the pretensions. People are losing all sense of proportion, all consciousness of the difference between what is permissible and what is indecent. The Duma goes much too far, makes itself virtually into a constituent assembly, and wants to create Russian legislation on the basis of ignoring the executive power called to rule the state by the will of the Monarch. Everyone seems to be gripped by some kind of psychosis, an aberration of all feeling. We should either lay down our arms, or firmly and impressively point out that there is a limit to desires, that a government exists in Russia, and that it will not allow its authority to be torn to shreds.

---

[6] The reference is to the French Revolution.
[7] "Novella" is used in a legal sense.

A. A. KHVOSTOV: A. V. Krivoshein is absolutely right! It is time to give warning. In fact, the idea of such a law could only be born in highly feverish brains, unless it is a crude tactical maneuver to force the government into the expected refusal and then shout about its [the government's] obscurantism. The question is so serious that the use of the monarchic veto would be fully justified in this case. One cannot allow the legal formation of an irresponsible organization made up of irresponsible men hiding under parliamentary immunity.

P. A. KHARITONOV: The course of action which has been suggested is practical and proper to the occasion: We should openly oppose this at all levels and, if it becomes necessary, we should address ourselves directly to His Imperial Majesty. The very fact that such an awkward project has been proposed is highly characteristic of our insane times. Just think—to what absurdity people can be led, who seem quite reasonable in daily life but who are acting under the influence of party goals and narrow tactical considerations. One should put all these gentlemen into the Council of Ministers so that they could take a look at the kind of frying pan these same ministers are being fried in, hourly. Probably, many of them would quickly give up their dreams of alluring [ministerial] portfolios.

PRINCE N. B. SHCHERBATOV: Yes, we must show our claws. Many do not understand words unless they are accompanied by a meaningful gesture.

I. L. GOREMYKIN: I also share the opinion of A. V. Krivoshein. If no one is opposed, let us settle on that.

The Chairman of the Council of Ministers asked the Minister of War what was the status of the law for the mobilization of soldiers of the second class that was being examined by the Duma. A. A. Polivanov answered that so far the question was dragging on in committee with no end in sight.

A. V. KRIVOSHEIN: This is also a tactical maneuver, in order to postpone the adjournment of the session. We too, in turn, should answer this by a tactical maneuver—ask the Duma publicly: Do the gentlemen popular representatives want to defend themselves against the Germans or do they consider it superfluous to send the army the necessary replacements? With all this, one should declare a minimum time-span for the completion of the work on the law. If our demand will not be fulfilled within this time, the Duma will inevitably have to be adjourned and the soldiers will have to be mobilized by a manifesto.

I. L. GOREMYKIN: I should like to ask the Minister of War to discuss this with the Duma in this sense, and to warn it that the government insists categorically [on the passing of the law].

A. A. POLIVANOV gave warning that Headquarters was working out, at the present time, the problem of expanding the war theater into the interior of the country up to the approximate line of Tver'-Tula: In this manner, yet another good bit of Mother Russia leaves the hands of government authority and enters into the undivided possession of the redheaded Danilov.[8] "I have pointed out that, from the point of view of the War Ministry, this measure will create great difficulties for its activities in preparing and training replacements. And I have drawn attention to the fact that such a question could hardly be decided without consultation and agreement with the government. It seems to me that the Council of Ministers should intervene and protest. What was already pretty bad [9] in Germany and Poland, will be a national disaster close to Tula and Tver."

PRINCE N. B. SHCHERBATOV: We should not only protest, but categorically declare that this is impossible. The picture in the military rear area is one of sickening outrages, anarchy, arbitrariness, and absence of authority. One cannot hand over the central provinces to be abused by the redheaded Danilov and his horde of rear-echelon heroes. We have accumulated enough sad experiences to be able to say that the abolition of normal authority serves the cause of revolution.

A. V. KRIVOSHEIN: Seriously, people are being gripped by some kind of mass psychosis, by the eclipse of all feelings and reason. The generals in Headquarters, instead of thinking about how to stop the German advance, are worrying about establishing safer places for themselves, in the rear. They are either incapable or unwilling to take into account that, besides Headquarters and generals and

---

[8] Lieutenant-General Nikolai Alexandrovich Danilov: known as *ryzhii* ("redhead"), to distinguish him from the "Black Danilov" (cf. note 5, Chap. I). During the war, Chief of Supply for the Northwestern Front.

[9] That is, the chaotic retreat.

ensigns, there is also a Russia whose patience cannot be tried to the very end. One is frightened for the future.

I. L. GOREMYKIN (addressing himself to the Minister of War): Do write to them, pretty sharply, that their proposal is complete nonsense and that the Council of Ministers does not allow even of the possibility of deepening the military zone at the rear and removing it from the competence of civilian authority. In the meantime, I will talk this over with His Majesty the Emperor and ask him to rein in the authors of this project.

A. A. POLIVANOV: But there is an even cuter little project afoot. This time it does not come directly from Headquarters, but from General-Adjutant Ivanov.[10] The Commander-in-Chief of the Southern Front finds it necessary, in order to achieve victory over the enemy, to evacuate, forcibly, a frontal zone one hundred versts deep.[11]

The arguments on this question are not written down in my notes in detail, but only the following general words: Unanimously considered impermissible. From the military point of view, a mass arrival of refugees restricts the movement of troops and [messes up] the zone of the immediate rear. From the general, State, point of view, the complete evacuation of the population with the [accompanying] destruction of property and general ruination is out of the question. Besides, it is done brutally and forcibly, including the killing, by punitive expeditions, of landowners who refuse to abandon their estates. The burning of buildings and crops is an extreme irritant, and the peasants are even arming in order to guard their property from destruction. Factories and plants, containing supplies of raw materials for the evacuation of which no measures are being taken, are also being destroyed.

PRINCE V. N. SHAKHOVSKOY: The systematic devastation of the frontal territories of the southwest forces one to think that the Supreme Command does not hope to recover this area for Russia

---

[10] General-Adjutant. The highest military honorific title, denoting Imperial favor and allowing its possessor to wear the Emperor's initials (instead of the badge of his rank) on his epaulettes. This title was borrowed by the Russians from German (Prussian) and Austrian usage.

[11] A *versta* is about a kilometer: 3,500 feet.

and wants to leave the enemy a total desert. Is the military situation so utterly hopeless?

A. A. POLIVANOV: The staffs have lost the ability to reason and to restrain their own actions. Everyone exists in some kind of madness. A military commander does not have the right to lose hope till the last minute. A retreat must always be regarded as temporary. A skillful leader, while retreating, is at the same time preparing his advance. With us, exactly the reverse has taken place.

A. V. KRIVOSHEIN: What is happening is simply monstrous! It's as if people were doing deliberately everything to ruin Russia, to push Russia into the abyss. No people ever saved themselves by ruining themselves.

PRINCE N. B. SHCHERBATOV: And I would add also—by moral degeneration. In the chaos of retreating wagon trains and military units, voluntary and involuntary refugees, of Jews chased on by whips—in the midst of this tired, hungry, abused mob, some kind of mad bacchanal is taking place. Drunkenness, robbery, debauchery are flowering. The reports which come to me state bluntly that the Cossacks and soldiers are deliberately dragging families of refugees behind them, in order to have women during the march to whom they give looted property. Thus they are able to have a good time. It seems to me one can't go much further. If Headquarters will not reject Ivanov's project, one must beg the Emperor to intervene in this outrageous mess.

It is decided to write to the Chief of Staff of the Supreme Commander, in a categorical tone, that the Council of Ministers considers wholesale evacuation and the destruction of property in districts abandoned or designated for abandonment to the enemy, absolutely impermissible.

I. L. GOREMYKIN: We shall write the letter together with Ivan Nikolaevich [Lodyzhensky], and besides this, I shall direct the Emperor's attention to this utter outrage. They're losing their heads completely at the front.

PRINCE N. B. SHCHERBATOV: Polish representatives have complained to me about the following: Twenty-four hours before the departure of our army from Warsaw, the gendarmes, at the orders of military authorities, arrested a whole mass of people—Poles and

Jews—on suspicion of pro-Austrian sympathies. No exceptions were made, even for minors. All these arrested people have been sent to the rear and put into prisons. I have checked this information, and it is quite accurate. The Poles are outraged because people were apparently arrested without discrimination, and they are requesting a reexamination of this action, which does not in any way accord, they claim, with the spirit of the address of the Chairman of the Council of Ministers on the day the Duma opened.[12] I should like to ask the Council of Ministers for instructions. What should be done in this case? The whole thing occurred within the theater of operations, and the Minister of Internal Affairs has no voice there.

S. D. SAZONOV: The men who are in control there are simply mad. Instead of leaving behind them a population well-disposed toward us, the gentlemen generals do everything possible to have our retreating troops followed by curses. I must say, a pretty good atmosphere is being created for the solution of Russo-Polish relations! The appeal of the Supreme Commander, the declaration of the government before the legislative chambers, the generally conciliatory direction of our policy on the Polish question—all this apparently is a lie, superficial, while the reality is the arbitrariness of the generals. I can imagine the impression on our Allies when they learn that babies are being put into jail for pro-Austrian sympathies. It is essential to dispose of this scandal with the utmost silence and speed. I will report to His Majesty that such military despotism makes it impossible to conduct any [foreign] policy.

It is agreed to release minors immediately, as well as those against whom there is no convincing evidence, and to report about the whole matter to the Emperor.

I. L. GOREMYKIN: I beg the Council of Ministers to discuss the problem of the press. It has allowed itself the devil knows what, lately!

A. V. KRIVOSHEIN: During my last report, His Majesty the Emperor spoke about this problem and expressed his dissatisfaction with the sharp tone of the newspapers and their interference in matters which are none of their business. In fact, our press has

---

[12] In this speech, Poland was promised self-government after the war ended.

violated all the boundaries, not only of what is permitted but of simple good taste. Until now, only the Moscow papers distinguished themselves in this way, but in the last few days the Petrograd ones also act as if they have jumped the leash. They have taken a position that would not be allowed in any republic, let alone in a monarchy, particularly in wartime. Continuous abuse, unfounded condemnation, the stirring up of public opinion against the government, the spreading of sensational rumors—all this, day after day, is acting on the psyche of 180 million people. After all, we have a military censorship law, and there are military censors, swarms of generals and ensigns, in the rear offices. Finally, we do have a special head of the Chief Administration of the Press. What is this whole Areopagus waiting for? One must take decisive steps and stir up those who need it.

PRINCE N. B. SHCHERBATOV: At the front, censorship is subject to the military authorities. The Minister of Internal Affairs and the head of the Chief Administration of the Press, as the Council of Ministers well knows, are plain and speechless onlookers at the front. The civil, preliminary, censorship was abolished long ago, and my ministry has no way to stop, in time, the publication of all the impudent lies and agitational articles which fill our newspapers.

P. A. KHARITONOV: If the generals, who have unlimited authority and who use it gladly on other occasions, do not wish to help the Ministry of Internal Affairs to deal with the banditry of the press, then one should send them to hell and replace them with others, more complacent.

A. A. KHVOSTOV: One should pay particular attention to articles which stir up unfounded public hopes and expectations. Here, there is deliberate lying—to announce things and then accuse the government or, still worse, to accuse the "influences." Now all the newspapers are shouting about a general amnesty which must take place, if not today then tomorrow, and about the return to the Duma of the five deputies convicted of participation in a conspiracy against the safety of the State and of defeatist propaganda.[13] This idea is

---

[13] Five Social-Democratic (Bolshevik) deputies were arrested despite their parliamentary immunity in the fall of 1914, and were convicted of conspiracy against the State on insufficient evidence in February, 1915.

being seriously discussed in workers' circles, and could become the basis of dangerous complications. After all, if we do not have armed uprisings of workers right now, it is only because they have no organization, and these five deputies were the chief organizers. One cannot allow the newspapers to print rumors designed for propagandistic purposes.

A. A. POLIVANOV: Everyone here is attacking the generals—that they are so bad at reining in the press. But they are military men, and not particularly skilled in political nuances. They understand their task in the way in which it was always framed for military censors—that is, not to allow the publication of anything which may be useful to the enemy.

A. V. KRIVOSHEIN: The stirring up of public anxiety and the spread of a revolutionary mood in the country is more useful to the enemy than any other sins of the press.

P. A. KHARITONOV: If the military censors are unable to figure this out, one should assign civil advisors to them and order the censors to obey them.

A. A. POLIVANOV: Absolutely correct. The generals cannot afford to start distinguishing the permissible from the impermissible, from the point of view of the changing interests of internal policy. They should be reinforced by people who are competent in these questions.

P. A. KHARITONOV: Yes, and they should be strictly ordered to follow such instructions. And if the generals do not want to obey, and refer to their independence of civilian authority, then one must report to His Imperial Majesty. Even if the Council of Ministers is helpless, there still must be some check over the gentlemen censor-generals.

A. A. KHVOSTOV: There is yet another and more practical method of attaining the goal. One should ask the Minister of Finance to put more pressure on the banks, on which the greater bulk of Russian independent newspapers depend.

P. L. BARK: I have spoken about it constantly, and I remind everyone of it constantly. It is difficult to put pressure on the banks, for they do not possess the necessary organization to influence the press, day by day.

P. A. KHARITONOV: There is still another action possible, one even more to our purpose—to close down two or three newspapers at once, so that they take thought and feel the problem in their own pockets.

P. L. BARK: It seems to me that the whole trouble is that, with polyarchy, anarchy is inevitable. The press takes advantage of it, and its desires and demands are known to everyone. To slap a couple of newspapers shut will be a sobering demonstration.

P. A. KHARITONOV: And one should slap down newspapers of various tendencies, right and left. *Zemshchina* and *Russkoe znamia* are no less harmful than the various *Dni, Raneo Utro* and similar organs.

S. D. SAZONOV: *Novoe* and *Vechernee Vremia* are also not very good. I consider them no less harmful than the various little sheets designed for sensationalism and for circulation build-up.

P. A. KHARITONOV: Both these newspapers are under special patronage, and military censorship will not raise a hand against them. Since the beginning of the war, the Suvorins[14] have constantly fawned before Headquarters, and therefore they [the censors] have been instructed not to touch them under any circumstances.

PRINCE N. B. SHCHERBATOV: P. A. Kharitonov's idea, that one should close down a few particularly violent newspapers, of various tendencies, is very useful. First of all, one maintains balance and impartiality, and, second of all, first a poke in the snoot and then a friendly chat. At the present, the majority are in such fine fettle that without an eloquent introduction they cannot be reasoned with.

A. V. KRIVOSHEIN: I would consider it best to reinforce military censorship with civilian officials and, at the same time, warn the newspapers that if they do not change their tone they will be ruthlessly punished, up to and including being closed down.

I. L. GOREMYKIN: We must request the Minister of Internal

---

[14] Boris Alekseevich and Mikhail Alekseevich Suvorins, brothers and owners of *Novoe Vremia* (*New Times*), the largest newspaper in Petrograd, founded by their father, the famous journalist A. S. Suvorin (1834-1912). Liberal in the beginning, the newspaper swung more and more to the right, chiefly on account of the lack of principles of the old Suvorin and his heirs. Boris, though the younger brother, ran the family business. At the beginning of the War, Boris opportunistically got on the bandwagon and demanded the elimination of all Germans, whether of Russian or foreign birth, from all areas of Russian life. In this he joined the program of the extreme Right.

Affairs to occupy himself with this question immediately, in agreement with the military authorities, and to force the press effectively within proper boundaries. Things cannot continue this way.

PRINCE N. B. SHCHERBATOV: Very well, we will take the necessary measures, and then the Duma will raise protests, questions, and scandals. What will we reply, when we know that we do not have a legal right to establish civilian censorship?

I. L. GOREMYKIN: The matter is sufficiently serious to extend a warning that interference from the Duma in this question could serve as cause for adjournment.

P. L BARK: I think that it will not be necessary to use such a threat. In the Duma they understand perfectly well that encouraging political passions and desires by the press isn't permissible in wartime. Everywhere abroad, both among our enemies and our Allies, even in republican France, the press is subject to the strictest regulation, and serves as a weapon against the enemy. If, despite all this, talk and rumors still arise, one can always reply that the measures are being taken at the demand of the military authorities in the interest of securing the military defense of the country.

I. L. GOREMYKIN: I do not particularly share P. L. Bark's optimism about the reasonableness of the Duma. In any event, let us see what will happen.

THE CHIEF OF CHANCELLERY read aloud a telegram from Bakherakht, our Ambassador in Switzerland, sent over by the Ministry of Foreign Affairs, concerning the immediate need for an official denial of rumors being spread in neutral countries by pro-German newspapers about the hopeless economic situation of Russia, and that Russia is on the brink of final bankruptcy.

At this point A. V. KRIVOSHEIN interrupted the reading of the telegram and exclaimed, "What is false about it? It's the absolute truth!"

P. L. BARK looked at him, not without reproach, but remained silent.

In my notes I have: "They're still very nervous. Polivanov remains mostly silent during the discussion, with an air of opposition. Samarin looks anxious and sad. Ignat'ev, for some reason, refrains from participating in the general exchange of opinions."

X

The Meeting of
18 August 1915

———◆———

I will begin with my conclusions: "A long meeting: A whole mass of questions. Great nervousness. Jumping from one problem to another, cutting short the discussion, and dodging any resolutions. Much was expressed that was interesting and characteristic. I wasn't strong enough to take minutes for so many hours. Nevertheless, I write it down if only to leave a trace in history, as V. N. Kokovtsev used to say. And will I have a chance, ever, to occupy myself with this history? If one is to judge the state of affairs by the conversations of the Council, then, instead of writing history, one will soon be hung from a lamp post."

PRINCE N. B. SHCHERBATOV: In Moscow, at Konovalov's,[1] there was a secret meeting of so-called progressive people—to put it simply, Cadets and fellow-travelers—to discuss the situation of the country. As I understand it, those assembled unanimously agreed

---

[1] Alexander Ivanovich Konovalov: born 1875; Progressive deputy to the 4th Duma; owner of large textile manufacturing business; very influential in industrial and commercial circles in Moscow. Entered the Provisional Government, after the revolution, as Minister of Trade and Industry; resigned in May, 1917, but re-entered the cabinet as Vice-Prime Minister in September, 1917.

to take advantage of the favorable situation in order to present demands for the formation of a government possessing full powers and the confidence of the country. The mood was most warlike, but under a patriotic flag. Apparently, the order was given for various localities to come forth with similar demands. The Moscow City Council is supposed to start first. I sent a telegram saying that the Moscow administration should not allow this question to be raised at the meeting of the [City] Council. I am afraid that the Council will go ahead anyway. How should one react then? In general, this assembly of Konovalov's is pregnant with consequences.

There was discussion concerning the difficult situation of the government, concerning the beginning of a decisive attack on the government, openly propagandized by the press, concerning the difficult and sharp complications which are forthcoming, and so on; but no particular measures were proposed. Again, one is gripped by a feeling of helplessness before the coming storm.

The dismissal of General Dzhunkovsky is a fact.[2] The impression it made on the public is a great one, because of the rumor which has spread that this dismissal was the consequence of an attempt to struggle with the "influences."

A. V. KRIVOSHEIN: The departure of Dzhunkovsky from the administration is an enormous scandal, not only for the government but even for the higher [authority]. He does not have the moral right to abandon his post because of personal dissatisfaction. It is not fitting for a military man, who also has the honor to be in the Suite of His Imperial Majesty,[3] to retire in wartime and when the State is in a difficult situation. The reference to [his] material circumstances was dragged in artificially. These circumstances can always be arranged, but one cannot allow oneself to demonstrate to

---

[2] Vladimir Fedorovich Dzhunkovsky: Major-General in the Suite of His Majesty; Vice-Minister of Internal Affairs and Chief of the Corps of Gendarmes from 1913 to August, 1915. Dismissed for presenting to Nicholas II an exposé of Rasputin's debauches in Moscow.

[3] The implication is that Dzhunkovsky, bearing the honorific title of Major-General in the Suite, and thus possessing the personal favor of the Emperor, had a particular personal obligation of loyalty, virtually in the feudal sense.

a point which acquires virtually a political character. If the statesmen who possess [public] sympathy are going to run away, then with whom is the government—which has been appointed by the Imperial will—going to be left, in its present composition? I always considered Dzhunkovsky a gentleman, and did not expect such an ill-mannered outburst from him.

Everybody was sad over this, and the discussion concluded with the ironic words of P. A. KHARITONOV: Well, nothing to be done—extraordinary times are what we live in!

A. A. POLIVANOV: I can report to the Council of Ministers that His Majesty has finally signed the orders appointing General Ianushkevich as assistant to the Viceroy of the Caucasus, and General Alekseev to the post of Chief of Staff of the Supreme Commander.

GENERAL EXCLAMATIONS: "Thank God!" "It was long overdue!" and so on.

P. A. KHARITONOV: Well, we should finish this up now, and we shall see later what is to happen.

A. D. SAMARIN: I am in full agreement with this wish. One should ask His Majesty for this.

A. V. KRIVOSHEIN: The removal of Ianushkevich is a great victory for the front. [But,] as the military say, it is not enough to win; it is necessary to use the victory skillfully.

A. A. POLIVANOV: The question of replacing Alekseev with General Evert at the front is being held up a little. At Headquarters they are having difficulty finding a name for the middle Front. This important argument focuses on two suggestions concerning the most useful and purposeful nomenclature—western Front or northwestern. One must hope that General Alekseev, with the decisiveness which is his in critical moments, will find an acceptable solution, and that the war which has been started in Headquarters will cease.

The Minister of War's remark, and his sarcasm, were noted by the Council of Ministers.

General P. A. Frolov came to the meeting, to which he had been invited in order to participate in the discussion of the problem of the press. I do not remember his post at that time—either he was Commander of the Petrograd military district, or he was chief of something or other at the northern Front, which was responsible for the fate of Petrograd.[4] I. L. GOREMYKIN drew his attention to the immediate necessity of putting an end to the debauchery of the newspapers, and to the need for forbidding the publication of articles and news which implant anxiety in the population, which undermine the authority of the government, and so forth.

P. A. FROLOV: The chaos in the press began with General Zvonnikov's circular which released military censors from the duty of checking the civilian aspects of printed works. The circular was, in turn, based on instructions from Headquarters. I have no authority to interfere in these matters, for the military censorship administration is not subject to me, as it is a central and not a local organization. His Majesty the Emperor ordered me to take measures, within the framework of my military authority, in the Petrograd military district. This I can do with the power that I have. His Majesty told me bluntly: "God knows what is being written in the newspapers! They must be properly reined in. One cannot continue to fight calmly at the front when this calm is daily poisoned by incredible rumors about the internal situation." This means, as I understand it, that I am the stick which must beat more harshly. But if one has to exact retribution, I want to aim well. This business is new to me—only yesterday was it put in my hands. I will assemble all the editors; I will speak to them frankly and try to persuade them. But if they do not meet me halfway, then I shall take recourse by applying the necessary punishments, including the forcible travel of the obdurate to areas far from the capital.[5] I very much want the help of the Ministry of Internal Affairs and the instructions of the Council of Ministers as to what I should primarily pay attention to. Then, there is also the forthcoming convening of a Special Commission, under the chairmanship of General

---

[4] This comment was obviously added by Iakhontov at a later date. General Sergei Petrovich Frolov: commanded the Petrograd military district from April 22, 1915 to September 14, 1915; After that date was Chief Quartermaster of the northern Front.

[5] The traditional euphemism for exile, frequently to Siberia.

Beliaev,[6] which will work out proper instructions for military censors.

A. V. KRIVOSHEIN: Are any written instructions possible in such a matter as censorship in wartime, other than common sense, patriotism, and thoughtfulness? None of us has ever been a censor, but we understand the essence of what is impermissible in the destructive work of the contemporary press. It seems to me that each military man should understand that internal peace is particularly important to the success of the war.

P. A. FROLOV: Yes, but these same military men are fighting at the front, and we have to work primarily with ensigns who are former lawyers or come from other liberal professions. The overwhelming majority of them understand internal peace in their own way.

I. L. GOREMYKIN: In any event, the sense of the Imperial order announced to us by General Frolov does not allow of any doubts. The press must be brought to order, at whatever cost. I request you, General, to take this most seriously and, without any committees, to occupy yourself with this question. As far as Zvonnikov[7] is concerned, I will speak with His Majesty. Where did that general pop up from, with his idiotic circulars? It's an outrage!

The exhaustion of the countryside by total mobilizations, or, as A. V. KRIVOSHEIN expressed it, "the requisitioning of the population of Russia for re-enforcement of the garrisons which are doing nothing in the rear," has complicated the problem of agricultural labor to the point that the harvest could become a catastrophe. Particularly hard hit is the Far East, where the wheat crop is a marvelous one, but is remaining in the fields. This question has occupied the Council of Ministers greatly, and the Council, reversing former practice, has recognized the possibility of using Yellow labor in the fields.[8] A. V. Krivoshein, who observed that he is

---

[6] General Mikhail Alekseevich Beliaev: Chief of the General Staff in 1914; Vice-Minister of War from June, 1915, though retaining his former post; from January 3, 1917, to the revolution—February 27, 1917—Minister of War.

[7] Lieutenant-General Aleksei Ivanovich Zvonnikov (1865-1919): military jurist; from the beginning of the war, chairman of the Petrograd military censorship commission.

[8] That is, the importation of Chinese agricultural workers from Manchuria.

adopting this measure most reluctantly but sees no other solution, was authorized to issue the necessary instructions.

A. A. POLIVANOV announced that His Majesty the Emperor deigned to express his consent to the Presidents of the Legislative Chambers presenting him with a welcoming address at the opening of the Special Conference on Defense and Supply; also, that the submission of a memorandum, by M. V. Rodzianko, in the name of the deputies of the Duma was considered acceptable.

A. V. KHVOSTOV: I expect little good from such *démarches* before the Tsar. They will only upset the Sovereign by some insolent behavior.

I. L. GOREMYKIN: They should be warned that the consequences might be most unpleasant for them.

Submitted by A. V. KRIVOSHEIN, the redaction of the Imperial Rescript for Grand Duke Nicholas on the occasion of the change in the supreme command was approved by the Council of Ministers without objections. It was decided to petition for the publication of this Rescript not in Petrograd, but on the spot, in Imperial Headquarters, at the moment His Majesty the Emperor entered on the direct leadership of military activities.

A. D. SAMARIN: Simultaneously with this petition of the Council of Ministers, I beg you to report to His Majesty my particular opinion that this Rescript should not be published anywhere, nor signed. My conscience does not allow me to give my sanction to an act which ruins Russia and the monarchy. I will never tire of repeating it.

[There followed a long discussion on the possible need to prepare for the evacuation of the industrial resources and artistic treasures of Petrograd, threatened by the German advance.—*Ed.*]

I. L. GOREMYKIN: Yes, God guards him who guards himself.[9]
It was decided to ask for General Ruzsky's opinion, and to return to this question in one of the forthcoming meetings.

A. D. SAMARIN: The Most Holy Synod, as the Council of Ministers knows, has appealed to the Orthodox people, in a special

---

[9] A Russian proverb.

epistle, to resort to fast and prayer because of the misfortunes that have befallen the motherland. It would appear that an Orthodox government should respond to this appeal by closing down all places of entertainment during the fast days.

General sympathy. The Minister of Internal Affairs is authorized to take the necessary measures for the 26th, 27th, 28th, and 29th of August.

A. V. KRIVOSHEIN: It seems to me that the problem of entertainment is acquiring general significance in our difficult times. Both in France and in England decisive steps have been taken about this, and public opinion itself rules out various café amusements.[10] While here everyone shouts "Everything for the war!"—but they refuse to renounce voluntarily their pleasures and their drunkenness. Hence, the government must interfere and stop these outrages. Hundreds of thousands are dying at the front and in the refugee trains, while the aquariums[11] blaze with light and resound with music.

PRINCE N. B. SHCHERBATOV: The question is not only one of principle, but a practical one also—the useless expenditure of electricity while there is not enough for the factories because of the shortage of fuel. And besides, quite unnecessary gatherings of people and seedbeds of gossip.

A. V. KRIVOSHEIN: One cannot manage without compulsory measures. I recall the anecdote about the French judge who asked all the respectable ladies to leave the hall at the hearing of a rather racy case and was shocked to see that no one left.

I. L. GOREMYKIN: Here one has to act differently: Suggest to the respectable people that they leave, and escort the nonrespectable people out.

A. D. SAMARIN: All these triumphant taverns are producing a highly negative impression on the people. I have had to listen to the sharpest remarks against a government which does not interfere with this, and allows this kind of debauchery in the capital.

P. A. KHARITONOV: On the other hand, one must try to under-

---

[10] A slight exaggeration, considering the amount of night life in Paris and London during the war.

[11] That is, night clubs.

stand the circumstances of the military men who return from the front—the desire to refresh the nerves and to forget the endless tension. It is forgivable for the youth to have a good time, when they risk their lives every minute.

A. V. KRIVOSHEIN: Yes, but this consideration does not change the basic question of the need for a healthier rear, and particularly in the capital of the Empire, which sets the tone for the whole country.

A. A. KHVOSTOV: One should establish a curfew after which all places of entertainment must be closed. One should also restrict restaurant hours. It is quite unnecessary that people sit there until morning and be served forbidden alcohol. Two hours for dinner, two for supper, and two for breakfast are quite sufficient.

I. L. GOREMYKIN: I, too, agree—the less entertainment, the fewer outrages. But A. A. Khvostov's idea, that it should be done gradually, is correct.

THE MINISTER OF INTERNAL AFFAIRS [Shcherbatov] is charged with discussing, with the military authorities of Petrograd, the issuance of compulsory instructions.

PRINCE N. B. SHCHERBATOV: Well, now we are talking about the epistle of the Holy Synod. Have the gentlemen members of the Council of Ministers noticed the article on this epistle in the *Vechernee Vremia*? It would be little enough to thrash Boris Suvorin for such a trick.

A. D. SAMARIN: The article is an outrageous one, and evokes justified anger that its author has not suffered exemplary punishment. In 1905, even the most extreme little newspapers did not allow themselves to use such a tone.

I. L. GOREMYKIN, A. V. KRIVOSHEIN AND A. A. POLIVANOV declared, with one voice, that the newspaper deserves immediate closure.

P. A. KHARITONOV: The respected Boris Suvorin has gone a little too far. He has been spoiled by his status as the unpunishable favorite of Headquarters. Now there is an end to that patronage. . . .

I. L. GOREMYKIN: It would be good to put that madman into a strait jacket. He has absolutely no idea of what he is doing. If we clamp down on *Vechernee Vremia*, it will sober up the other newspapers as well. They will pull in their heads, and not dare to touch questions which cannot serve as subjects for *démarches* and ill-mannered articles.

PRINCE N. B. SHCHERBATOV: It would be embarrassing to begin with Suvorin. There is already a rumor in the public about the government's dissatisfaction with his irreconcilable position on the question of German influence. Undoubtedly, the closing down of his newspaper will be quickly explained by this dissatisfaction.

I. L. GOREMYKIN: The simplest way would be for the Minister of Internal Affairs [Shcherbatov] to call Boris Suvorin in and rinse his head properly. If he continues to misbehave, then one can send him off somewhere, pretty far away. In general, the Ministry of Internal Affairs must pay particular attention to the press. Otherwise it is beginning to get to a point where only the devil knows what's going on.

XI

The Meeting of
19 August 1915

—————◆—————

THE MINISTER OF INTERNAL AFFAIRS [Shcherbatov] reported on the growing public excitement in Moscow in connection with the Konovalov meeting. An immediate echo of this meeting was the resolution by the Moscow City Council, containing many points: in favor of a government possessing the confidence of the country, of a greeting to be addressed to the Grand Duke the Supreme Commander, of an Imperial audience for the representatives of the Moscow City Council, and so forth. Unfortunately, I did not record Prince Shcherbatov's report in detail, and I do not have the resolutions of the Moscow Council at hand. At the end I noted: "The discussion had a particularly heated, even sharp, character. They spoke so quickly, interrupting each other, that one had to catch everything in flight. Not a discussion, but a cross-fire argument.

I. L. GOREMYKIN: The report of the Minister of Internal Affairs deserves serious attention. So-called public figures are beginning to take a course of action that necessitates giving them a proper rebuff.

PRINCE N. B. SHCHERBATOV: The demands of the Moscow Council for an Imperial audience are impermissible both in form and in substance. One cannot conduct political conversations with the Tsar, over the heads of the government and the legislative institutions. We must immediately take the most decisive measures, either in one direction or the other. It cannot continue this way any longer. Either there is a government or there isn't. I do not see a third possibility.

A. A. KHVOSTOV: There exist legally justifiable reasons for the cancellation of the resolutions of the Moscow City Council. Thereby the announced petition would fall away by itself.

I. L. GOREMYKIN: That's an extreme measure. It is better, in this case, to avoid using a formalistic reason. We must decide, substantively, whether or not it is desirable that Chelnokov[1] be received in Tsarskoe Selo for the submission of the Moscow resolution.

P. A. KHARITONOV: A question every aspect of which is pregnant with consequences. One should not forget that the Muscovites are speaking under the banner of loyal emotions.

I. L. GOREMYKIN: The question is, of course, a ticklish one. But I fully agree with the Minister of Internal Affairs that one cannot conduct political conversations with the Tsar over the heads of the government and the legislative institutions. We must, in some way, support His Majesty the Emperor at this difficult moment and find a solution which will ease his situation.

PRINCE N. B. SHCHERBATOV: One can foresee that Moscow will be followed by other towns and that the Emperor will be literally swamped by hundreds of petitions.

I. L. GOREMYKIN: The simplest way, of course, would be not to answer all these chatterers, and not to pay any attention to them as long as they are poking their noses into a sphere outside their competence.

A. A. POLIVANOV: I cannot agree with the oversimplified solution of a question of the greatest political importance which has been suggested by the Chairman of the Council of Ministers. It is

---

[1] Mikhail Vasilevich Chelnokov: Member of the Duma from 1906; Cadet deputy to the 2nd, 3rd, and 4th Dumas; elected Mayor of Moscow in 1914; also elected President of the Union of Towns in 1914; owner of four brick-making factories; a member of a wealthy industrial family.

important to keep in mind that the city government of the first capital [2] is announcing, to all of Russia, its unshakable confidence in the Supreme Commander, the Grand Duke, as the leader of our armies against the enemies. We must draw the attention of His Majesty to this, and beg him to postpone the change of command and his departure for Headquarters. Otherwise, the change-over, coming immediately after the Moscow resolution, will make a very negative impression and will be interpreted as a kind of challenge. Besides, what is so impermissible or revolutionary in the resolution? A government which is based on the confidence of the population—this, after all, is the normal State order.

s. d. sazonov: The events in Moscow convince me, still more, of the necessity of postponing, in any way possible, the issue of command. It is necessary that neither the Grand Duke nor His Majesty the Emperor move and that everything appear as of old, on the surface at least. In the meantime, His Majesty should receive Chelnokov as the Moscow city head, and not as the representative of the Council, and, in conversation with him, try to soften the sharpness of the issues. In such a conversation, the Emperor could ask Chelnokov to speak his mind about the times we are living through, and in this way the Emperor could ignore the collective demands and the resolution itself. More correctly, not ignore, but pass over with silence.

a. d. samarin: The mood in Moscow serves as a vivid and quick example for what I have constantly said in the Council of Ministers. The change of command threatens the gravest consequences for our motherland. The resolution of the Moscow City Council, in the contemporary context of heightened and sharpened emotions in Russia, is actually quite moderate. It would be a mistake to regard it as a simple political *démarche* against the existing government. It is caused by anxiety for the fate of the State, and an expression of this anxiety is the affirmation of profound confidence in the Grand Duke. This one cannot refuse to consider; one cannot simply dismiss it. One also cannot use the measure recommended by the Minister of Justice [Khvostov]: namely, the

---

[2] Moscow was called the "first capital" (*Pervoprestol'naia*) because it had been the earlier one.

voiding of the Council's resolution. This would be, forgive me, simply too rude and improper, especially because the resolution speaks of continuing the war to the death. Such a wish cannot be answered either by cancelling it or by silence. One also cannot refuse to receive the Moscow city head. This would be an undeserved insult to Moscow, the first capital of the Empire. Since the first days of the war, Moscow has frequently proved its patriotism. It deserves the right to express to the Tsar its anxiety for the future of the motherland in a critical time. For me, the problem is not simply whether one should or should not receive the representative of the first capital, but how one should receive him, and what one should say to him during the reception. It seems to me that one should not postpone the audience, but should arrange it as soon as possible, in order to avoid unnecessary rumors and discontent. The reception itself should be particularly gracious and favorable. In the course of the conversation, His Majesty could express his gratitude to Moscow for the sentiments which it has expressed; he could state his full confidence in the sincerity of its wishes; he could announce that the Tsar understands the necessity for public confidence in the government; he is occupied with this matter and, under his direction, everything has been done and will continue to be done, and so forth.

I. L. GOREMYKIN: That is, A. D. Samarin suggests that we should neither fight nor make peace.

A. D. SAMARIN: That formulation does not quite convey my thought. I would add just one other word—"to caress." And then, in the report to His Majesty the Emperor, I would emphasize that the resolution of the Moscow City Council cannot be regarded as in any way an arrogantly revolutionary one, that one cannot deny the necessity that the government possess the country's confidence, and that the words addressed by the Council to the Grand Duke serve as yet another confirmation of the impossibility of changing command under present circumstances.

P. A. KHARITONOV: I consider the most important point in the resolution of the Moscow City Council to be the address to the Grand Duke, exactly now, when the Emperor's decision is known to all. Hence this address is placed there deliberately, as a sort of warning. This cannot be ignored. In the course of the war, Moscow has become a focus of public activity, and her voice is a reflection of a significant part of the Russian population. We must explain this to His Majesty, and, if it is not too late, attempt once again to dissuade him from undertaking the immediate execution of his decision. As far as the audience is concerned, it is quite necessary, in my opinion. One should never provoke geese deliberately.

A. V. KRIVOSHEIN: The report of the Minister of Internal Affairs [Shcherbatov] has shaken me deeply. It is in complete accord with the private news I have received from Moscow. The mood there is a very heightened one, and one can expect consequences which would hopelessly complicate the internal situation and which could create conditions which would make the conduct of the war hopeless. In any event, the government should, at all costs, avoid actions which might increase public irritability. From this point of view, I find that the reception of the Moscow city head is quite inevitable and that it should be set up in the way pointed out by A. D. Samarin. But I cannot hide from the Council of Ministers my opinion that the issue is, in principle, far broader and more significant. Undoubtedly, Moscow will be followed by other towns and *zemstvos,* and by public organizations with similar wishes and demands. In what kind of a situation will we find ourselves when not only the press and the Military-Industrial Committee but the entire organized Russian public is loudly demanding a government possessing public confidence? I do not wish to touch on personal feelings, but, from the point of view of the interests of State administration and the organization of defense, such a situation is quite impossible. In any event, it cannot go on for very long. One must find a way out, ahead of time, and one must settle on a definite decision and a plan of action. One must either react with force and with faith—in one's own power, in the possibility of achieving success—or one must openly embark on a course of acquiring moral confidence for the government. It is my deepest conviction that we are capable of neither the one nor the other. The conclusion from all this is clear: We must state all this openly to the Emperor, who is not conscious of the existing situation and who is not aware of the condition his government (and, hence, all the affairs of government administration) is in; we must open the Monarch's eyes to the extraordinary acuteness of the present moment, and to the fact that much of the fate of our motherland will depend on one or the other solution. This is our sacred duty in the historic moment in which we live. We must tell His Majesty that the internal situation, as it exists (to dig about in its causes and origins is now too late, and useless, anyway)—these conditions allow of only two solutions: either a strong military dictatorship, if one can find a suitable person, or reconciliation with the public. Our Cabinet does not correspond to public hopes and demands, and it must give way to another in which the country can believe. To delay, to continue to hold on in the middle and wait out events, is impossible. The atmosphere is becoming graver with every hour. The decision to take over the command, which has become known everywhere, has served to increase the nervousness of various circles of the population. I completely agree that this decision is, as A. D. Samarin has said, a fatal one. An enormous risk, the results of which cannot be predicted even approximately, is concealed in it; one can only foresee that they will be most difficult for Russia and for the success of the war. This is not the time to risk rejecting the overwhelming majority. We must ask His Majesty to meet with us, and we must beg him to renounce removing the Grand Duke and, at the same time, to change, fundamentally, the character of internal policy. I hesitated for a long time before I finally came to such a conclusion, but right now every day is like a year. The situation is changing with dizzying speed. From all sides, one is forced to listen to the grimmest prediction [of what will happen] if no decisive steps are taken to calm public anxiety. This is said by people whose loyalty to the Monarch cannot be doubted. I was visited by Count Kokovtsev, who firmly and insistently drew my attention to the fact that things cannot go on this way any longer, that irritation and dissatisfaction are increasing everywhere, and that ominous rumors are coming from Moscow. One cannot, after all, dismiss the fact that the Moscow City Council's resolution of confidence in the Grand Duke was unanimous. Even Shmakov[3] and his followers voted for the resolution. Under the circumstances, it would be difficult to label it a revolutionary one. Not revolu-

---

[3] Aleksei Semenovich Shmakov; lawyer; extreme anti-Semite; leader of the extreme right wing in the Moscow City Council.

tion, but infinite fear for the future! We must honestly, without concealment and euphemisms, explain to the Emperor that the step he has thought up is, besides everything else, an enormous risk for the dynasty. As most loyal servants of the Russian Tsar to whom the fate of our motherland is tied, we are forced to say that the dismissal of the Grand Duke is impossible, and that we cannot answer for order and safety in the country. Nevertheless, it is undoubtedly true that the matter has gone too far and that a complete reversal of his decision would reflect on the Monarch's prestige. A compromise is quite possible: The Tsar assumes Supreme Command and appoints the Grand Duke as his assistant. Before this basic issue, all else is petty detail which can be arranged when this question is decided. It must be done at once. It is dangerous to play so long with fire. We must be firm and insistent before His Imperial Majesty. If necessary, we should not only beg but demand. Let the Tsar cut off our heads, let him exile us to distant places and deprive us of title, rank, and decorations (unfortunately, he will not do this); but in the event that our presentation is rejected, we must, in the interests of the motherland, announce to him that, in all conscience, we can no longer serve him.

PRINCE V. N. SHAKHOVSKOY: A. V. Krivoshein's formulation exhausts the problem. We are at the turning point, on which the whole future course of events depends. It is our duty to be firm before the Tsar in the consciousness of our uprightness. We must tell His Majesty that thus far, public wishes in general, and the Moscow ones in particular, have remained moderate and are clothed in respectful forms. In the past, demands have been both more extreme and more sharply presented. Hence, to dismiss all of them, all at once, would be dangerous. One cannot refuse to consider the fact that the defeats at the front have created a revolutionary mood in the country. And as long as the rumors of the Grand Duke's dismissal sharpen and heighten such moods, one must renounce it [the dismissal], if not forever, at least for a time. The compromise suggested by A. V. Krivoshein solves the problem quite painlessly in all respects.

A. A. POLIVANOV: It was said here at one time that public opinion was beginning to get accustomed to the idea of removing the Grand Duke from the High Command. Perhaps this is so (though the Moscow resolution is a vivid refutation), but as far as the front is concerned, I can testify to the opposite. This morning I was visited by an officer of one of the more prominent infantry guard regiments, who has come from the front and who asked me if it is true that the Grand Duke is being replaced. I answered that it was possible, but that he would be replaced by a person of much higher standing. The officer bowed low to me and left silently. According to the news reaching the War Ministry, the dismissal of the Grand Duke is being discussed in the trenches, and the soldiers are saying that their last defender, a man who can control the generals and the officers, is being taken away from them. With such moods in the rear and at the front, the dismissal of the Grand Duke and the entry of the Emperor upon the Supreme Command is pregnant with all kinds of events. As the lesser of two evils, A. V. Krivoshein's idea is quite acceptable.

s. d. sazonov: The thought of such a combination is in the air and will have a calming effect.

a. d. samarin: I also welcome the suggested combination. The presence of the Emperor at the opening of the Special Conference on Defense would be an excellent moment for its fulfillment. His Imperial Majesty could tell those assembled that he is going to the army to work hand-in-hand with the Grand Duke. I am sure that such an announcement would give joy to everyone and would relieve the anxiety in the hearts of many. Is it possible that the Council of Ministers is so powerless and so lacking in prestige in the eyes of its Monarch that it could not achieve the acceptance of so saving a compromise?

count p. n. ignat'ev: I will consider it my duty to inform His Majesty that among the university youth there is unrest, springing from sympathy for the Grand Duke and from the recognition of the undesirability of his dismissal, as he is the one leader capable of standing up against the Germans. The Rector of the Petrograd University has asked me to postpone the opening of the [academic] session, as he is afraid of the likelihood of various student escapades and protests.

a. d. samarin: And what impression will be made on the religious public, when they cease to mention the Grand Duke in the prayers in the churches? After all, for a whole year he has been prayed for, as Supreme Commander. The attention of His Majesty the Emperor should be drawn to this detail, too.

I. L. GOREMYKIN: Retaining my former view that His Majesty's decision is unchanged and cannot be weakened by persuasion, I will yet not oppose a new attempt to influence His Majesty. But I must tell the Council of Ministers that in any conversation with the Emperor one must be most careful, of speaking about the aura of the Grand Duke as leader. To do so, not only will not help, but will, on the contrary, decisively worsen the issue.

P. A. KHARITONOV: It would seem that there are already enough arguments, such as the risk to the dynasty and the danger of revolutionary movement in the country. However, we live in such a time that the impossible exists . . .

Finally, it was agreed that it was necessary to petition for an immediate assembly of the Council of Ministers under the chairmanship of His Majesty the Emperor, in order to discuss the following questions, in accordance with the formula suggested by A. V. Krivoshein: (A) the procedure for executing the Imperial will concerning the Supreme Command; (B) the evacuation of Petrograd; and (C) the future internal policy: namely, either a firm policy or a policy of moving toward meeting public desires. Bringing forth this last point, A. V. KRIVOSHEIN added: "The golden mean irritates everyone."

The conversation touched again on the Duma, which is going further and further, and by its speeches, is sowing dissatisfaction and chaos. It is twisting itself from a legislative institution virtually into a constituent assembly. Such intentions are in direct contradiction with its legislative work and are transforming the Duma into a platform for agitation.

A. V. KRIVOSHEIN: I have been visited by members of the Duma belonging to various parties, and they tell me that the Duma has exhausted the material for its Session and that, because of this, an anxious mood is developing in it. The hopelessness of trying to establish relations with the government, the question of the change of command, the incoming reports about the flood of refugees, the general dissatisfaction, the popular expectation of help from the Duma, the agitation in the press, and so on—all this, combined, can push the Duma to decisions and actions which will affect the defense adversely. I was told bluntly that the speeches on parliamentary questions, and the resolutions which follow, may take on an openly revolutionary character. Word-making carries one away, and there is no end to it. It is time, finally, to think through the question of the date of adjournment of the Session. Aside from the political considerations, one must take into account the fact that a whole pile of measures, evoked by war conditions, remain without resolution because the government is deprived of the possibility of using Article 87. But when deciding about the Duma, one must simultaneously also decide the question of further policy of which I have already spoken today.

I. L. GOREMYKIN: We have already decided that this problem will be raised at the meeting under Imperial chairmanship. We shall talk about the Duma then, also.

A. A. POLIVANOV: Before one adjourns the Duma, it is necessary to get the law on the mobilization of factories through it. This measure is absolutely and immediately necessary for defense. But its essence is such that to carry it out without the sanction of the legislative bodies is hardly possible in the present confused times. In any event, I would not dare use Article 87 for such a ticklish issue.

P. A. KHARITONOV: Well, and I would prefer exactly this expedient if, in general, one cannot escape such an extraordinary measure as mobilization of factories. I am quite sure that it has no chance of getting through the Duma. After all, the problem involved is neither more nor less than the question of involuntary personal service. In itself, considering the tendencies reigning in the Duma, the question of such service would become a basis for undesirable speeches and agitational *démarches*. Besides, the labor question is also involved in this, so the whole mess will be started. At present it would be more prudent, precisely in the interests of defense, to postpone this problem until a calmer moment, and in no event to connect it with the cessation of the Sessions of the legislative bodies.

I. L. GOREMYKIN: Let us not dwell on details until the basic question is decided. Let us see what His Majesty the Emperor tells us, and then we can return to the statement of the Minister of War [Polivanov].

THE CHIEF OF CHANCELLERY [Lodyzhensky] announced a tele-gram from Headquarters concerning the preparation for the evacu-ation of Kiev, which is being recognized as inevitable by General-Adjutant Ivanov. Necessary military instructions have been given to General Mavrin by the Commander-in-Chief of the Southern Front. Headquarters suggests that the necessary instructions be handed down by the civilian ministries.

P. A. KHARITONOV: Just a moment! What's going on? Does this mean that Kiev is threatened by enemy occupation? Or are we again dealing with a manifestation of the generals' panic?

A. A. POLIVANOV: I think that the State Comptroller [Khari-tonov] is correct in his supposition. The plans and intentions of Headquarters are unknown to me, as it is considered unnecessary to keep the Minister of War informed of the course of events. But insofar as it is possible for me to think on military matters, I am convinced that there is no direct danger to Kiev and that the conversations about its evacuation are, to say the least, premature.

P. A. KHARITONOV: Then how dare General Ivanov give some kind of instructions to General Mavrin, and how come Headquarters did not stop him and did not consult the Council of Ministers ahead of time, on a question of such colossal importance as the evacuation of Kiev? For all we know, one fine day we will find out that one brave general has ordered another general to evacuate Petrograd. The devil knows what's going on here! After all, one cannot upset a whole region because of someone's frightened fancy. Kiev is not Chernovitsy or some little Galician village. The abandonment of the Mother of Russian Cities[4] will echo over all Russia and can have consequences which will cause not only General Ivanov and [his] Mavrin to suffer. I am furious over our helplessness before this re-treating bravery of the generals. One must put an end to this flighti-ness, or one must abolish the government and hand over its func-tions to some military man who's not inclined to think about State interests. I refuse to discuss the question raised in the telegram until we know exactly on what grounds Ivanov gave orders to Mavrin, and exactly how far they have gone.

PRINCE N. B. SHCHERBATOV: In general, what is going on with

---

[4] Kiev's traditional title.

evacuation is simply unbelievable. The military authorities have completely lost their heads and all their common sense. Chaos and disorder are created everywhere, as if on purpose. All local life is being turned upside down. It is really, finally, necessary to take some measures to regularize the relations between military and civil authorities. It is impossible, in such an extraordinarily complicated matter as evacuation, which touches all our existence deeply, to concentrate all dispositions in the hands of the military. They're utterly ignorant of the situation in the central provinces, and yet they direct waves of refugees according to their whim. In my opinion, a centralization of the evacuation question in the hands of the civil authority is inevitable, with the military participating only as experts.

A. V. KRIVOSHEIN: Yes, unbelievable conditions are in fact being created by the removal of a part of Russia [to serve] as the theatre of military actions. Some kind of *oprichnina* and *zemshchina!* [5] In any event, as far as Kiev is concerned, one must protest most energetically and not allow this question to be settled without the sanction of the Council of Ministers. After all, the question involves an ancient Russian shrine.

S. D. SAZONOV: This whole story outrages me profoundly. The Minister of War expresses the opinion that there is no danger threatening Kiev, while the bewildered gentlemen generals want to evacuate it, to abandon it to Austrian abuse. I can imagine the impression on our Allies, when they find out about the abandonment of Kiev, the center of an enormous grain-growing region.

After a long exchange of opinions in the spirit of these statements, it was decided to ask Headquarters urgently what instructions were given by Ivanov to Mavrin, and to request it to abstain from taking any final steps in the matter of the evacuation of Kiev without the preliminary agreement of the Council of Ministers.

After the approval of the draft of the Imperial address for the opening of the Special Conference on Defense, submitted by A. V.

---

[5] The division of the state instituted by Ivan the Terrible during his struggle with the aristocracy in the sixteenth century. In theory, Ivan created two separate and parallel governments for two separate societies.

Krivoshein, the whole last part of the meeting was devoted to the demands of the Allies for the dispatch of Russian gold to America to guarantee payments for contracts, and for credit operations. The conversation was largely technical. But particular statements touched upon the general question of the behavior of the Allies toward us, and deserve to be noted in order to characterize the difficulties of the time.

[There followed a discussion, on a rather primitive level, of the financial arrangements and requirements among the Allies and of the problems posed by the need to export Russian gold reserves. —*Ed.*]

XII

The Meeting of
21 August 1915

---◦◉◦---

On the 20th of August, at 9 o'clock in the evening, a meeting of the Council of Ministers took place in Tsarskoe Selo, under Imperial chairmanship. Neither the Chief of Chancellery nor his assistant attended such meetings. What took place in Tsarskoe Selo, unfortunately, was not noted down by me. Noted are only the words of I. L. GOREMYKIN to I. N. Lodyzhensky the next day: "Yesterday it became clear that His Majesty the Emperor remains on the right, while the Council of Ministers is rapidly shifting to the left, with the current."

The conclusion of my notations of the 21st of August is the following: "Judging by the mood, the long-awaited meeting with the Tsar did not fulfill the expectations of the majority of the Council. In the debate on Chelnokov's telegram there was a sense of helplessness and powerlessness. Everybody's nerves must be in pretty bad shape if they speak in such a tone. Yes, it really looks as if everything were coming closer to the all-deciding lamp post."

Apparently, His Majesty has instructed the Council of Ministers to draft an answer to the most-loyal [1] telegram of the Moscow City Head, Chelnokov, transmitting the Moscow Council's resolutions on its confidence in the Grand Duke, Nikolai Nikolaevich, on a strong government based on the confidence of the public, and so on. Suggesting that this question be studied, I. L. GOREMYKIN declared: I think that in answering this telegram one can restrict oneself to the expression of Imperial gratitude for loyal feelings.

S. D. SAZONOV: No, that would be too little and would sound ironic. The issue lies not in most loyal feelings, but in the fact that the telegram was written with the blood of men who are suffering for their motherland. The most proper thing would be to fulfill the desires of the Moscow Council which are, in essence, quite justified. It would hardly be possible to contend that the government should not be strong and should not base itself on public confidence.

PRINCE N. B. SHCHERBATOV: We must foresee that, after the Moscow telegram, hundreds of similar telegrams will come from all the towns and *zemstvos*. If one is to regard the Moscow expressions as revolutionary, one will have to close down not only the Moscow City Council but all local public organizations. The nature of the reply to Moscow is of very great importance. It decides the direction of internal policy. One of the two: One must either be silent and ignore public demands, or one must go openly forward to meet them. I cannot envisage any half-measures. In this particular case, one cannot slough it off with even the most gracious gratitude.

S. D. SAZONOV: Quite correct. The situation is becoming most serious. One cannot restrict oneself to gratitude, for the question does not involve a New Year's congratulation but the fate of a State. But one cannot resort to silence either, for it can have very serious consequences. Moscow is not a child whose serious question one can dodge by silence.

COUNT P. N. IGNAT'EV: I, too, find that it would be improper to answer by dodging. It is hardly permissible, under present conditions and with rather heightened moods everywhere, to give rise to conclusions that the Tsar denies the need for a government which is at one with the country. In my opinion one must reply to the

---

[1] This was the official term for any address by a subject to the Emperor.

effect that the Tsar understands perfectly, and values the patriotic feelings which directed the Moscow local government, that the heart of Russia feels correctly, that the Tsar thinks and worries about questions of organization of authority which are making Russian people anxious, and so forth and so forth—in this vein. In a word, one must, in the content of the answer to Moscow, *"faire bonne mine au mauvais jeu."*

A. A. KHVOSTOV: It seems to me that it would be premature to speak about the government in the telegram. After all, as every one remembers, His Majesty has postponed this question. It is to be considered in connection with the report which the Council of Ministers must submit to the Emperor on the government program and on the problems which are created by the change in command.

A. A. POLIVANOV: The situation is becoming so threatening that the answer to Moscow should be exhaustive. Russia will have to read, in this answer, what awaits her in the near future.

I. K. GRIGOROVICH: I also think so. In a critical situation, one cannot play blindman's buff; one must act quickly and decisively. For a whole month we have been stamping around in one spot. One cannot behave this way in war time, when the enemy is making his way into the interior of Russia.

A. D. SAMARIN: One must respond to Moscow's painful anxiety about the change of command. Yesterday the Emperor told us that he trusts the Grand Duke, but as for those who surround him . . .

S. D. SAZONOV: Yes, but what stylist can blend confidence in the Grand Duke with his appointment to the Caucasus? Such "confidence" is traumatic. People will begin to say that our Tsar is perfidious. It will be better to avoid touching on the question of the Grand Duke in our reply.

P. L. BARK: I do not quite agree with S. D. Sazonov's apprehensions. Everyone knows that Nikolai Nikolaevich's transfer to the Caucasus is a decided matter. One must emphasize that this decision was not born of personal motives, and one must emphasize that the confidence of the Tsar in the Grand Duke is unshakable and that the Tsar does not differ with the country in the evaluation of his military feats. Then one must express, most vividly, that His Majesty the Emperor has the greatest confidence in Moscow, believes in the sincerity of its anxiety, and expects loyal subjects to be fully united at this difficult time. In my opinion, one cannot leave unanswered, not just the Muscovite, but the all-Russian plea for firm authority and government. One must mention, in the telegram, that His Majesty the Emperor has given orders on the direction of government activity in agreement with public desires. One can end it with an Imperial appeal to all loyal subjects to carry out their duty to the end.

PRINCE N. B. SHCHERBATOV: We will write all this in a telegram to the Moscow City Council, and tomorrow the Emperor will be snowed under by thousands of telegrams from all corners of the Russian land.

A. D. SAMARIN: Moscow is not some corner of the Russian land, but the first capital, the heart of Russia, which always beats with particular force in times of national trouble. We can talk about other telegrams later, when they are received. But Moscow must be set apart, and she must be answered well. One also cannot slight the Moscow merchants—they are a historic class, a famous one, the voice of which is heard by many, far from Moscow.

I. L. GOREMYKIN: If we keep being diverted into general questions all the time, we will never finish and we will not execute the Imperial order. We must submit to His Majesty some kind of answer to the Moscow telegram.

S. D. SAZONOV: Not *some kind* of an answer, but a deeply and thoroughly thought-out one. I hope that the Chairman will not impede the Council of Ministers from interpreting the Monarch's will in this way, and from fulfilling it conscientiously and deliberately.

I. K. GRIGOROVICH: We know, from His Majesty the Emperor's statement yesterday, that despite everything, he is leaving for Headquarters to take over the Supreme Command. The Council of Ministers, or at least the majority of its members, consider that this act worsens considerably an internal situation which is already virtually hopeless. If our pleas, and our convictions, did not influence the Emperor yesterday, then it is our duty to make one more final attempt—to submit to His Imperial Majesty a written report expressing our opinion on the change of command, on the danger to the dynasty, and so forth.

I. L. GOREMYKIN: His Majesty the Emperor said yesterday, quite definitely, that he is leaving for Mogilev in a few days and will announce his will there. What kind of written reports are possible? It is impermissible that the Council of Ministers should bother the

Tsar in a historic hour of his life, and should agitate uselessly an infinitely tortured man. It was not easy for the Emperor to make this decision, but once it is made—he will not relinquish it.

I. K. GRIGOROVICH: I do not consider myself justified to take the responsibility for this decision, and, as a most loyal servant of my Tsar, I must tell him: Do not take this irrevocable step; do not touch the Grand Duke; postpone the execution of your decision.

S. D. SAZONOV: In this crisis into which Russia is being dragged, our duty is to say honestly to the Tsar that in this situation, as it is developing, we cannot rule the country, that in all conscience we are powerless to serve him, that we are harmful to our motherland.

I. L. GOREMYKIN: That is, to put it simply, you want to present an ultimatum to your Tsar.

S. D. SAZONOV: For us in Russia, there are no ultimatums. For us only most-loyal pleas are possible. Let us not argue about words. The substance is more important in the terrible time that is coming. The issue is not one of ultimatums, but lies in the fact that one must make a last attempt before it is too late to open the Tsar's eyes to the depth of the risk for Russia, to warn him about the fatal danger, and to tell him honestly that the government cannot fulfill its function when it does not possess the Emperor's confidence.

PRINCE N. B. SHCHERBATOV: The Navy Minister's [Grigorovich's] idea is absolutely correct. One must submit a written report to His Majesty, and explain that a government which has neither the confidence of the bearer of supreme power, nor of the army, nor of the towns, nor of the *zemstvos,* nor of the gentry, nor of the merchants, nor of the workers—not only cannot work, it cannot even exist! It is an evident absurdity! We, sitting here, are like Don Quixotes!

PRINCE V. N. SHAKHOVSKOY: A most important point for the redaction of this report: One must by all means avoid in it any shading which would suggest the idea of a strike. His Majesty the Emperor uttered this word yesterday.

S. D. SAZONOV: It cannot refer to the Council of Ministers. Such suspicion must fall away from us. If we speak of the impossibility of continuing service, it is only because, under present circumstances, so correctly characterized by Prince Shcherbatov, our work is not only useless but directly harmful. I am sure that if P. A. Kharitonov would undertake to write up the journal of the Council of Ministers, he would find the proper expression for our thoughts.

P. A. KHARITONOV: My mind is so chaotic after yesterday's meeting in Tsarskoe Selo that I couldn't put two lines together. How can I undertake this general diplomacy? Let me come to a little!

I. L. GOREMYKIN: While I am Chairman, I cannot allow the submission to His Imperial Majesty of a journal with such contents, in the name of the Council of Ministers.

S. D. SAZONOV: Then we, that is, the majority of the Council of Ministers, reserve for ourselves the freedom of action to convey our opinion for the information of His Majesty the Emperor.

I. L. GOREMYKIN: I do not find it possible to interfere with your personal *démarches*.

COUNT P. N. IGNAT'EV: I agree that we must inform the Emperor of our opinion, and that it is necessary to do so in writing. We must absolve ourselves from the reproach that we were silent in a moment of the greatest danger for Russia.

S. D. SAZONOV: I can, in no way, share the point of view expressed yesterday by our Chairman, that if His Majesty the Emperor deigns to run the risk, then it is not up to us to warn him about it.

A. D. SAMARIN: Let us speak quite openly among ourselves; the times are such that no reservations are possible. The issue is the fate of Russia, and we are the participants in a great tragedy. We must explain ourselves to the end. You, Ivan Longinovich [Goremykin], apparently do not sympathize with the aspirations of many members of the Council of Ministers to dissuade His Majesty the Emperor at any price, to restrain him from a step which we feel, in all conscience, to be fatal for Russia and for the dynasty. Yesterday, in the Imperial presence, you said that petitions like the Moscow ones are dictated by the desire to create opposition to the removal of the Grand Duke and, hence, to guarantee him some kind of a special position. I think I am not incorrect in conveying your thought. But after all, we too are petitioning. That means that, in your eyes, we too are in opposition and we too are pursuing some hidden goals. I find it difficult to carry the discussion any further until this basic question is cleared up.

I. L. GOREMYKIN: I have never concealed, and I am not now concealing my opinion, and I will gladly answer a frank question with frankness. Many of those present here will confirm for you, Alexander Dimitrovich [Samarin], that from the beginning of the war I was definitely opposed to the Emperor's intention to assume personal command of the army. I felt the same later, as the Council of Ministers knows, when His Majesty warned me about the dismissal of the Grand Duke. But His Majesty did not deign to agree with my reasons and with the reasons of the Council of Ministers. Then I understood that the Imperial will is inflexible, and I felt myself duty-bound to bow before it as before the inevitable and to give all my strength to help my Tsar in a difficult moment. Everyone now knows about His Majesty's decision. They know, also, that this decision is irrevocable. It follows that the agitation that is going on around this question, and which is being connected with the demand for a Cabinet possessing public confidence—that is, for a limitation of the Tsar's power—is nothing but the aspiration of leftist circles who use the name of the Grand Duke to discredit His Majesty the Emperor.

A. D. SAMARIN: In the Moscow City Council it was not only the leftists, but all the deputies unanimously, including even Shmakov, who participated in the writing of the resolution of confidence in the Grand Duke. It is difficult to consider that Council, with its present make-up, a leftist one.

PRINCE N. B. SHCHERBATOV: I fully agree with A. D. Samarin about the Moscow Council. Its attitude toward the Grand Duke is not an attitude of a particular party, but an expression of the deadly fear of all Russian society before the act of the Emperor—his taking on himself the Supreme Command and removing that person who is considered (whether justly or not, is another matter) to be the only one capable of withstanding the German invasion.

I. L. GOREMYKIN: I cannot agree with such an idealization of motives. In my opinion, the exaggerated faith in the Grand Duke, and all this noise around his name, is nothing else but a political attack against the Tsar. The Grand Duke is only a means.

PRINCE N. B. SHCHERBATOV: Those [who use the Grand Duke as an excuse] are not more than five per cent [of the population].

S. D. SAZONOV: Both the Left and the Cadets are trembling for their own skins. They are terrified of a revolutionary outburst, and of the impossibility of continuing the war. They are afraid that the change of command will call forth such an explosion.

A. D. SAMARIN: Hence, you, Ivan Longinovich [Goremykin], think that those protesting against the dismissal of the Grand Duke are doing it for selfish reasons? But one cannot, after all, accuse all

Russia of such motives. Everyone is protesting, including the majority of the members of the Council of Ministers.

I. L. GOREMYKIN: I am not speaking about all Russia, which is not shouting, but is going on about its business. I am speaking of those leftist politicians who want to creat difficulties for the monarchy, and who are taking advantage of the misfortunes of Russia. The Minister of Internal Affairs [Shcherbatov] himself spoke about this when he reported to us on the Konovalov meeting and warned us that there would be a *démarche* by the Moscow Council. I repeat, the name of the Grand Duke has been deliberately chosen as a unifying slogan for the opposition. Believe me, if His Majesty the Emperor could now renounce his decision, and the Grand Duke were to remain, the leftists would arrange for triumphant and ceremonious greetings for Nikolai Nikolaevich as the savior of Russia. Against whom? Against the Tsar.

S. D. SAZONOV: We categorically oppose such an interpretation of public activity. It is not a result of intrigue; it is a cry for help. We, too, must join this cry.

I. L. GOREMYKIN: To your requests the Emperor has answered clearly and decisively: "I am going to Headquarters." With these words the question is closed.

S. D. SAZONOV: It is clear that you and we speak different languages. The majority of us, after the meeting yesterday in Tsarskoe Selo, had a strong impression of significant discord between us. I find it necessary to state this quite openly. We diverge radically in the evaluation of the present situation, and about the means of struggling with the approaching storm.

I. L. GOREMYKIN: I beg all of you to report to His Majesty the Emperor on my unfitness, and on the necessity of replacing me by a man more suitable to the demands of the present. I will be grateful to you from the bottom of my heart for such a service.

PRINCE N. B. SHCHERBATOV: The issue regarding the government is far broader. We, all of us together, are unfit to govern Russia in the existing situation. When one needs basses, one cannot substitute tenors. I, and many of my colleagues in the Council of Ministers, definitely feel that it is impossible to work when the tendency from above is clearly contradictory to the demands of the time. Either dictatorship or a policy of reconciliation is necessary. I, for one, find myself absolutely unsuitable, either for one or the other.

Our duty is to tell the Emperor that, in order to save the State from the greatest perils, one must move either to the left or to the right. The internal situation of the country does not allow for continued sitting between two chairs.

s. d. sazonov: I am completely in agreement with Prince Shcherbatov. As Minister of Foreign Affairs, I must warn His Majesty the Emperor that I am not capable of conducting foreign policy and preserving the unity of the alliance in a situation of [such] internal confusion. It is my duty to say that this alliance is precious to us, for without it we will perish quickly and would have perished long ago. For this, I must say, it is necessary to openly embark on one or another policy and follow it inflexibly.

i. l. goremykin: Tell His Majesty, also, that to this end it is necessary to remove Goremykin. I have constantly begged His Imperial Majesty to shift the responsibility from my old shoulders to younger ones. Even yesterday I repeated to the Emperor that I will bow low to whoever replaces me at this difficult post. But under present circumstances, I myself will not submit a resignation, and I will stand by the Tsar until he himself finds it necessary to dismiss me.

s. d. sazonov: The issue is not one of honor, but of the preservation of one's moral face before all Russia. When the motherland is in danger, gentlemanly behavior toward the Monarch may be beautiful, but it is harmful to immeasurably broader interests. We are not preparing to make a demonstration before the Tsar, but to warn him away from a fatal step, by our unanimous declaration. We declare: The interests of the State, its very being, require a change of policy which must be executed by new people.

i. l. goremykin: I am not interfering with your particular declarations. Report to His Majesty everything that your reason and your conscience order you to. In my mind, His Majesty the Emperor is the Anointed of God, the Hereditary Bearer of Supreme Power. He personifies Russia. He is forty-seven years old; he reigns and he disposes over the fate of the Russian people not as of yesterday. When the will of such a man is manifested and the path of action irrevocably taken, loyal subjects must submit, no matter what the consequences. And then there is only the Will of God. So I think, and in this knowledge I will die.

prince n. b. shcherbatov: Not one military commander, not

one commander of a ship, would allow the Emperor to expose himself to obvious danger.

I. L. GOREMYKIN: And if he, the Supreme Leader, orders it?

A. A. POLIVANOV: The captain of a ship will still not allow it, even if he has to use force. This has been foreseen by law. There is the case of Emperor Nicholas I. He submitted, though he knew how to command.

S. D. SAZONOV: Unfortunately, we have neither the authority nor the opportunities of a ship's captain. For us only one thing remains—to state to His Imperial Majesty firmly and definitely: You are leading yourself and Russia to ruin; our conscience, our patriotic duty, will not allow us to help you in this; find yourself new servants who can be more useful to you in this new atmosphere.

A. A. POLIVANOV: Tomorrow His Majesty the Emperor will open, and then greet, the Special Conference on Defense. Everyone is expecting a soothing word. Everyone knows that the pledge of success against the enemy and the very possibility of victory rest in the union of all forces in the country, in the devoted work of public organizations and workers. But how can one achieve this union, this passion, when the overwhelming majority is not in sympathy with the change of command, nor with the course of internal policy, nor with the government called upon to conduct this policy? How can men work when they have neither faith nor confidence in their leaders? One must attempt, once again, to explain this to the Tsar, to convince him that the situation can only be saved by a policy conciliatory to society. The present shaky and flimsy dams are not capable of forestalling catastrophe.

I. K. GRIGOROVICH: It is not a secret that the army does not trust us either, and is awaiting changes.

COUNT P. N. IGNAT'EV: Yes, and moreover the army has stopped being an army and has become the people-in-arms.

I. L. GOREMYKIN: The substance of our discussion amounts to the fact that my point of view is archaic and harmful. Do me the very great favor—convince His Imperial Majesty to dismiss me. But I cannot renounce my own understanding of my duty to serve my Tsar, the Anointed of God. At the door of the tomb is it too late for me to change my convictions.

A. D. SAMARIN: Undoubtedly, there is a basic divergence of views between us. You hear, in the general voice of the country, only the desire to create opposition to His Majesty the Emperor for the sake of political aspirations, while we consider that in this voice is manifested the healthy, correct feeling created not by other aspirations, but by anxiety for the motherland. We believe in this feeling, in essence, and we find that the government cannot be useful to its Emperor and to the motherland without the confidence of the well-meaning mass of society.

PRINCE N. B. SHCHERBATOV: Both Samarin and I are former provincial leaders of the nobility.[2] So far, no one has considered us left-wing, and we do not think of ourselves that way. But neither of us can understand, in any sense, a situation in the State in which the monarch and his government are in radical discord with the whole well-meaning public (it isn't worthwhile speaking of the revolutionary intrigues), with the gentry, merchants, towns, *zemstvos,* and even the army. If, higher up, there is no wish to consider our opinion, it is our duty to leave.

I. L. GOREMYKIN: When His Imperial Majesty is in danger, from whatever source, I do not consider it morally right for me to declare to him: "I can no longer serve the Emperor." For a half-century I have been accustomed to understand my duty to serve the monarch in this way, and I will not renounce this rule until the end.

PRINCE N. B. SHCHERBATOV: And I cannot understand how I can continue to serve, if my views do not correspond to the views of the one who is the source of my authority. How can I direct my authority against those with whom I agree? His Majesty the Emperor is not the Lord God. He can make mistakes.

I. L. GOREMYKIN: Even if the Tsar were mistaken, to abandon him in a threatening moment, to worsen the difficult position of the Throne—I cannot do this.

PRINCE N. B. SHCHERBATOV: The country does not believe that the Council of Ministers—the closest servants of the Tsar—is not able to undo the fatal step. We pleaded verbally; let us try, for the last time, to plead in writing. Future historians will exonerate us of the accusations which now pour down on us from all sides. Perhaps a written statement will make a greater impression on the

---

[2] The nobility of each province elected one of its members as leader (*predvoditel'*) for a three-year term.

Emperor and will force him to think about it, at the last moment.

I. L. GOREMYKIN: I am not interfering with the form of your address to the Emperor. But what will your written report achieve? The Emperor will not change his mind and he will not agree to the resignation of virtually the whole Council of Ministers; he will order you to remain at your posts. What then?

S. D. SAZONOV: Then, that which I will constantly repeat to the Tsar: I cannot conduct foreign policy under threat of internal revolution. After all, we do live in an age when one cannot, even if one does not consider or respect opinions, refuse to respect people, particularly when these people are ministers and speak of the impossibility of continuing to serve.

I. L. GOREMYKIN: My conscience does not permit such a method of action. I cannot demand my dismissal at a moment when all should unite around the Throne and defend the Tsar from the danger which threatens. Achieve my resignation and I will be deeply grateful. No matter how weak my forces, I will still be able to serve the Tsar as a private individual.

A. D. SAMARIN: I, too, love my Tsar, am deeply devoted to the monarchy, and have proved it with all my activity. But if the Tsar acts to the detriment of Russia, then I cannot follow him submissively.

I. L. GOREMYKIN: In the times we live in, I consider a demand for dismissal and disobedience to the will of the Tsar as an unpatriotic act. It would not be for the benefit of Russia, but for the opponents of the Throne. Perhaps my view is archaic, but I cannot change it and do not find it necessary to do so. I would like to note that this whole question of command and of some special kind of government is being deliberately exaggerated. In my opinion, for the Emperor to renounce his decision and to retain the Grand Duke at Headquarters at this time would be much more fateful than the entrance of His Majesty upon personal command of the troops.

A. D. SAMARIN: Unfortunately, exactly this point of view was observable in your speeches to His Majesty yesterday. You have touched upon the sickly strand in the attitude of the Emperor toward the Grand Duke—the feeling of competitiveness. Perhaps it was your words that called forth the sharp statement that he is going to Headquarters in the next few days.

s. d. sazonov: I was watching the Emperor, and I saw clearly, on his face, how excited he was by your words about the triumph of a Grand Duke returning to the supreme command, and to the effect that all those who are for the Grand Duke are thereby in opposition to the Tsar. A worse service to the struggle against the Emperor's fatal decision you could not have offered.

i. l. goremykin: Do report to His Majesty on my unfitness and my lack of understanding of State interests.

prince n. b. shcherbatov: We go further. We all consider ourselves unfit, if in over three whole weeks we have been unable to break down the Tsar's obstinacy.

p. a. kharitonov: For the majority of the members of the Council of Ministers the question is quite clear: If the will of the Tsar is not harmful to Russia, it must be obeyed; but if this will threatens Russia with great misfortunes and evils, then one must refuse to execute it and one must leave. We serve not only the Tsar, but Russia as well.

i. l. goremykin: In my conception, these ideas are inseparable. Here is the root of our discord.

p. a. kharitonov: Yes, this is the root. In contradistinction to your opinion, we feel that one should not obey blindly, that one cannot participate in something in which one sees the beginning of ruin for our motherland.

s. d. sazonov: I would add that we can sacrifice everything for the Tsar except our conscience.

a. d. samarin: The Russian Tsar requires the service of thinking men, not a slavish execution of orders. The Tsar can punish us, but we must tell him the truth. We could never forgive ourselves our silence at a time when the fate of our motherland is at stake.

i. l. goremykin: Our discussion is acquiring a hopeless character. I beg you not to distort my words. I did not speak of slavish obedience. My opinion amounts to the fact that the will of the Tsar is the will of Russia, that the Tsar and Russia are inseparable, that we owe obedience to this will, and that a Russian cannot abandon his Tsar at the crossroads, no matter how difficult it may be personally.

s. d. sazonov: If one develops your thought further, the inevitable conclusion is that the words of the Tsar are as sacred as the words of the Gospel. Do not forget that the popularity of the Tsar, and his prestige in the eyes of the people have been considerably shaken. It is difficult, in the present climate, to prove the coincidence of the will of Russia and of the Tsar. What one notices is exactly the reverse phenomenon.

I. L. GOREMYKIN: In my understanding of the essence of the Russian monarchy, the will of the Tsar must be obeyed like commands of the Gospel.

S. D. SAZONOV: Then there remains one thing only: to drown oneself. I do not want this and do not consider it necessary. I do not see my duty in bowing down, but in warning the Tsar and trying to restrain him from a course which is fatal for my motherland. Declarations in the name of the Council of Ministers will sound much more authoritative. Hence, I prefer not to declare myself individually, but in cooperation with those who think like me.

A. A. KHVOSTOV: I have refrained from participating in the argument over the essence and dimensions of the monarch's power throughout the discussion. For me, this question is decided at the moment of one's oath. For myself, I consider it absolutely impermissible to submit to the Tsar a demand for dismissal. Therefore I will sign neither the journal, nor the report, nor any other declaration. The renewal of the discussion about the government is premature. The Emperor has not pronounced his final word and decision on this question. He has postponed it until our submission of a program. It is our duty to work out such a program immediately, in order to end the uncertainty of a situation which only breeds arguments.

A. D. SAMARIN: The main lines of this policy have been emerging quite clearly in today's discussion, in the opinion of the majority of the members of the Council of Ministers, if we consider it necessary to listen to the unanimous voice of the country and to select from public demands those which are acceptable in substance and which do not infringe upon the bases of the State's existence. We believe that, in the face of the fatal danger threatening the motherland, there are neither leftists nor rightists nor indifferent ones, and that all are united in a single desire to save Russia from ruin. Individual intriguers and politicking cliques are drowned in the general patriotic *élan*. We consider that this passion should be handled, not by the establishment of a dictatorship, but by our being well-disposed toward it.

A. A. KHVOSTOV: I doubt the correctness of this analysis and of the conclusions. Of course, one cannot deny the presence of a patriotic movement and of selfless anxiety for Russia. But as always during periods of public movement, it is joined by various shady characters who use the moment to catch fish in muddy waters. Those who shout the loudest cover themselves with the beautiful cloak of patriotism in order to achieve their party aspirations and weaken the forces which oppose a wartime *coup d'état*. I do not know whether the Council of Ministers is aware of the rather characteristic fact that the most violent patriots and adherents of public demands asked for active support from the Moscow workers but were unsuccessful, receiving the answer that the factories will function until the achievement of final victory. Such addresses are not only an unpatriotic act but are legally criminal. In Petrograd, the situation among the workers is far worse, and here such *démarches* could eventuate in an armed uprising, which is being prepared, but as yet, thank God, has not ripened. I also have substantive doubts. In my opinion, the policy of concessions is incorrect in general, and quite impermissible in wartime. Demands are being presented for changes in the State structure, not because these changes are necessary for the organization of victory but because the military misfortunes have weakened the position of the authorities and one can now act against them with a knife at the throat. Today one will satisfy some demands; tomorrow new ones, which go still further, will be announced. The policy of concessions has not led to any good anywhere in the world; it has always dragged the country down an inclined plane. If I did not express all my doubts yesterday at the meeting with the Emperor, it was only because I did not feel morally right about undermining his confidence in the conclusions of the majority of my colleagues in the Cabinet. My doubts correspond in substance with His Majesty's point of view, and my spark could have started a fire. But at today's meeting I do not consider it necessary to disguise my doubts.

A. D. SAMARIN: We hear only of your doubts, but you apparently do not as yet have your own opinion.

A. A. KHVOSTOV: I am looking for a solution, and I doubt sincerely, and this is why I cannot join in the categorical statements of the other members of the Council of Ministers. The appeals which come from Guchkov, from the left parties in the Duma, from the Konovalov meeting, and from the public organizations led by the participants of that meeting are clearly aimed toward a *coup d'état*. Under wartime conditions, such a coup would inevitably be followed by the complete dissolution of State administration and by the destruction of the fatherland. Therefore, I shall fight them [the opposition] with my dying breath. Let the Tsar judge me, but this is what my conscience tells me.

s. d. SAZONOV: You state frankly that you believe neither the whole of Russian society nor the Duma, summoned by the will of the Monarch. And the Duma answers that it, for its part, does not believe in us. How can the State mechanism function under such conditions? Such a situation is intolerable! Hence, we consider that the solution lies in reconciliation, in the creation of a Cabinet in which no one would feel *a priori* distrust toward the legislative chambers, and the membership of which would be equal to the struggle against the tendencies, not only from below but from above, which are fatal for Russia.

i. l. GOREMYKIN: I repeat for the tenth time: Plead with the Emperor to throw me out. But believe me, you will forestall nothing by your concessions, and achieve nothing. It is absolutely clear that all the parties of revolution are using military misfortunes to strengthen their attack against the government and to limit monarchic power.

a. a. KHVOSTOV: No matter what you concede, it will all be the same. The Messrs. Chkheidzes and Kerenskys[3] will be dissatisfied, and will not cease to stir up public irritation by various promises.

s. d. SAZONOV: What do we care about the desires and understanding of all these insignificant Kerenskys, Chkheidzes, and other revolutionaries! We're not worried about them, but about Russia, which is being pushed into the embrace of these gentlemen!

---

[3] Alexander Fedorovich Kerensky (1881-   ): lawyer; deputy to the 4th Duma; leader of the Trudovic group. Kerensky was one of the great orators in the Duma; as a lawyer he specialized in defending political cases. After the revolution, he entered the Provisional Government as Minister of Justice, the only Socialist in the cabinet; at the same time, he was Vice-Chairman of the Council of Soldiers' and Workers' Deputies. In May, 1917, he became Minister of War and the Navy; in July, he became Prime Minister and remained in office until the Bolshevik revolution in October, 1917.

The Trudovic group was a political party of the revolutionary Left, the least radical of that grouping. The basic program was that of the social revolutionaries, the peasant-oriented Socialists. The *trudovic*—based on the root *trud* ("work")—position was not very doctrinaire.

*　*　*

My notes ended at this point. Apparently, I simply didn't have the strength to go on, as the writing of the last lines is more and more uneven and illegible.

The Most-subject[4] letter was sent over the signature of all members of the Council with the exception of A. A. Khvostov and, if I am not mistaken, Prince V. N. Shakovskoy. The Minister of War and the Navy Minister did not sign, as their military status did not permit them to participate in any collective actions, but they conveyed to His Majesty their full agreement with the thoughts expressed in the letter. This document was not presented to I. L. Goremykin, but was handed to the Emperor. I myself never saw the letter or a copy of it, and its content is unknown to me.

Text of the Collective Letter of the Ministers[5]

Most Gracious Sovereign

Do not blame us for our daring and frank address to You. Our most-loyal duty, our love for You and the Motherland, and our anxious awareness of the foreboding significance of current events, forced us to do so.

Yesterday, at the meeting of the Council of Ministers under Your personal chairmanship, we submitted to You our unanimous plea that Grand Duke Nikolai Nikolaevich be not removed from participation in the supreme command of the army. But we fear that Your Imperial Majesty did not deign to condescend to the plea which is ours and, we dare think, that of all the Russia loyal to You.

We dare, once again, to tell You, Sovereign, that the decision you have taken, according to our most thoughtful consideration, threatens Russia, You, and Your dynasty with the direst consequences.

During the same meeting a basic difference of opinion emerged, between the Chairman of the Council of Ministers and ourselves, in the evaluation of the events taking place in the country and in the determination of the proper course of action for the government. Such a situation, impermissible at any time, is disastrous in these days.

Finding ourselves in such circumstances, we are losing our faith in the possibility of serving You and the Motherland with any consciousness of utility.

---

[4] Vsepoddanneishee—in the most subject-like humility.

[5] I. V. Gessen, editor of the *Archive of the Russian Revolution,* wrote this note in Berlin, in 1926.

Your Imperial Majesty's most-loyal subjects:

PETER KHARITONOV, ALEXANDER KRIVOSHEIN, SERGEI SAZONOV, PETER BARK, PRINCE N. SHCHERBATOV, ALEXANDER SAMARIN, COUNT PAUL IGNAT'EV, PRINCE VSEVOLOD SHAKHOVSKOY.*

21 August, 1915

* The signature indicates that Iakhontov was mistaken in thinking that Shakhovskoy had refused to sign the letter.

In the end, they returned to the Moscow telegram and charged A. D. Samarin with composing the draft of an answer. Written out by him at once, the draft was approved by the Council of Ministers in the course of further discussion, and then signed by His Majesty the Emperor. I have preserved its redaction in a clipping from *Pravitel'stvenny Vestnik,*[6] which printed the following:

In answer to the telegram of the Moscow City Head with the known resolutions of the Council, the City Head had the joy of receiving from His Majesty the Emperor the following reply: "I heartily thank the Moscow City Council for its most loyal emotions, expressed to me unanimously. I particularly value them in these present difficult days for our motherland. I trust in their sincerity and I fully share the thought that now, when all the forces should be directed to one goal—victory over the enemy—the union of the Tsar and his government with the people is particularly necessary.

Before the adjournment of the meeting, the end of which was dedicated to a discussion of current affairs (which are not of general interest, now) I. L. GOREMYKIN warned that, in the next few days, the bloc being formed among the members of the State Council and the Duma will submit a unified program to the Council of Ministers which, according to an Imperial order, is to be examined [by the Council].[7]

From the meeting of August 21st, besides S. V. Rukhlov, A. V. Krivoshein was also absent.

---

[6] The official government bulletin.

[7] The Progressive Bloc, made up of a coalition of moderate rightist, center, and nonradical leftist parties of both legislative chambers, formed in the summer of 1915. It had a majority in the Duma and represented, in essence, the opposition of society to the government. Its demands can be seen as the demands of the nonrevolutionary majority of society. Its program is duplicated on pp. 188 *ff.* of the text.

XIII

The Meeting of
24 August 1915

A. POLIVANOV: I have received a message from Headquarters that the Commander-in-Chief of the southern Front insists upon the execution of the evacuation of Kiev. His reason is that his armies are too small to withstand the enemy, which has enormous superiority in artillery and supplies and a high morale based on universal successes. Besides, General-Adjutant Ivanov considers that it is necessary, in order to prepare for further struggle, to widen the rear area, freeing it of unnecessary elements. All these considerations are supported by Headquarters.

PRINCE N. B. SHCHERBATOV: In other words, a new migration of peoples is demanded from us. All the districts close to the rear zone are overflowing with refugees. Pskov, Smolensk, Minsk, Chernigov, Poltava, not to speak of district towns and villages—everything is crowded to the limit. Hence, for the convenience of the general, retreating before an inspired enemy, it is necessary to dislodge this human wave, this hungry and angry flock of locusts which has managed somehow, in some way, to settle down, and chase it into the interior provinces. And this is how one is expected to be Minister of Internal Affairs and uphold public order and calm! The Emperor goes to the front, and the first consequence is the abandonment of the Mother of Russian Cities. It will make a nice impression! I categorically protest against the execution of General Ivanov's plans. It is better to perish in a final battle than to sign, ourselves, Russia's death warrant.

A. A. POLIVANOV: In substance, I agree fully with Prince Shcherbatov. But, returning to the problem of Kiev, I must say that I would be most hesitant to leave this question completely in the hands of the army rear echelon. One should create a special, competent, and authoritative committee which should be charged with the whole matter of the evacuation of Kiev. The chief voice in it should belong to the representatives of the ministries.

A. V. KRIVOSHEIN: As always, when in conflict with a proposal from the front, I feel, in this case too, the greatest confusion. One general or another, or a third, thinks up something, but one cannot see an over-all conception. There is no planning in the face of an advancing enemy, but some haphazard kind of accommodation to circumstances. We act not as men being tried by misfortunes, but blindly. One is frightened for the fatherland. One must finally, after all, decide on a plan for the conduct of the war, to be worked out with the participation and common forces of all the military commanders. One must beg His Imperial Majesty to undertake this elementary measure, the calling together of a military council, about which no one has thought or wished to think for thirteen months. Is it possible that even now they are not thinking about it in Headquarters? Historians will not believe it, that Russia conducted the war blindly and hence came to the edge of ruin—that millions of men were unconsciously sacrificed for the arrogance of some and the criminality of others. What is going on at Headquarters is a universal outrage and horror.

A. A. POLIVANOV: Since the 11th of July, I have constantly insisted before His Imperial Majesty the Emperor that an immediate convocation of a council of war is a necessity. You know what answer was given to this. On the eve of His Majesty's departure, I again reported on it, emphasizing the necessity of clearing up the organization of the rear, because our staffs apparently feel restricted in Russia. The Emperor promised to think about a military council after a closer acquaintance with the situation on the spot. One must beg His Majesty to face this question in view of the new demands for evacuation from the Front. I cannot understand why such an elementary thing as a council of war calls for so much delay and restraint.

P. A. KHARITONOV: It would be good for the Emperor to see in person what goes on in the evacuation. A complete outrage justified by nothing. It would not be difficult to regularize the matter, if one took its direction from the hands of flighty ensigns and placed it in the hands of experienced administrators. From all sides I get complaints, via the Comptroller's Department, that people are being ruined without reason, and that, with some systematization, one could eliminate a mass of unnecessary complications. I think the same is being said to the other ministries. Cadres of opposition are being created from the ranks of government civil servants. And really, how can one remain calm and obedient to the law, when one sees how uselessly one's property is being destroyed, when panic is sown by the stupidity and in many cases the criminality of many heroes of the rear, and thus suffering is created for many which is justified by nothing.

A. V. KRIVOSHEIN: The State Comptroller [Kharitonov] is absolutely right. The gentlemen ensigns are digging the grave of Russian statehood and are spawning enemies everywhere. Panic is being created, not only in Kiev but also in Odessa. Indescribable scenes of stupidity are taking place there, I have been told. It's easy for the military—they have special trains standing ready, loaded with all their junk, including canaries. But what about civil servants and the mere inhabitants? As a matter of fact, one begins to feel like climbing walls. Our defenders skip out, with all conveniences, well before the imaginary danger, and leave peaceful civilians to their fate and complete ruination. It is our duty to reiterate untiringly to His Imperial Majesty the necessity of assembling a united council composed of the government and the military commanders. The task of this council: the working out of a plan for the further conduct of the war and the establishment of a firm plan for carrying out evacuations. Let Headquarters establish, well beforehand, the regions subject to evacuation, and let the evacuation itself be carried out by competent and responsible organs. Otherwise, we will never get out of this blind alley.

P. A. KHARITONOV: One must explain to the Emperor that the senseless ruination of people cannot be tolerated.

A. V. KRIVOSHEIN: I am prepared to ruin myself for a cure, if

I have been advised by competent doctors at a concilium, but I am not prepared to submit to the decision of medical assistants. Let knowledgeable and authoritative leaders say that Odessa must be abandoned to its fate in order to pursue the conduct of the war. But when this is said by saviors of the fatherland who specialize in evacuationary maneuvers, then I will yell and be outraged.

A. A. POLIVANOV: According to the intelligence at Headquarters, the enemy intends to exert pressure on Odessa via Balta, for the purpose of threatening Rumania.

A. V. KRIVOSHEIN: And at such a moment, His Majesty the Emperor, moved by religious feeling, despite the passionate pleas of nearly all of Russia, takes the Supreme Command upon himself! What horror! What blindness!

A. A. NERATOV (the Vice-Minister of Foreign Affairs): Curious! where did the Central Powers get so many troops?

A. A. POLIVANOV: The issue does not lie in the number of troops, but in skillful leadership and in military art. As far as Kiev is concerned, then, the Council of Ministers will most abjectly beg, first, that a military council be assembled; then, depending on its decision, the issue of whether it is necessary to abandon this center will become clear.

A. V. KRIVOSHEIN: I would request that a form of address more fitting to the importance of the occasion be chosen. It is not necessary to beg, but to most loyally insist. It is impossible to leave the matter of evacuation subject to the accidents of local Fronts. One must mark out a course and follow a general plan confirmed after consultation with responsible people. Gentlemen, after all, it is impossible to make all Russia rise, and move her toward an unknown destination for unknown reasons. If this continues this way, soon only Siberia will be left for the habitation of Russians not dressed in military uniforms. We have the right to say to our Emperor that Russia was created and built over a thousand years, and that it is being wiped off the face of the earth in one moment by various brave warriors who are acting in accordance with unknown orders. This is madness.

At the conclusion of the debate, it was decided to send to His Imperial Majesty a telegram of the following content (jotted down right then):

The evacuation of Kiev, because of its enormous economic and political importance, can be allowed only under extreme duress; it cannot be allowed to take place on the order of local military authorities in the person of General Ivanov, but only according to a general plan of the campaign which must be worked out at a military council; such evacuations of designated districts should take place on the orders of competent authorities, with the participation of military representatives functioning only as experts on military matters.

COUNT P. N. IGNAT'EV: In connection with the decision just taken, how should the Ministry of Public Education react to General Mavrin's demands for the closing down of all educational institutions in Kiev and for their evacuation before September 10th?

A. D. SAMARIN: This problem also affects the religious department. The Metropolitan of Kiev writes to me that they are demanding that he move all ecclesiastical schools out before September 15th.

P. A. KHARITONOV: Closing down the schools only increases the panic in the city.

I. L. GOREMYKIN: Studies would be useless anyway, when all of life is so upset. It is better to send the youth further away from the life of the rear area.

A. D. SAMARIN: I would consider it most proper to close down the schools without evacuating their equipment. After all, the Germans won't start destroying textbooks and classroom equipment which they do not need. If they so wish, the parents can concern themselves with the evacuation of their children to the inner provinces, where one must guarantee them the opportunity to continue their education.

A. V. KRIVOSHEIN: And with all this, one must stop all postponements of the mobilization of students. I agree fully with our Chairman's opinion that, under present conditions, it is difficult to expect any utility from study. Everyone must now go to the front to defend the motherland. This is more important than textbooks.

A. A. POLIVANOV: I welcome A. V. Krivoshein's suggestion about abolishing deferments. The army needs a flow of educated people for the speeded-up preparation of officers. Our losses in the officer corps are colossal, and they must be made up at any price.

It was decided to assign this question to be worked out immediately, with the participation of the ministries concerned.

* * *

PRINCE N. B. SHCHERBATOV: The Central Military-Industrial Committee, headed by Guchkov, resolved to resort to elections in the factory districts in order to get representatives into the workers' section [of the Committee]. From a formal point of view, this resolution is based on far too broad an interpretation of the decree establishing the Committee. Yet substantively, considering present moods, it is most difficult to oppose this interpretation. The whole affair is being conducted under a patriotic banner and in the name of defense. How, then, can one react and take repressive measures?

PRINCE V. N. SHAKHOVSKOY: I am afraid that the leaders of the workers will use the elections as an excuse to agitate. Their attitude towards the Guchkov Committee is negative, but they will not refuse to create a workers' cell in it. It is much too tempting to form a center for the organization of workers under legal auspices. One must open Guchkov's eyes for him—where his Committee, and the creation of a workers' section in it, is leading him.

A. A. KHVOSTOV: Guchkov will not believe us in any event. But one cannot ignore this plan. It creates a possibility for the workers to fill the gaps in their organization, which was shattered by the arrest of the leftist members of the Duma.

A. A. POLIVANOV: But after all, one cannot deny that mobilization of industry is impossible without the cooperation of the workers. If that is so, it would be most careless to stir up the workers by denying them participation in a guiding organization.

The Ministers of Internal Affairs [Shcherbatov] and of Trade [Shakhovskoy] were authorized to explore this issue in its fullest context and to report to the Council of Ministers.

A. V. KRIVOSHEIN: The ministries must submit their budgets to the Duma by September 1st. If we do so, we have excluded the possibility of ending the Session of the Duma. We must decide this question right now. What is more advantageous for us from the political point of view: an immediate adjournment or a new postponement? Practically speaking, at the present time, and with the present relations between the government and the Duma, it is hopeless to get any laws through the Duma. Yet Article 87 does not apply, and therefore everything waits, now, when every minute is precious. Such a situation is impossible. Sessions without any legislative material transform the Duma into a political meeting on current events; and its tribune, into a tribune for antigovernment propaganda. I am being told by many delegates, even leftists, that the Duma has begun to roll impetuously down an inclined plane.

I. L. GOREMYKIN: I have, in my possession, a decree on the adjournment of the legislative bodies which has been signed by His Majesty and on which I may enter the date. I beg the Council of Ministers to express itself on the issue raised by A. V. Krivoshein.

A. A. KHVOSTOV: I must warn everyone that, as I have been told by M. V. Rodzianko, the idea of presenting the Minister of Justice [Khvostov] with a demonstrative parliamentary question about Gregory Rasputin and all the abnormalities connected with the latter, is very popular among the deputies in the event of a premature adjournment of the Duma. It is difficult to predict how this question will be put, but we cannot shut their mouths, and there will be an incredible scandal. According to Rodzianko, the only way to forestall such a scandal is for the Minister of Justice to prefer charges against Rasputin and imprison him. I have studied the issue from this point of view and have become convinced that there is no evidence which would allow legal intervention.

I. L. GOREMYKIN: I am convinced that Rodzianko has invented all this in order to frighten us. Knowing against whom it is directed and what consequences it would have, no one in the Duma would dare ask such a question. In any event, the government does not have to bother with such threats.

A. V. KRIVOSHEIN: Quite right. The chief basis at the present time is the absence of any legislative material before the Duma, and, in connection with this reason—should we submit our budgets, which would be exactly this kind of legislative material and therefore would be a formal excuse to oppose adjournment?

PRINCE V. N. SHAKHOVSKOY: If the Duma has done everything for which it was summoned, then I do not understand why one should wait. One must publish the decree [of adjournment] in advance of the legal deadline for the submission of the budgets.

PRINCE N. B. SHCHERBATOV: No, not all of our legislative projects have been finished. There is the motion on a special conference on refugees; the sanction of the Duma is necessary for this, as we would otherwise be left without any elected representatives from the legislative bodies. The presence of such representatives is absolutely necessary in order to remove the whole responsibility for the horrors in the life of the refugees from the government and in order to share this responsibility with the Duma.

A. V. KRIVOSHEIN: I think we can get together with them on this issue and that they will let it go through without delay. The need for a special conference, with the participation of the representatives of the public, is too self-evident.

P. A. KHARITONOV: The Duma has cured us of optimism. She is being guided, not by general interests but by party considerations. If people find out that the adjournment is being postponed because of the refugees, then the law will be delayed as long as necessary from the viewpoint of political calculations.

I. L. GOREMYKIN: The issue is not the specific legislation, but the determination of the date of adjournment based on general State considerations. It is most important to decide when is it best to publish the decree: before the assumption of the supreme command by His Majesty, or afterward. I am inclined to the second alternative.

(It is interesting that the decree on this assumption had already been signed and made public in Headquarters the day before: that is, on the 25th of August. Headquarters did not find it necessary, however, to inform the Council of Ministers of this fact.) [Note by Iakhontov]

A. V. KRIVOSHEIN: I am afraid this may delay matters. I think the adjournment should take place before the 1st of September: that is, before the submissions of the budgets in any event. One should agree with the Presidium [of the Duma] concerning the specific day. In general, both the internal and external situations are such, right now, that our parting with the Duma should be done nicely, properly, with some previous notice rather than suddenly, like a cold shower.

I. L. GOREMYKIN: I am ready to discuss this with Rodzianko and Kulomzin.[1] As the reason, I will point out that everything for which the legislative bodies have been summoned has been done.

P. A. KHARITONOV: In other words, the conversation should have the character of a consultation, rather than of an announcement of

---

[1] Anatoly Nikolaevich Kulomzin (1838-1924): old gentry family; member of the State Council from 1902; President of the State Council in 1915-16.

a decision already taken. One can be certain that Rodzianko will rear up on his hind legs and insist that the salvation of Russia lies only in the Duma.

I. L. GOREMYKIN: I know that some Duma circles express fear that popular unrest may prove to be stronger than the Duma and that the latter's absence will only hasten the explosion. In general, a great deal of nonsense is being chattered there.

A. A. KHVOSTOV: I think that one can no longer be slow about the adjournment. Correctly or not, the change in the supreme command is connected with the expectation of an explosion of unrest. If riots really break out, then it will be difficult to resort to adjournment and the government will end up tied hand-and-foot. It would be more prudent, therefore, for the Emperor to assume the command after the adjournment of the legislative bodies.

A. A. POLIVANOV: I consider, that, in any event, the date of adjournment should be determined in the course of preliminary, and, as A. V. Krivoshein said, "well-intentioned" discussions. They should be conducted, not with Rodzianko alone but with other well-intentioned deputies.

I. L. GOREMYKIN: Who are they, these well-wishers?

A. A. POLIVANOV: Did the Chairman of the Council of Ministers not interest himself in this question earlier, and did he not take steps [to be able] to answer it?

PRINCE N. B. SHCHERBATOV: I, too, would deem it necessary to involve other deputies besides Rodzianko in these conversations. In no case can he be regarded as the moral representative of the Duma. It would be most proper to invite the whole Presidium.

A. V. KRIVOSHEIN: No matter whom you invite, the answer will be inevitably negative. Even the Balashev[2] people will not dare to say openly that it is time to adjourn the Duma. This is a question for the Supreme Authority. The conversations have only a diplomatic significance.

I. L. GOREMYKIN: I request the Council of Ministers to express itself on the date of adjournment. As far as the preliminary conversations—whose usefulness, up to a point, I do not deny—are con-

---

[2] Petr Nikolaevich Balashev: deputy to the 3rd and 4th Dumas; member of the Nationalist Party; rich landowner; leader of his party and of the moderate Right in the Duma.

cerned, I will conduct them with those whom I will consider necessary to invite.

COUNT P. N. IGNAT'EV: It is difficult to express oneself before we know the outcome of the conversations, and, in general, before the whole internal situation at the moment of adjournment is clear. For example, the possibility that the Duma will refuse to obey and will continue to meet is not to be excluded.

I. L. GOREMYKIN: That would be direct opposition to Supreme Authority. Then the conversation would be a different one. Then one would not conduct negotiations, but would act.

PRINCE N. B. SHCHERBATOV: It is unlikely that the deputies will dare direct disobedience. After all, the enormous majority are cowards and are trembling for their own hides. But violent scenes, appeals, protests, and similar *démarches* are inevitable. If even the Imperial Yacht Club on Morskaia Street is revolutionary and demands changes, then one can expect anything and any kind of hysteria from the Duma.

A. V. KRIVOSHEIN: The question of the change of command complicates the issue enormously. It is dangerous to associate two causes for disorders: this change and the adjournment of the Duma. The first of these is particularly risky. One should direct His Majesty's attention to this coincidence, and beg him to postpone the change of command until the effect of the adjournment of the Duma has abated. One should wire the Emperor about this.

A. A. KHVOSTOV: I have been told that Mr. Miliukov openly boasts that all the strings are in his hands, and that, on the day the supreme command changes, he has only to press a button and riots will break out all over Russia.

I. L. GOREMYKIN: Miliukov can talk any kind of nonsense and fantasy he wishes. I believe so much in the Russian people and in its patriotism that I do not even tolerate the notion that it would answer its Tsar with riots, particularly in wartime. And if separate little groups of intriguers begin to make mischief, there are enough police for them and there is no need to consider them.

A. D. SAMARIN: All this is quite conjectural. The majority of us think differently than you, Ivan Longinovich [Goremykin]. In an affair of State, particularly when the very existence of the State is being gambled, it is the duty of the government to exhaust all means of forestalling disaster. I think that the question of the

Duma, right now, has extraordinary importance and that it should be decided with the direct participation of His Majesty. In my opinion, we should ask the Emperor to summon the Council of Ministers for this purpose, and discuss, at a meeting in the Imperial Presence, both the date of adjournment and the date of the assumption of command. The motive for such a request is the one which has been indicated by A. V. Krivoshein: namely, the dangerous coincidence of two causes of trouble.

I. L. GOREMYKIN: I find it impossible to burden the Emperor once more with a question that he has decided finally, a fact about which he personally informed the Council of Ministers. Neither can I write him about the danger of riots and frighten him unnecessarily, for I do not share these fears. They are being exaggerated by Miliukov and the rest of that crowd for the purpose of instilling fear.

PRINCE N. B. SHCHERBATOV: The expectation of disorders is found not only in Miliukov, but also within the political police and the gendarmes. Intense propaganda is being generated in the garrisons and in the hospitals, with the excuses of the change of command and the defense of the Duma against the attacks of the bureaucracy. My ministry is daily receiving reports to the effect that universal rioting is inevitable two or three days after the adjournment of the Duma.

P. A. KHARITONOV: Not only the Yacht Club, but the United Gentry is protesting and demanding changes. Even Strukov,[3] who can be accused of anything but liberalism, demands, in the name of the United Gentry, that ministers be chosen from society.

A. V. KRIVOSHEIN: This great statesman probably has mixed-up notions. It is doubtful that he understands the word "society" in the same sense as the Moscow City Council. It is interesting that, according to this point of view, we do not belong to society.

I. L. GOREMYKIN: Among all the various resolutions, one cannot reject the resolution of the United Gentry. And it reads that, in the present universal unsteadiness of minds, speeches of the left-wing deputies in the Duma and abuses by the press are creating confusion and spreading disorder.

---

[3] Ananii Petrovich Strukov: rich landowner and right-wing member of the State Council; very influential in the United Gentry.

* * *

(My notes are interrupted at this point. It is noted that the question of the adjournment of legislative bodies is to be postponed until it can be considered in the light of the program of a bloc of various parties being formed in the Duma; a program which is to be considered by the Council of Ministers.)

A. V. KRIVOSHEIN: And I still repeat that one cannot stay in the middle. One must act in one way or another. If one is to fear everything, then everything will be lost.

The MINISTER OF INTERNAL AFFAIRS announced that the well-known resolution of the Moscow City Council had spread all over Russia, and that now, or in the near future, one could expect similar resolutions from all cities. "What's to be done, how should one react?" asks PRINCE N. B. SHCHERBATOV: According to the information received by me these last few days from various governors, Town Councils intend to send deputies to the Tsar with prescriptions for the salvation of Russia modelled on the sample confirmed at the Konovalov meeting. Such resolutions are not in accordance with the law on Town Councils and they can be protested.

After long discussion, in the course of which the split in the Council of Ministers on the meaning and significance of the internal situation in the country emerged still more strongly, it was decided not to use the power of protest against Town resolutions similar to the Moscow one; it was decided to direct the problem of deputations in the normal way, through the Minister of the Imperial Court.

I. L. GOREMYKIN: We have spoken repeatedly about the absolutely impermissible activities of the daily press. Nevertheless the outrages do not cease. I consider it my duty to remind you of the Imperial Resolution of the year 1906, which resembles our own time. His Majesty pointed out, at that time, that in a revolutionary period one cannot be guided only by law in dealing with the abuses of the press, and that one cannot allow the emission of poison into the people to go unpunished. I would particularly beg the Minister of Internal Affairs to pay attention to these words. In one way or another, the issue of the press must be pushed off this dead spot.

XIV

The Meeting of
26 August 1915

---◆---

I. L. GOREMYKIN: Today, we must finish with the question of the adjournment of the legislative bodies. This question is very important, complicated, and badly delayed. I request the Council of Ministers to express its final opinion as to the day of adjournment. A. V. Krivoshein, who has left for Moscow, has expressed his opinion on the necessity and urgency of an adjournment. What do the other members of the Council of Ministers think about this?

A. A. POLIVANOV: But at the last meeting it was decided to discuss this first with Rodzianko and well-meaning deputies. It would be most important to know the results of these negotiations. Otherwise, I find it difficult to answer the question that has been put.

I. L. GOREMYKIN: I have not conducted any negotiations as yet. I find them superfluous before the Council of Ministers decides on the day of adjournment. If one starts to talk with Rodzianko, that chatterer will immediately announce it all over the place. I will talk with him after the date has been definitely set.

S. D. SAZONOV: I have profound and substantive doubts. How convenient is it, from the government's point of view, under the present circumstances, to resort to an adjournment of the Duma?

Such action will undoubtedly evoke disorders, not only among the public organizations, unions, and establishments which lean toward the Duma, but also among the workers. Even though these last are connected with the Duma artificially, and not organically, they could not ignore such a convenient occasion for demonstrations. The majority of the members of the Duma, themselves, feel that the adjournment is necessary by reason of the present situation. Nevertheless, they are restrained by fears of increased unrest in the factories and of sharp *démarches* which might have bloody consequences. How will all this affect the defense effort and the further conduct of the war? One must weigh this question from all sides. Perhaps it will be necessary to admit that a troublesome Duma is a lesser evil than workers' disorders in the absence of the Duma.

I. K. GRIGOROVICH: According to my information, disorders are inevitable if the Duma is adjourned. The workers are in a very bad mood. The Germans are conducting very potent propaganda and are pouring funds into the antigovernment organizations. The situation is particularly acute at the Putilov factory.[1] What is taking place there is an Italian strike: [slow-down] The workers stand at their machines, but they don't do anything and demand a twenty per cent raise. Obviously, one must fear that both the demands and the method of action will change the moment there is an excuse for more decisive *démarches*. I very much fear that the adjournment of the Duma will have very adverse repercussions on the internal situation of Russia.

A. A. POLIVANOV: One cannot ignore the mood in the public organizations and in the factories. Do not forget that the whole defense effort rests on society and on the workers. If both the former and the latter are driven to despair, what will this lead to? One must remember also the words spoken by His Majesty the Emperor when he opened the Special Conference on Defense: "The Tsar relies on the whole country." The consequences of the adjournment of the Duma will demolish such expectations. One must think all this through. There is an old saying: Measure seven times before you cut once. If the Council of Ministers still decides that the adjournment is necessary, then we must work out both the reasons

---

[1] The largest armament factory in St. Petersburg.

for it and the procedure. It is important to give this act a façade which would soften the impression and squelch unnecessary rumors and interpretations.

P. A. KHARITONOV: The way the Minister of War [Polivanov] suggests posing the issue appears to me to be correct. From this point of view, it is important to find out, precisely, whether all the legislation submitted by the government was passed in this Session. I speak, of course, of the more important measures: for example, the Special Conference on Refugees, the income tax, and others.

I. L. GOREMYKIN: The income tax is not a measure evoked by military necessity and it can well wait for the next Session. As for the Conference on Refugees, this question is being delayed in the Duma deliberately. Besides, even if this legislation were passed, the election of the representatives of the Duma to the conference would still be dragged out. It is the story about the white calf.[2] Actually the matter does not have enough substantive importance to warrant delaying because of it, a measure required by general State considerations.

PRINCE N. B. SHCHERBATOV: The participation of the representatives of the Duma in the Special Conference on Refugees is insurance for the government against biased attacks in this delicate matter.

I. L. GOREMYKIN: What kind of insurance is it? The entire onus will be piled up on the government anyway! The Committee on Defense consists of elected people and possesses unlimited authority, and we alone are cursed for all the insufficiencies of supply, nevertheless.

S. D. SAZONOV: I have not finished with my doubts. Our desire to acquaint ourselves with the program of the bloc has become known to everyone. Is it profitable to adjourn the Duma without having discussed, with its majority, the acceptability of this program? What kind of impression will be created by this way of acting? Today one decision; tomorrow another. Today, the well-intentioned decision to converse; tomorrow—dispersal, without a word.

I. L. GOREMYKIN: We are not talking of dispersal, but of an adjournment until November.

S. D. SAZONOV: The issue is not in the form but in the sub-

---

[2] The reference is to a Russian folk story in which endless promises and endless waiting occur.

stance, or rather, in the political impression made by this government action. I personally vote for the necessity of negotiating with the representatives of the bloc. Their program undoubtedly has a twist to it and is virtually designed for the next fifteen years. It should be examined in detail, discussed, and one should pick out that which is acceptable in substance and which applies to wartime conditions. I am convinced that it will be possible to agree, for there is much in the program which the government would not protest. And then, having agreed, and having promised to realize the things decided on, one can even adjourn [the Duma]. The deputies would then go home, aware that their voice had been heard and that the government is willing to meet their just demands. It would be a very great mistake to reject everything, all at once, and hence give the adjournment a forcible character. This would, first of all, affect the workers' districts and would complicate an internal situation which is already virtually hopeless.

I. L. GOREMYKIN: Such conversations would lead nowhere anyway. It is incorrect to assume that the workers' movement is connected with the adjournment of the Duma. It has existed and will go on existing, independent of the existence of the Duma. The problem for the leaders of the workers is their lack of organization, which was smashed by the arrest of the five members of the Duma. I beg you not to digress from the basic issue—the determination of the date for ending the session.

S. D. SAZONOV: I am searching for this date by trying to evaluate the whole context of the political situation. The development of the workers' movement in its historical perspective is not relevant to this matter. There is a practical question before us: How will the factories and plants react to the adjournment of the Duma at the present moment? The majority of the members of the Council of Ministers believes that a sharpening of the mood amongst the workers will be a direct consequence of such an action and will, in turn, affect both the general situation in the country and the defense effort.

I. L. GOREMYKIN: I agree that the adjournment will be used for agitational purposes. But even if the Duma were to remain [in session] we would have no guarantees against flare-ups among the workers. The moment their leaders organize themselves and become conscious of their own strength, they will call the workers out for demonstrations on any pretext, even with the help of provocations. Whether we go along with the bloc or without it is irrelevant for the workers' movement. And one can struggle with this movement by other means, and up to now the Ministry of Internal Affairs has managed.

s. d. sazonov: I am of a different opinion, and I believe that it is impermissible to reject all of society in time of the greatest war, and that what is necessary is the union of all levels of the population. However, I speak futilely, as the question has apparently been decided without us. I simply don't understand, however, why it was necessary to assemble the Council of Ministers and waste time on conversations which, obviously, cannot accomplish anything.

i. l. goremykin: No one has decided anything in advance. I began by asking the Council of Ministers to express itself. Our deliberations will be reported fully to His Majesty the Emperor, who will decide what is to be done. If it pleases you to associate the question of adjournment with the program of the bloc, then let us discuss the program. Insofar as I have had an opportunity to acquaint myself with it, not everything in the program should be rejected, but some of the demands are absolutely unacceptable.

s. d. sazonov: That means, judging by your words, that not everything in the desires of the bloc is rejected *en masse,* and there are points on which one can agree?

i. l. goremykin: Yes. As far as the program is concerned, a part can be accepted by the government for its future actions. As far as the bloc itself is concerned, however, I find any conversations with it impossible for the government. We can deal only with legislative bodies, and not with an accidental union of their separate representatives. Such an organization is not provided for by law.

s. d. sazonov: Then I utterly fail to understand the purpose of today's discussion. One can examine the program, but one cannot talk with the organization which has worked out this program! One can talk with the separate members of the bloc, but one cannot talk with the bloc itself! Men, whose hearts ache for their motherland, seek the unity of the most active nonrevolutionary elements of the country—and they are declared an illegal assembly and are ignored. This is a dangerous tactic and an enormous political mistake. The government cannot exist in a vacuum and rely on the police alone. I will keep on repeating this until the very end.

I. L. GOREMYKIN: The bloc has been created to grab power. Anyway, it will fall apart and all its participants will end up squabbling with each other.

S. D. SAZONOV: And I believe that, in the name of general State interests, this bloc, essentially a moderate one, should be supported by us. If this one falls apart, we will get one which is much further to the left. What will happen then? Whom will that profit? Not Russia, in any event.

A. A. POLIVANOV: And how will this reflect on our defense effort, on our struggle against the enemy who is carefully following our internal disorders and disorganization?

S. D. SAZONOV: It is dangerous to provoke the left, to challenge it to nonparliamentary means of struggle. I insist on the necessity of not rejecting blindly the wishes of the bloc and on agreeing with it about that which is acceptable to the government. What is the point of worsening relations which are bad enough already, without any purpose?

I. L. GOREMYKIN: And I consider the bloc itself, as an organization overlapping the two chambers, unacceptable. Its badly concealed aim is the limitation of the power of the Tsar. Against this I will fight to the last.

S. D. SAZONOV: It is better for us not to start conjecturing. Otherwise our exchange of opinions may stray very far from the point.

I. L. GOREMYKIN: I am only answering questions, and I would be very glad if we were to return to the only issue which I have posed—the day of adjournment of the Duma and of the State Council for the autumn vacation.

S. D. SAZONOV: If you insist, I am prepared to discuss the issue, but beginning with the conclusion. An adjournment is necessary, but, in order to achieve it, it is essential to get together with the organization which represents all of the antirevolutionary Duma.

PRINCE N. V. SHAKHOVSKOY: I thought that the question of adjournment had already been decided by us, in principle, the last time, and that, moreover, we had recognized that it was desirable to achieve it before the 1st of September: namely, before the submission of the budgets by the ministries. It remains, therefore, to agree on the date. This should be determined before our conversation with Rodzianko and the deputies, for one should not show them our cards ahead of time and give them the opportunity to prepare undesirable *démarches*. Now I will say a few words on the substance. Considering the present climate, both the continuation of the Duma and its adjournment are equally dangerous. The Duma is not legislating, but holding political meetings, stirring up the country and the workers. Its adjournment may, or may not, prove to be the starting point for an outburst of disorders. Of these two evils, I choose the lesser and I vote for immediate adjournment, even tomorrow. But it should be done in a nice way: One should discuss their program with the representatives of the bloc, one should agree on that which is acceptable, and so on. With such actions of a conciliatory character, we will open a way out for the deputies themselves, who are yearning for adjournment because they recognize the hopelessness of their situation and are afraid of becoming, in the end, toys in the hands of leftist elements.

PRINCE N. B. SHCHERBATOV: It is my opinion that we should adjourn the Duma right away, both because of the approach of September 1st—the date of the submission of the budgets—and because of the worsening relations between the Duma and the government, or, to put it more strongly, because of the discord between these two sides. This discord is affecting the course of events very negatively, and is irritating the whole country. It is impossible to allow this situation to continue. But it is important to get the adjournment through properly, without quarrels and causes for scandal. It is regrettable that, up to now, the government has not negotiated with the bloc. It is impossible to deny that the program is sewn together with basting thread and that it would be easy to demolish it. But I agree with the view that to do this would be unprofitable for the government, for it would place it face-to-face with leftist tendencies and would force into these tendencies many who are obviously nonrevolutionary. The program itself undoubtedly has been deliberately contrived in order to bargain and to discover how far the government is willing to go. The determination of this aspect will also determine the future make-up of the bloc, which has, at present, a temporary character, being a union of people of various parties, a union evoked by fears of a social revolution if the present uncertainty is to continue. Our silence, our ignoring of the bloc could affect the mood of an enormous majority of the well-intentioned part of the Duma most negatively. One cannot allow it to go home insulted and angered by our lack of attention, for this would manifest itself both in the provinces and at the front, where quite a number of the members of the Duma work in various organizations. In a word, all considerations lead to the conclusion that one should talk with the deputies in a peaceful and friendly way, before adjournment. My attention has been drawn to the necessity for this by many deputies, and by Rodzianko himself. He, by the way, is more angry than anyone else over the fact that the government does not take him seriously. Having negotiated, having agreed on separate points of the program, we will have created a nucleus sympathetic to us— even if only a couple of hundred deputies—and then one can get the adjournment through painlessly. The hiatus in the Session of the legislative bodies should be devoted to the passing of laws and reforms agreed upon with the deputies, by using Article 87. This activity would raise the prestige of the government in the country, which would know that we are acting in accordance with our agreement with the deputies. It will be easier for us to govern and to achieve that which is demanded by the extraordinary circumstances of the war.

I. L. GOREMYKIN: You are forgetting that one of the basic desires of the bloc is a lengthy Session.

PRINCE N. B. SHCHERBATOV: That's only for public consumption.

S. D. SAZONOV: The majority of the Duma is definitely against a lengthy Session.

I. L. GOREMYKIN: Yes, but they will never confess it publicly.

S. D. SAZONOV: But neither will they impede us from ending the Session, and, if need be, they will support us. For this, it is necessary to have conversations ahead of time and to determine, together, the program of activity during the vacation period.

P. A. KHARITONOV: I, too, am for adjournment, but with the qualifications which have just been stated. The program of the bloc must be discussed, together [with its representatives] and the unacceptable stricken out.

I. L. GOREMYKIN: We'd have to strike out three-quarters of it.

PRINCE N. B. SHCHERBATOV: We have not yet examined the program in detail, and at the moment it is difficult to say what should be excluded. In any event, the program, even in a cut-down form, will serve as a basis for conversation and for identifying those who are sympathetic. Those unwilling to compromise will withdraw, and we will tighten up the nucleus and go hand-in-hand with it.

A. A. KHVOSTOV: I don't believe very much in all this, but I will not object to preliminary discussions.

I. L. GOREMYKIN: The conversations must not be binding on the government. One cannot undertake any formal obligations right now. The times don't allow it.

P. A. KHARITONOV: No one is speaking of this now. The question right now is of information, not of agreement. The program serves as a basis for an off-the-record union, and any conversation about it should be limited to an off-the-record exchange of views.

I. L. GOREMYKIN: Conversations of this kind must be conducted by the head of the government.

P. A. KHARITONOV: Quite correct as far as definitive negotiations are concerned. But it would be more prudent to have the preliminary conversation conducted by individual authorized persons.

I. L. GOREMYKIN: We will return to this detail later. Now we must examine the program of the bloc as a whole, and agree on it among ourselves.

(As a supplement to these present notes I have preserved a copy of the program which was discussed in the meeting. I am reproducing it in full. This is necessary to the understanding of the later discussion [note by Iakhontov].)

On the 25th of August, 1915, representatives of factions and groups of the Duma and of the State Council signed a program of agreement creating a Progressive Bloc. It was entered upon by the Progressive Nationalists, the Center group, the Zemtsy-Octobrists, the Left Octobrists, the Progressives, and the Cadets of the Duma; and by the Academic group, the Center, and, conditionally, by the nonaffiliated group of the State Council. The final text of the program is as follows:

The undersigned representatives of parties and groups of the State Council and of the Duma, basing themselves on the conviction that only a strong, firm, and active government can lead the fatherland to victory, and that such a government can only be one which is based on public confidence and capable of organizing the active cooperation of all citizens, have come to the unanimous conclusion that the most important and essential task of creating such a government cannot be accomplished without the fulfillment of the following requirements:

The creation of a united government made up of persons who have the confidence of the country and are in agreement with the legislative bodies concerning the immediate execution of a definite program.

A definite abandonment of the methods of administration used up to now, which were based on distrust of public participation.

In particular: (a) strict legality in administration; (b) the abolition of the dichotomy of military and civil authorities in questions which are not directly connected with the conduct of military operations; (c) changes in the personnel of local administrations; (d) a rational and consistent policy directed to the preservation of internal peace and the elimination of discord among nationalities and classes.

The following measures, both administrative and legislative, must be taken to achieve such a policy:

1. By means of Monarchic Grace, the termination of all cases based on accusations of purely political and religious crimes which are not of a generally criminal character; the liberation from punishment and the restoration in their rights (including the right of participating in the elections to the Duma and to the *Zemstvo* and town organizations, and so forth) of persons convicted of such crimes; the mitigation of the fate of all others convicted of political and religious crimes, with the exception of spies and traitors.

2. The return of all those administratively exiled for political reasons.

3. The complete and definitive termination of all persecutions for religious beliefs, on no matter what pretexts, and the abrogation of all circulars designed to limit and distort the meaning of the Decree of April 17, 1905.[3]

4. The solution of the Russo-Polish question: namely, the abrogation of all limitations of the rights of Poles in all of Russia; the immediate drafting of a law for the autonomy of the Polish Tsardom and its submission to the legislative bodies; and the simultaneous re-examination of the legislation on Polish land ownership.[4]

5. The entrance on the path of abrogation of the limitations on the rights of Jews: in particular, further steps to abrogate the zone of settlement; making it easier to enter educational institutions; the annulment of limitations in the choice of profession; the restoration of a Jewish press.

6. Conciliatory policy in the Finnish question: in particular, a change of personnel in the administration and the Senate, and the cessation of the persecutions of officials.

---

[3] This act was entitled "On the strengthening of the bases of religious toleration."

[4] Poles were forbidden to acquire estates in the eastern areas of Russian Poland populated by Orthodox peasants. The legal name of Russian Poland was *Tsarstvo Polskoe* ("the Polish Tsardom") which the Emperor ruled as Tsar of Poland, an office created by Alexander I.

7. The restoration of a Ukrainian press; the immediate re-examination of the cases of inhabitants of Galicia who were arrested and exiled; and the liberation of those who have been victimized by the persecution.[5]

8. The restoration of the activities of labor unions and the cessation of persecution of workers' representatives in medical insurance cooperatives on suspicion of belonging to illegal parties; the restoration of a labor press.

9. The agreement of the government with the legislative bodies on the most rapid passing of:

(a) All legislation having a close relation to national defense, to the supply of the armies, to the care of the wounded, to the organization of the lot of refugees, and to other questions directly connected with the war;

(b) The following program of legislation directed to the organization of the country for victory and for the maintenance of internal peace: the equalization of the peasants, as to their rights, with all other social classes; the introduction of *volost' zemstvo;* the change in the *Zemstvo* Decree of 1890;[6] the change of the Law of 1892 on towns;[7] the introduction of *zemstvo* organizations on the peripheries—namely, in Siberia, Archangel Province, the Don territory, the Caucasus, and so forth;[8] legislation on cooperatives, on vacations for salespeople, on the betterment of the situation of post and telegraph employees, on the confirmation and the perpetuity of temperance, on *zemstvo* and town assemblies and unions, on the regulations of the census, on the introduction of justices of the peace in those provinces where this measure was postponed because of financial considerations, and on the accomplishment of those legislative

---

[5] The center of Ukrainian nationalism was in Galicia, a part of the western Ukraine within the Austro-Hungarian Empire, whose government encouraged this nationalism as a balance to Austrian Poland and against Russia.

[6] The Progressive Bloc's demand for the organization of the *zemstvo* not only on the county (*uezd*) level but on the *volost'* level had serious implications. While the county organization insured gentry dominance in the local self-government, the *volost'* was purely a peasant unit.

The 1890 law on the *zemstvo,* part of the reaction under Alexander III, required that all appointments and all decisions of the *zemstvo* be approved by the provincial governor.

[7] Similarly, the 1892 law on towns, restricted local self-government by imposing administrative control on elections (by the Emperor for Moscow and St. Petersburg; in other towns by the Minister of Internal Affairs and the provincial governors), and by restricting the suffrage to owners of houses, land, or businesses.

[8] The *zemstvo* organization was, originally, introduced as an experiment only in the central provinces, the government constantly promising to extend this right of local self-government.

measures which may be found necessary for the administrative execution of the program outlined above.

Signed—On the part of the Progressive Nationalist Group: Count V. A. Bobrinsky;[9] on the part of the faction of the Center, V. N. L'vov;[10] on the part of the faction of *Zemstvo* Octobrists, I. I. Dmitriukov;[11] on the part of the Union of the 17th of October, S. I. Shidlovsky;[12] on the part of the faction of the Progressives, I. N. Efremov; on the part of the faction of Popular Freedom [Cadets], P. N. Miliukov; on the part of the Academic Group of the State Council, D. D. Grimm; and on the part of the group of the Center of the State Council, Baron V. Meller-Zakomel'sky.

I. L. GOREMYKIN: The beginning of the program adds up to some fancy language on which we will not waste any time.

A. A. POLIVANOV: This "fancy language" contains the whole essence of the desires of the public about the government. Can one pass them by so contemptuously?

I. L. GOREMYKIN: It is not possible for the Council of Ministers to discuss demands which amount to the limitation of Imperial power. The program will be submitted to His Majesty the Emperor, and it is up to His Majesty, alone, to make one or another decision. I request the Council of Ministers to address itself to the specific points of the program. The first point has in mind a broad amnesty. I believe that, in time of war, it is not possible to allow the rear to be cluttered up with jailbirds, even political ones. It will only lead to additional disorders and outrages.

PRINCE N. B. SHCHERBATOV: The whole point is the demand for the restoration of political rights. The main concern is for the

---

[9] Count Vladimir Alekseevich Bobrinsky: born 1867; Nationalist deputy to the 2nd, 3rd, and 4th Dumas; large landowner; county leader of the nobility; Vice-Chairman of the Nationalist Party in the Duma; one of the leaders of the neo-Slav movement (a modern form of pan-Slavism) in 1908.

[10] Vladimir Nikolaevich L'vov; deputy to the 3rd and 4th Dumas; at various times, member of the Octobrist, the Nationalist and then the Center parties; influential in the center groupings of the Duma and in Church circles.

[11] Ivan Ivanovich Dmitriukov: Octobrist deputy to the 3rd and 4th Dumas; elected Secretary of the 4th Duma.

[12] Sergei Illiodorovich Shidlovsky: Octobrist deputy to the 3rd and 4th Dumas; 1905-06, director of the Department of Agriculture; chairman of the Duma Octobrist group and representative of the Left Octobrists in the Progressive Bloc.

Vyborzhtsy[13] and for the five members of the Duma convicted in the spring. As far as the *Vyborzhtsy* are concerned, I would not argue— it's ten years old now. But one cannot amnesty the members of the Duma—they are the organizing center of the workers' movement in its most dangerous forms.

A. A. KHVOSTOV: Now Guchkov's Military-Industrial Committee is becoming such a center.

PRINCE N. B. SHCHERBATOV: The more reason not to reinforce it by the addition of experienced men. I would also be against a general amnesty. One should limit oneself to a gradual procedure. From the point of view of creating a political effect, it would be most purposeful, in the beginning, to select some of the most prominent gentlemen and be very nice to them. One can agree with the bloc, in the sense that they should make up a list of those to be amnestied and we will look it over and gradually take care of it.

A. A. KHVOSTOV: The re-examination of political cases has gone on continuously in the Ministry of Justice. Since I took over the Ministry, many cases have been dismissed by means of Monarchic Grace, and quite a few of these gentlemen are walking around free.

PRINCE N. B. SHCHERBATOV: Yes, I know this, but the public does not know it. One must advertise it. Take a dozen or two particularly beloved liberators and let them out, all at once, into the light of day, publicizing it in all the newspapers as the Tsar's mercy. In a word, what is now being done secretly should be done very loudly and at a faster tempo. Of course, the final selection would be in the hands of the government, and the bloc could only recommend.

Everyone agreed on the undesirability of a general amnesty, accepting the point of view of Prince N. B. Shcherbatov on the *Vyborzhtsy* and on further tactics.

I. L. GOREMYKIN: The suggestion of the Minister of Internal

---

[13] *Vyborzhtsy*—those who were in Vyborg, Finland. Upon the dissolution of the 1st Duma, in July, 1906 (as it proved to be too radical), the Cadets and the radical Left deputies (some 200 in all) went to Vyborg. Finland, though a part of the Russian Empire, possessed a constitution which protected the deputies against administrative repressions. There the deputies appealed to the population of Russia not to pay taxes or serve in the army until a new Duma was summoned; this appeal was signed by 180 deputies. In December, 1907, the deputies were tried, condemned to three months in prison, and permanently deprived of the right to vote and to be elected.

Affairs [Shcherbatov] can also be applied to the second point of the program. In connection with administrative exiles—not a general measure, but a re-examination of individual cases.

s. d. sazonov: Thousands of people are sitting, for no reason, in various distant places. This is a disgrace! Everyone knows that administrative arbitrariness was the method of Prince Shcherbatov's predecessor [Maklakov]. One must end all this and re-examine Maklakov's actions.

p. a. kharitonov: The government has already embarked on this course, having finished the affair of Burtsev.[14]

prince n. b. shcherbatov: One can find hundreds of Burtsevs, both in Russia and abroad.

s. d. sazonov: Yes, find them, and, without hesitation, ease their situation. We must remove this stain of unjustified arbitrariness and despotism from ourselves.

i. l. goremykin: We proclaimed religious toleration a long time ago.

s. d. sazonov: In theory, but not in practice. With us, circulars are more potent than [Imperial] manifestos.

p. a. kharitonov: Everyone is particularly irritated by the circulars on the Catholic question, which are designed for the struggle against the Poles. They serve as a pretext for arbitrariness and total outrages. It was time to put a stop to this long ago.

i. l. goremykin: Of course, there are quite a few outrages. But what do you suggest be done when men shield themselves with religion in order to obtain political goals and act to the detriment of Russian interests?

s. d. sazonov: For this, we have the courts.

prince n. b. shcherbatov: Undoubtedly much should be re-examined and abolished. Preliminary work on this is already going on in my Ministry. Nevertheless, a general measure is hardly possible, even in this matter. For instance, how is one to manage with the Baptists, among whom German influence and sympathies are clearly visible?

---

[14] Vladimir L'vovich Burtsev (1862-1936): journalist; spent many years in France, in political exile; involved with the Social-Revolutionary Party; returned to Russia at the beginning of World War I out of patriotic motives, and was arrested by the government.

* * *

It was acknowledged that administrative regulations on religious matters should be re-examined in the positive sense, with a qualification that the interests of Orthodoxy be safeguarded.

I. L. GOREMYKIN: On the Polish question, much has been done and is being done. The wishes expressed in the program coincide with the government declaration in the Duma. What else does the bloc want?

P. A. KHARITONOV: The hidden purpose here—to remove all limitations in matters of land ownership in the areas being safeguarded from Polish penetration. It seems to me that, in this case, government policy does not allow for any concessions.

The Council of Ministers unanimously agreed with the conclusion of the State Comptroller [Kharitonov].

I. L. GOREMYKIN: I must warn the Council of Ministers that the Emperor has repeatedly said that he will not undertake anything, by himself, on the Jewish question. Hence, only one way is possible—in the Duma. If she can manage it, let her try to deal with equal rights. She won't get very far with it.

PRINCE N. B. SHCHERBATOV: The Duma will never dare raise the issue of equal rights for the Jews. Nothing will come of it except scandals. It is another matter to abolish unnecessary, avoidable, and outmoded restrictions. We should not allow this method of action to slip out of our own hands. The abolition of the Zone of Settlement in respect to the towns had an effect which was not only political, but financial. Let's look, for example, at the Jewish press; it is undoubtedly a thousand times less harmful than the labor press. The Jewish newspapers are available only to Jews; the labor ones, to the whole mass of the population. Nevertheless, Headquarters is afraid to touch the labor press, and has completely forbidden a Jewish one —including journals for children—on the pretext that Jewish newspapers print so-called advertisements which really service the German intelligence. I am in favor of an end to such persecution. Let the Jews, if they so wish, read the news in their own tongue, and spend money on their own publications rather than on influencing Russian organs.

COUNT P. N. IGNAT'EV: As far as the educational institutions are concerned, there are no objections to following the course of further privileges for Jews, particularly in their areas of settlement.

Our progressive circles attach much importance, in principle, to this question. Our consent to loosen the existing constraints will make a very good impression on the bloc.

A. A. KHVOSTOV: I would say the same thing about the legal profession.[15]

It was decided to discuss the bloc's program on the Jewish question in the spirit of consenting to a policy of gradual re-examination of the restrictive laws and administrative regulations.

I. L. GOREMYKIN: On the Finnish question, the Council of Ministers instructed the Governor-General to soften his policy, even before the Duma expressed its wishes. Various reliefs have been made for Svinkhuvud.[16]

P. A. KHARITONOV: The problem is that Frantz Alexandrovich Zein himself is not particularly loved by the public and by the Duma. One can expect open requests for his replacement by a man more suitable to the present climate.

S. D. SAZONOV: I do not think that the bloc will bother with such petty details. It is not likely that it will make personal attacks.

A. A. KHVOSTOV: Most likely they will raise the question of general all-Imperial legislation according to the Law of June 17th.[17]

I. L. GOREMYKIN: While the war is going on is not the time to occupy oneself with such basic questions. And after the war—we will see what happens.

The principle of benevolence in Finnish policy did not meet with objections but it was considered undesirable, in order not to commit the government, to undertake any obligations for an im-

---

[15] The Jews were limited to a percentage of total admissions to high schools and universities. They were also limited in their choice of professions; though they could be legal assistants, they could not be lawyers, recognized as such by the government, without having been converted.

[16] P. Svinkhuvud, Finnish political figure; headed the first government of independent Finland after the Russian Revolution.

[17] The Law of June 17, 1910, on the Grand Duchy of Finland, dealt with the procedure for issuing laws which concerned Finland and measures which were of general all-Russian significance. Since the Russian Emperor ruled Finland as Grand Duke of Finland, the country, constitutionally, had separate legislation. At the same time, as Emperor, the ruler could impose certain general measures in order to preserve administrative uniformity. This situation led to constant friction and Finnish dissatisfaction. The law was issued in the period of reaction following the revolution of 1905, and was intended to diminish the autonomy guaranteed to Finland by the 1905 constitution.

mediate re-examination of legislation on the Grand Duchy of Finland.

The restoration of a Ukrainian press was considered permissible, insofar as the question did not include separatist Ukrainophile organs. And, as far as the imprisoned Galicians were concerned, instructions had been handed down before the bloc had raised this question.

I. L. GOREMYKIN: How does the Council of Ministers view the question of labor unions and of the labor press?

PRINCE V. N. SHAKHOVSKOY: From the viewpoint of the administration concerned with industry, I wholeheartedly welcome the restoration of the activity of labor unions as legal organizations under the control of the authorities. As far as the medical insurance cooperatives are concerned, I can say that their destruction by the military authorities and the provincial administration is one of the chief causes of discontent and unrest among the workers. One must hand down categorical instructions about this.

A. A. KHVOSTOV: It is no secret that the medical insurance cooperatives serve as a center for the organization which is directing the workers' movement. Complaints against persecution are all hypocritical, and are a demagogic trick. The banner of humanitarianism cannot serve as a shield for antigovernment activity and the preparation of social revolution.

PRINCE V. N. SHAKHOVSKOY: The divergence of the medical insurance cooperatives (one must note that it is rather rare) from their chief function is a consequence of the closing down of the labor unions. The restoration of the latter will facilitate the task of watching the labor movement. It is easier to struggle against an enemy that is out in the open, than against an underground, or against the conspiratorial activity of medical insurance cooperatives.

A. A. KHVOSTOV: To allow labor unions will give the leaders of the workers the opportunity to develop a network over all of Russia. It will be harder to watch over them, and the administration will be limited in its possibilities of dealing with them.

P. A. KHARITONOV: Nevertheless I am in favor of allowing labor unions. It would serve as a vivid example of the softening of government policy and of its change in favor of fulfilling public wishes. It seems to me that, in practice, it would be easier to supervise unions which are acting openly. Such supervision is now accomplished only by the political police. But after their legalization, one can involve members of the administration and of the factory inspectorate in this supervision as well. Clearly one comes out ahead.

PRINCE V. N. SHAKHOVSKOY: I must explain that the labor unions have not been legally prohibited. If they are not functioning now, it is only because of prohibitions based on extraordinary authorizations. One must say that, in most cases, the closing was done without sufficient reason by various jaunty generals and over-eager governors.

PRINCE N. B. SHCHERBATOV: One cannot deny that absolute arbitrariness has triumphed over the unions in the provinces. It is far more to the liking of the generals and the governors to close down unpleasant organizations than to mess around with them and to be responsible for them: Everything is closed, no assemblies, no legal *démarches,* and everything is quiet on Shipka.[18] One must stop such an outrageous development of the system of official (so-called) "well-being." I believe that labor unions should be permitted. The whole issue amounts to the problem of supervision in order to stop divergences and arrest criminal agitators. Let the various administrators on the spot work a little and worry a little. It is unthinkable for the Ministry of Internal Affairs alone to carry out such a program, since the largest industrial centers are outside its jurisdiction and depend on military authority. Yet, in this question, a unity of practice is necessary.

P. A. KHARITONOV: In our conversation with the bloc, it would be better not to pursue the details of this question too far. One should be reserved and substantively benevolent.

S. D. SAZONOV: That is the reverse of the way Maklakov behaved; in such questions he was both unbenevolent and uncontrolled.

It was decided that it was possible to permit labor unions, and to conduct the discussion on the program of the bloc in the sense outlined by the State Comptroller [Kharitonov].

Concerning the last point of the program, the Council of Min-

---

[18] The reference is to the Russo-Turkish War of 1876-78; the Russians were held up at the Shipka Pass for a long time, and their assaults were repulsed with great losses. These were concealed by the government, which kept reporting that "everything is quiet on Shipka."

isters found that, in principle, it did not contain anything unacceptable. Of the enumerated legislative projects, some have already been passed, some have been lying around the Duma for a long time without any action [on them]. The questions which have been raised anew will be worked out by the government in time, and in the normal manner. It may be possible to agree with the bloc that the more urgent matters be decided by the Council of Ministers during the interruption of the legislative session by means of Article 87 of the Basic State Laws.

s. d. sazonov: Thank you for the reading. Now it has become clear that there are no irreconcilable disagreements on practical issues between the government and the bloc. Judging by the exchange of opinions which has just taken place in the Council of Ministers, one can see that five-sixths of the bloc's program can be incorporated into the program of the government.

i. l. goremykin: I cannot agree with such a formulation. The government may execute one or another measure, if it considers it useful in particular cases, but it is impossible to accept the whole program of the bloc and tie one's own hands in wartime.

s. d. sazonov: No one is talking about tying one's hands by a formal agreement. The issue is only getting together with the bloc and, by means of mutual concessions, achieving mutual support.

i. l. goremykin: That means we will simply engage in chattering with the bloc. And on this chatter the day of adjournment of the Duma is to depend?

s. d. sazonov: Yes. We will show that the government is not prejudiced, is not rejecting public elements, and is parting on good terms with them, after an agreement.

i. l. goremykin: It is too early to think of an agreement as long as they [the bloc] have not shown their cards. So far, only an informative exchange of views is permissible. Not an official conversation, but an off-the-record one.

i. k. grigorovich: Such a conversation should be entrusted to the Minister of Internal Affairs [Shcherbatov] with the participation of some of the members of the Council of Ministers.

s. d. sazonov: The results of this conversation will then be conveyed to the Chairman of the Council of Ministers who, if he finds it necessary, will enter into personal negotiations.

a. a. polivanov: In general, one should arrange the whole

affair nicely. Much will depend on the impression made by these conversations. From the viewpoint of defense, the help of the country is most important; and this help will be assured only if there is mutual trust and a rejection of prejudice. His Imperial Majesty deigned to pay attention to this and pointed out the necessity of common efforts on the part of public organizations. One should be as benevolent and as conciliatory as possible with the representatives of these organizations, who are part of the bloc.

PRINCE N. B. SHCHERBATOV: If we could manage to attract to our side, against the Messrs. Kerenskys, even 200 members of the bloc, we would have a pretty big force which could play an enormous political role. The government could afford to concede something for the sake of this.

S. D. SAZONOV: If one manages all this nicely and gives them a little way out, the Cadets will be the first to come to an agreement. Miliukov is the greatest bourgeois, and he fears a social revolution more than anything else. And, in general, the majority of the Cadets are trembling for their fortunes.

I. L. GOREMYKIN: Well, we'll see who proves right. How then shall we decide about the adjournment of the Duma? In any event, the decision must precede the conversation with the members of the bloc. The last time, we said the session must be adjourned before the date of the submission of the budgets—that is, before September 1st—and today is already the 26th of August.

All the Members of the Council of Ministers, unanimously, voted for a most rapid adjournment, and for the realization, without postponement, of the conversations with the representatives of the bloc.

P. A. KHARITONOV: It would seem to me to be hardly correct to tie the question of adjournment to the 1st of September. An agreement with the members of the bloc is too essential to be made to depend on a few days. One can sacrifice them, in order to obtain better results. An adjournment with an agreement, or without one —that makes an enormous difference.

A. A. KHVOSTOV: Nevertheless, one must hurry in order to forestall a question about Rasputin which is ripening in the Duma.

I. L. GOREMYKIN: I, too, consider that the adjournment cannot be postponed. Both the political situation, and the need to use Article 87 to pass measures arising from military interests, make this necessary. In any event, the decree should be published not later than Saturday, August 31st.

s. d. sazonov: And I agree with the State Comptroller [Kharitonov] and find that one or two days cannot harm. One should make haste, but one should not decide *a priori*.

a. a. polivanov: I join the Minister of Foreign Affairs [Sazonov] in this. The final date can only be determined after the conversations with the bloc.

a. d. samarin: I beg your pardon, I was a little late in coming to the meeting and I did not hear the beginning. In what context is it planned to conduct negotiations with the bloc; that is, will any promises be offered in the name of the government?

prince n. b. shcherbatov: No promises, for the moment. The issue is reduced to an informative conversation and to the determination of the mood. The material obtained in this manner will be the subject of discussion in the Council of Ministers.

a. d. samarin: What significance will this kind of a conversation have for the bloc, then? It will be said that only individual ministers are participating, and not the government, and that such individual initiative is fruitless.

s. d. sazonov: The representatives of the bloc will know that this exchange of opinions will be conveyed to the Council of Ministers, which will then make its decisions according to the circumstances. In any event, the conversation is absolutely necessary in order to agree about adjournment and to make it peaceful.

i. l. goremykin: Whether they agree or not, the interruption of the Session is inevitable. It is required by State interests.

a. d. samarin: This [adjournment] is the prerogative of the Monarch and there is no need to run after the bloc about it.

a. a. khvostov: It is important to indicate to them the views of the government. Let everyone know that the government is not denying the necessity of certain changes in the methods of administration and in the direction of internal policy.

prince n. b. shcherbatov: The very fact of the meeting and of the conversation will create a certain atmosphere in public opinion.

a. d. samarin: Anyway, no one will believe in it. Public opinion awaits something else.

a. a. polivanov: The conversation with the bloc will help to establish a program on the basis of which an agreement is possible.

A. D. SAMARIN: The word "agreement" cannot be used in relation to such a ragtag group, which is not united internally and the majority of which is motivated by base desires to grab power at any cost. No matter what skin he pulls over himself, Miliukov will always remain a revolutionary in my eyes until he exonerates himself of his speeches abroad.[19]

S. D. SAZONOV: Then what should be done, in your opinion?

A. D. SAMARIN: One should listen to the voice of those men who are well-intentioned and who are sincerely suffering in their hearts for the motherland. There are not a few, if not many of those, outside the bloc. Such voices should provide the material for the planning of a government program which should be announced in the Duma on the day the adjournment is announced.

A. A. POLIVANOV: But who are these people? How shall one find them and choose them? Within the bloc, we are dealing with people honored by election to legislative institutions, prominent political and public figures.

A. D. SAMARIN: I am against an agreement, against binding obligations, and not against conversations with the bloc. But only an informative and off-the-record one, not commissioned by the Council of Ministers. And in the Duma the views of the government on further tasks should be announced, rather than a program in agreement with the bloc. I would put it this way: The whole attention of the government is focused on the war and its requirements, which have first priority; in general, however, we will act and work on such-and-such premises.

S. D. SAZONOV: Well, it's exactly these that we have not been able to think up for the longest time.

A. D. SAMARIN: In order to think up something concrete, one has to determine the changing mood of the country and be informed as to its real desires.

PRINCE N. B. SHCHERBATOV: Yes, this is a correct formulation. But in order to conduct the conversations with the bloc, one requires some guiding instructions from the Council of Ministers. Such in-

---

[19] It is hard to determine to which speeches of Miliukov Samarin is referring. Most probably, Miliukov's lectures in the United States in 1903, though this seems to be harking very far back.

structions would not be announced to the representatives of the bloc, but be designed for the representatives of the Council of Ministers who are authorized to conduct the conversations.

A. A. KHVOSTOV: I also am not building up big hopes about this meeting with the representatives of the bloc, but I think that one cannot allow them to reach the conclusion that the government spits on them. There is nothing to be done; one has to manage them and let them understand that their ideas are not being rejected *in toto*. I would not even object to speaking with them to the effect that the declaration of a government program is not being rejected in principle, but that there is no time, right now, to make one up, because it is necessary to interrupt the Session of the legislative bodies in order to execute measures whose urgency does not allow the sanctions normally required.

I. L. GOREMYKIN: We have already agreed about various points in the bloc's program, and we will not return to them. I beg the State Comptroller [Kharitonov] to take on himself the conduct of the discussions with the representatives of the bloc, with the participation of the Minister of Justice [Khvostov], the Minister of Internal Affairs [Shcherbatov], and the Minister of Trade [Shakhovskoy]. And as for the purpose of the conversation: information, the creation of an atmosphere which would allow us to part not as enemies but as friends (this last I do not believe). There can be no question of any agreement now. If the situation will not be unfavorable then, one can resume the negotiations in November.

A. A. POLIVANOV: Nevertheless, I would like to be told definitely: Will there, or will there not be, a government declaration to the legislative bodies in connection with their adjournment? In other words, does the government intend to declare its plans to the Duma or does it plan to let it go on vacation in silence?

P. A. KHARITONOV: Apparently, our Chairman does not wish to anticipate this question and discuss it today. It appears to me, too, that it is more useful to postpone the question until we know the results of the conversations with the bloc. No matter how difficult the task of negotiations with political and public figures is, these days, I do not find it right for myself to evade the suggestion of Ivan Longinovich [Goremykin].

A. D. SAMARIN: I was not present at the beginning and could not express myself concerning a declaration [of program]. It seems to me that such behavior toward the Duma would be most desirable. It would be particularly important in order to calm down the country, which is very nervous about the government and its relations with the Duma. Everyone will see that the parting is a good one, ending with a salutation. And the essence of our declaration, which should be a brief one, can be reduced to the following: The legislative projects arising from military circumstances and submitted by the government have been passed, and therefore the Session is being adjourned in order to give the deputies the opportunity to work in their localities and at the front; at the present time, all our thoughts and strength must be focused on the task of bringing the war to a victorious end; compared to this task, everything else is secondary; then one can refer to the speech of the Chairman of the Council of Ministers at the opening of the legislative bodies on the 19th of July, one can confirm it, and supplement it by whatever useful [material] can be extracted from public opinion. Hence, one would preserve the continuity of government policy during recent times and, at the same time, one would take a step forward toward meeting public wishes.

P. A. KHARITONOV: And then this declaration should be repeated in the State Council.

S. D. SAZONOV: An excellent idea! I am in complete sympathy with such a declaration, both in the Duma and in the Council.

A. A. POLIVANOV: It is self-evident that to adjourn the legislative bodies in silence would be simply indecent under the present circumstances.

PRINCE V. N. SHAKHOVSKOY: Here, there is a possible danger. After the declaration, debates will be opened, orators will begin to sign up, and passionate criticism and various *démarches* against the government will commence. All this will create unnecessary noise and delay the adjournment.

S. D. SAZONOV: One can agree ahead of time about not allowing debate. Rodzianko can read the decree [of adjournment] immediately after the speech of the Chairman of the Council of Ministers, and the whole thing is over.

A. A. KHVOSTOV: The Presidium would never dare to agree to such a procedure.

S. D. SAZONOV: Well, if Rodzianko refuses, the government would have a right to walk out of the session *en masse*.

P. A. KHARITONOV: Well, that would not be very nice. Instead of a reconciliation, a final break. I can just imagine what would be said after our demonstrative exodus, and how the newspapers would scream about it all over the place. No, it is better to think of something else, or even to refuse to appear, if the Presidium does not agree to forbid a debate.

I. L. GOREMYKIN: This is a very serious problem. I will think about it. Let's not get involved in it now. We have more urgent matters. In any event, I beg P. A. Kharitonov very much to hurry the arrangements for the conversation with the representatives of the bloc.

I. L. GOREMYKIN: General Frolov, whom I have invited for the discussion of the issue of the press, has come to our meeting. Our newspapers have gone quite mad. Even in 1905 they did not permit themselves the outrages that they do now. The military authorities must take all measures to calm down the press. And the Ministry of Internal Affairs is obligated to help them in this. One cannot tolerate the present outrages. Everything is directed towards undermining the prestige of the government. As an example, take the daily discussions about new cabinets, with public representatives and without them. Among government employees, there is complete confusion and uncertainty. At the front, too, the unhealthy impression exists that there is no stability in the rear. One must end this newspaper lying. This is not the moment for licentiousness in the press. This is not freedom of speech but the devil knows what!

S. D. SAZONOV: And what about yesterday's dispatch about an attempt on [the life of] Grand Duke Nicholas? A despicable achievement of a most despicable reporter. The Allied representatives have asked me about this. There was no attempt of any kind. It was all an evil-minded fantasy to arouse public anxiety. How come the military censorship lets such news through?

I. L. GOREMYKIN: I beg General Frolov to pay attention to this fact and, in general, to get after the press in a decisive way. I warn you, General, if this situation does not change, you can expect great troubles.

P. A. FROLOV: I don't doubt the troubles, and I expect them.

I. L. GOREMYKIN: Don't expect them; just cross out more of this newspaper nonsense.

P. A. FROLOV: I'm only the executor. The directives are issued by Headquarters and the Central Military-Censorship Committee, which is under the jurisdiction of the Ministry of War.

A. A. POLIVANOV: It is the task of the Ministry of War to follow the law on military censorship, according to which, what is forbidden for publication in the press is indicated in a list. Hence we are required to be guided by the list, on which there is no injunction against publishing news about new cabinets with the participation of public representatives. It is difficult for the military to distinguish all the nuances of the desirable or the undesirable, considering the varying tendencies in the government. The Ministry of War must be above politics. They are none of its business.

I. L. GOREMYKIN: In present wartime conditions, politics are inseparable from military affairs. Even the military say that it is the people-in-arms, and not the regular army, which is fighting.

S. D. SAZONOV: Military censorship is understood very broadly in Germany and is not divided up by ministries. The interests of the State are common to all [ministries].

PRINCE N. B. SHCHERBATOV: The dispatch about the attempt on the Grand Duke is the result of an unfortunate oversight. But, considering the present abnormal status of censorship, such deliberate or involuntary oversights are inevitable. The whole business is not unified and, in various places, practice is infinitely varied. In some places they allow one to write only about abstractions and to publish only theatrical news, and in the neighboring districts a labor press of the most impossible tendency is being encouraged. The Ministry of Internal Affairs has, for a long time, been proposing that military censorship be centralized in Petrograd, in a central organ, which would send out directives to be absolutely obeyed everywhere; but General Ianushkevich saw in this a threat to the prerogatives of Headquarters and refused categorically. The Ministry of Internal Affairs is helpless before the decision of Headquarters. Perhaps the Council of Ministers can get more favorable action.

A. A. POLIVANOV: This issue has already been raised in the Ministry of War, and will be discussed in a special commission with the participation of representatives of the Ministry of Internal Affairs.

I. L. GOREMYKIN: One must hurry. What's the point of all these commissions? Every hour is precious right now.

PRINCE N. B. SHCHERBATOV: Well, our Chairman has emphasized quite a few times, both today and earlier, that the Ministry of Internal Affairs is insufficiently energetic about the press. But what can I do, after all, when I am only a guest in Petrograd, and everything depends on the military authorities? The excesses of the press have evoked from us an address to Headquarters about the necessity of instructing military censors in a more broadened interpretation of their tasks, in the interest of maintaining internal order. In answer to this, an instruction came from Headquarters, over the signature of Ianushkevich, that military censorship cannot interfere in civilian affairs. It is this instruction which has served as a basis for the present license. In Moscow, which is not as yet within the theatre of operations, I must say we are also helpless. Pre-publication censorship was abolished long ago, and we cannot impede the publication of undesirable articles and news in the press. We have only one means—the right of punishment and of closing the newspapers.

I. L. GOREMYKIN: Well, go ahead and use this right. The publishers don't like it when their pocketbook is hurt, and they will pull in their tails. And as far as the military censorship is concerned, I will talk about this with His Majesty the Emperor. If the law interferes with the maintenance of State interests, then the law can be changed.

PRINCE N. B. SHCHERBATOV: The imposition of fines and the closing of newspapers evokes parliamentary questions and scandals in the Duma, which in turn help to popularize the organs of the press which are being punished.

I. L. GOREMYKIN: Well, exactly, in a few days the Duma will not be able to impede you anymore.

PRINCE N. B. SHCHERBATOV: Then we'll be able to manage.

I. L. GOREMYKIN: One must immediately think through, and put through, measures so that similar incidents do not happen again in the press. I request the Minister of Internal Affairs [Shcherbatov] to get together on this with the Minister of War [Polivanov], and with General Frolov. If necessary, I will get instructions from His Majesty concerning the theatre of operations. In general, one has to act energetically. It is time to pass from words to deeds. His Majesty is extremely dissatisfied that the government has not been able to curb newspaper agitation in so long a time. This could result in great troubles for the Ministry of Internal Affairs. I direct the attention of Prince N. B. Shcherbatov to the necessity of showing his power to the press, and, until new measures are found, to levy monetary fines. And I request General Frolov to impose a fine today on the newspaper which allowed itself to print self-evident lies about the attempt against the Grand Duke.

P. A. FROLOV: I will find out which newspaper published this dispatch first, and will give it the maximum fine, with an explanation of the reason for this punishment.

S. D. SAZONOV: This lie was printed by Boriska[20] Suvorin in his lousy *Vechernee Vremia*.

P. A. FROLOV: Well, we will slap Boriska down, then. It is evident that he wrote this while drunk. After all, that is his usual state.

I. L. GOREMYKIN: Once again, I request all the ministers to struggle, in every way, against the agitation of the press. In this situation, the interests involved are so essential that we cannot be stopped by formalities and legalisms. It is quite clear that military censors cannot remain indifferent about newspapers when they stir up the army and sow confusion in the country. If they can't figure all this out, then they should be immediately supplemented, without any committees, by civil and diplomatic officials. Such a dissolute press as we have would not be allowed in any republic.

A. A. POLIVANOV: It would not be allowed [in any republic] by law.

I. L. GOREMYKIN: When necessary they [republics] supplement the law, or quickly issue a new one. I repeat, it is not possible to delay any longer—one must act. This is necessary for the war and for the defense effort. When the war will end—then we will see what happens.

After the discussion of a few more issues which are no longer of general interest, the meeting was adjourned. I had noted: "Polivanov is mostly silent and once in a while snaps out. His sharpness toward Ivan Longinovich [Goremykin] passes all bounds of propriety. Despite all his correctness, the old man [Goremykin] is barely controlling himself. It is unclear what Polivanov is aiming at and what he wants. Looking through Guchkov's eyeglasses, he is fasci-

---

[20] *Boriska*—contemptuous diminutive of "Boris."

nated with society, and sees salvation only in it. But then, why did he, before the beginning of the meeting, ironically report on the endless word-making of the independent representatives in the Special Conference on Defense? Even though he is Minister of War, this is a strange personality, not to say a suspicious one. Oh, dear little Mother Russia, things are not easy for you!

XV

The Meeting of
28 August 1915

---◈---

On the 27th of August, an encounter with the representatives of the Progressive Bloc took place at P. A. Kharitonov's. Among these representatives, according to my notes: Miliukov, Dmitriukov, S. Shidlovsky, and Efremov. The results of the gathering were reported by the State Comptroller as follows:

P. A. KHARITONOV: At the outset, I warned those assembled that our encounter had a private character, that it was not binding on anyone, and that the purpose of the conversation was purely informative. The discussion followed the bloc's program in the order of sequence of its own exposition. First of all, we touched upon the program's desires concerning the government. To my question— how can this desire be achieved, since the appointment of ministers is the prerogative of the Monarch, who is not legally bound in any way about this—everyone answered that the issue can be reduced to the appointment by His Imperial Majesty of a person possessing public confidence, who, in turn, would be charged with using his own discretion to compose a Cabinet, and who would also be charged with establishing clear mutual relations with the Duma. Concerning the second wish—about the methods of administration —it was said that it is organically connected with the first. Then, the following emerged concerning the points of the program: The amnesty is conceived as a particular, rather than a general one, and they mainly have in mind the *Vyborzhtsy* and persons deprived of voting rights. Broader demands are submitted on the issue of an amnesty for the administrative exiles. Here one can clearly see the premise that this kind of exile is nothing but a manifestation of arbitrary despotism and that all these cases should be liquidated, insofar that there are no court decisions. The freedom of religion is understood in approximately the same way as we discussed it the last time. On the Polish question, there was a suggestion for a partial execution of autonomy as the Polish territories are cleared of the enemy. When our side pointed out that the removal of limitations on Polish land ownership is equivalent to the obvious danger of the Polonization of the Western area, the answers were evasive: Of course one will not be able to act; yes, of course, one could not act all at once; one would have to act gradually, depending upon conditions, and so forth; one must make a gesture, by beginning a re-examination of the restrictive legislation, which [re-examination] might even go on for the time being without any concrete results. It is interesting that even Miliukov did not press this issue, and expressed himself with great diplomatic caution—that is, to put it simply, neither for nor against. On the other hand, Miliukov insisted on the desirability of giving Polish landowners equal rights [with Russian ones] to borrow from the Gentry Land Bank. On the Jewish question also, one did not observe particular decisiveness in the sense of immediate equal rights. Our fears of pogroms in rural districts were not contradicted. The essence of the demands—further steps on the path of softening the régime for Jews, but gradually, not all at once. For Finland, the demand is for a benevolent administration, for which General Zein is regarded as totally and essentially unsuitable. Even more objections are raised against Borovitinov, the Chief of the Governor-General's Chancellery, who, according to some of the representatives, is very bad and tactless; his provocative tone irritates the Finns and creates dissatisfaction even in Sweden. His removal is particularly urgent. As far as the Law of the 17th of July[1] is concerned, they did not insist on its annulment;

---

[1] This is a misprint or a mistake; the law is that of June 17, 1910 (cf. note 7, Chap. XIV).

only Miliukov took the stand of the Social-Democratic faction, which has worked out a law on this by right of Duma initiative. The question of the imprisoned Galicians was dropped in view of the measures already undertaken by the government. As for the press, the desire can be phrased as meaning that immediate relief should be given to the Ukrainian press but not to the Ukrainophilic one, or, in other words, to local newspapers in the local language but not to political organs of separatist tendency supported by the Austrians. Dmitriukov was the main speaker on the labor question. One could not note any irreconcilable differences with the general considerations noted by the Council of Ministers at the last meeting, and an agreement, apparently, can be reached. The list of legislation did not evoke any particular discussion. As far as one could gather from rather vague hints, the whole issue boils down to the fact that the government should undertake the obligation to get the laws approved by the Duma through the State Council with the fewest possible changes. Summarizing our general impression of yesterday's conversation, one can say the following: The bloc is strong while it is united; its present make-up is artificial and hardly durable; the agreement on which it is based is not one of principle, but is evoked by considerations of the moment: in a word, it is a temporary organization; its program is based on compromises; one can foresee that, in the future, its demands will be broader and of a different character.

s. d. sazonov: And what kind of an impression did the Duma deputies have of this conversation, in your opinion? What do you think: Will they go along with at least a temporary agreement with the government?

p. a. kharitonov: Their behavior toward us was highly correct and reserved. One did not feel any confidence toward us as official personages; in any event none was manifested. Undoubtedly, however, they went away somewhat satisfied with the general mood of the conversation, without a consciousness of irreconcilable contradictions, and with the impression that the government can, in many ways, meet the desires of the bloc.

prince n. b. shcherbatov: It is interesting to note that during the conversation, the government was blamed for the secretiveness of its activity. We forgive political [activists], we clean up the administration, we carry out various improvements—but all this passes quite unnoticed by the vast majority of the country. In a word, our actions do not have any political effect.

s. d. sazonov: Therefore the conversation was informative to both sides, and the representatives of the bloc do not have a feeling of hopelessness about the government. One may think that, after all this, the deputies of the Duma will adjourn less angrily and less excitedly. This, after all, is a big step forward.

p. a. kharitonov: I would be afraid to state this so categorically. But undoubtedly, the meeting was not pointless, and one can extract some value out of it for the future.

prince n. b. shcherbatov: I also think that one can now hope that the adjournment will take place more smoothly.

i. l. goremykin: Whether the Duma will adjourn quietly, or with a scandal, makes no difference. Workers' disorders will take place irrespectively if the leaders are ready for action. But I am convinced that everything will go well and that the fears are exaggerated.

s. d. sazonov: The issue is not the readiness of the labor leaders, but that the tension and irritation in the legislative chamber, if not pacified in time, can create serious conflicts which will adversely affect the country and the conduct of the war.

i. l. goremykin: It's all the same; it's all nonsense. The Duma does not interest anyone except the newspapers, and it has bored everyone with its chatter.

s. d. sazonov: And I insist categorically that my question is not "all the same" and not "nonsense." While I am in the Council of Ministers, I will keep on repeating that, without good relations with the legislative chambers, no government, no matter how self-confident, can govern the country, and that one or another mood of the deputies influences the psychology of the public. It is the duty of a wise government to foresee threatening consequences, and not to act hastily.

i. l. goremykin: I, as Chairman of the Council, prescribe the issues to be discussed by the Council of Ministers. I find that the question of the adjournment of the legislative chambers is substantively exhausted and that further debates are superfluous. I now ask the gentlemen members of the Council of Ministers to express themselves definitely: Should one end the Session, when, and with what procedure?

S. D. SAZONOV: I cannot express myself on this question until I find out what impressions were received by those of my colleagues whom the Council of Ministers authorized to conduct the negotiations with the representatives of the bloc.

I. L. GOREMYKIN: If the participants of the conversation find it possible to give some kind of information, then I find no objection to it.

P. A. KHARITONOV: As far as I could discover from occasional remarks, the bloc isn't even thinking of the possibility of adjournment now, when we have begun conversations with it.

A. A. KHVOSTOV: I, too, have the same impression. Apparently they do feel that there is a basis for further discussions, after all.

PRINCE V. N. SHAKHOVSKOY: My impression is the same. The representatives of the bloc understood that the government is not rejecting the program of the bloc as a whole, and that one can still bargain.

S. D. SAZONOV: There can't even be any talk of the acceptability of the program as a whole. I am convinced that the magician himself, Pavel Nikolaevich Miliukov, agrees.

P. A. KHARITONOV: Two more words of explanation: I have said that one could feel no confidence in us among the representatives of the bloc. It seems to me that the root of this distrust lies in the lack of assurance that the government, despite the commenced negotiations, has given up thought of adjournment. They did not want to put this question to us bluntly, but one could sense it throughout the conversation.

S. D. SAZONOV: Therefore one can conclude, from your words, that adjournment at this time will make a bad impression and that the deputies will leave even more irritated.

P. A. KHARITONOV answers with a vague gesture of his hands.

I. L. GOREMYKIN: In the present circumstances, both external and internal, this is not the time neither to make peace nor to fight. One must act. Otherwise everything will collapse. If the bloc continues to devise new delays and refuses to give a straight answer, then God be with it. There is no need for the government to follow the bloc. I call for a vote on the issue of adjournment and ask the Council of Ministers to decide this question. (Addressing the Minister of Justice): Your opinion on this issue?

A. A. KHVOSTOV: The sooner one can wind up this dragged-out

issue, the better. All life has stopped. I have doubts only about the Special Conference on Refugees. This legislation was created by military circumstances, and was submitted by the government. It is important to get it through in the normal way and to allow an opportunity for electing members for it [the Conference] from the legislative bodies. If one can get this whole procedure through before Tuesday, then I would be in favor of a postponement till that date.

P. A. KHARITONOV: I share that opinion. We cannot allow ourselves to be reproached for the fact that the government itself submits legislation caused by military circumstances and itself does not allow opportunity for passing it.

A. A. KHVOSTOV: And if the deputies start to delay this on purpose, it would mean that one cannot deal nicely with them, and then one has to simply chase them out.

S. D. SAZONOV: I'm also in favor of adjournment, but with all the qualifications which I have repeated since the very moment this question arose.

A. A. POLIVANOV: I am also for adjournment, but I beg you to allow me to motivate this. The ultimate success of our struggle against the Germans is wholly dependent on the means of defense, on ample supplies for our armies. His Imperial Majesty considers this preparatory task largely dependent on the united and energetic work of the public organizations. The words uttered by the Emperor in his address to the Special Conference on Defense leave no room for doubt, and were received with joy by the country. It is the duty of the government to help this work, and to allow no actions which would create increased dissatisfaction in public circles, and *démarches* by the workers. Under these circumstances, the adjournment of the Session should be achieved in such a way that the members of the Duma are not made into open enemies of the government, for their influence in the public organizations is undoubtedly great. I would say that it is great not only in organizations in the rear, but at the front also. In the evaluation of issues of general political importance it is essential, these days, to consider the echo which one or another act might produce in the army. One should not forget that the army is now quite different from the one which marched forth at the beginning of the war. The regular troops are badly thinned out and have been absorbed into the mass of the armed people, as it is now fashionable to call them, badly trained and not imbued with the spirit of military discipline. In particular, one must note that the officer corps, being filled up with speeded-up promotions and ensigns from the reserve, is not aloof from politics and even from politicking. Hence, the question of adjournment cannot be decided without first deciding on the particular form of this act. In substance, I have no doubts that an infinite prolongation of the Session is useless and impermissible and that the adjournment should take place in the nearest future. The determination of the final day should be connected with the passage of the legislation on refugees and with the election of representatives of the legislative bodies to the Refugee Conference, this matter having been agreed on with the Presidiums of the State Council and of the Duma. Then, at the last meeting, before the publication of the Imperial decree on adjournment, the Chairman of the Council of Ministers should speak in both chambers; [he should make] an official declaration, in a benevolent tone, and point out that there are no irreconcilable differences with the bloc. This declaration should be brief, and yet it would be useful to motivate the adjournment itself by considerations, not of principle, but of a practical nature.

PRINCE V. N. SHAKHOVSKOY: I have no doubts that an immediate adjournment is necessary. I'm in full agreement with the Minister of War [Polivanov] that this act should be given a form which would eliminate unnecessary trouble between the Duma and the government. I would like to add that it would be a mistake to connect the issue of adjournment with the possibility of workers' disorders. These two issues are independent of each other. Whether the Duma is sitting or not, we will still not be able to avoid labor unrest and disorders. There will always be a pretext for them. The gentlemen leaders of the labor masses have always had the possibility of using a method which is beloved by underground organizations—provocation, with the transference of responsibility for it onto the government.

PRINCE N. B. SHCHERBATOV: I share the opinion on the necessity of immediate adjournment, but on condition that the Duma be allowed an opportunity to finish quickly examining the legislation on refugees, and to conduct elections of its representatives to the Conference. This Conference is essential to the Ministry of Internal Affairs. After all, one is forced to spend hundreds of millions on this refugee business, and without any forms and regulations. All this will serve as a cause for various reproaches, against which the presence of elected representatives of the legislative chambers will act as insurance. One must agree with the Presidium and the party leaders on the passage of the legislation on the Conference in the Duma, and determine, together with them, the date of the publication of the decree of adjournment. As for the appearance of the government on closing day in the Duma, I find it highly desirable from the general political point of view. One should keep in mind the fact that, lately, the stock of the Duma has fallen badly in the country, and does not rate very high. At the same time, the population has become convinced that the government is standing aside, hiding behind military circumstances, and does not want to do anything. Therefore an appearance before the legislative bodies is in the interest of the government itself; in this way it can inform everyone of its work and further intentions. This is the more important because, in general, the program of the Progressive Bloc is acceptable, in large measure, and departs from the government point of view only in particular questions. Hearing of all this, many of those who are hesitating will take a conciliatory position.

COUNT P. N. IGNAT'EV: An indefinite Session is, of course, impossible, and the adjournment must take place very soon. But, as the Minister of War [Polivanov] has said correctly, the whole question boils down to the form and procedure of adjournment—that is: Will this act take place in a pleasant or in an unfriendly atmosphere? In such anxious times, this [unfriendly] kind of atmosphere could be most dangerous. It would prove to the country that the legislative bodies are unable to work or agree with the government; or, more correctly, that the government is unable to agree with the Duma at a moment when all forces and all thoughts should be concentrated on defense. If we sever relations finally with the 4th Duma, this would confirm the fact that the government and popular representation are incompatible in principle.[2] It would then become necessary, in the near future, to announce new elections, which will take place in such an atmosphere that there will be no possibility at all of getting along with the 5th Duma. Such an outlook evokes a frightful feeling, and I am definitely in favor of

---

[2] This is a reference to the fact that the 4th Duma was elected on such a restricted suffrage base (established by the electoral law of June, 1907) that, if the government could not work with the 4th Duma, it could not work with any parliamentary body at all.

rounding all sharp corners and reaching an agreement with the Duma now. The adjournment should be the result of agreement with influential deputies.

A. V. KRIVOSHEIN: I am ready to join in the opinion which was so vividly presented by A. A. Polivanov. But another question poses itself: What is the possible form and substance of a government declaration in the Duma which is to avoid mentioning the definite and real conflict between the government and public opinion? No matter what we say, no matter what we promise, no matter how we play along with the Progressive Bloc and with society—no one will believe us a penny's worth anyway. After all, the demands of the Duma and of the whole country are reducible to the issue not of a program but of which people are to be entrusted with power. Hence, it seems to me that the focus of our consideration should be not on the search for this or that day for the adjournment of the Duma, but on the posing of questions of principle: the attitude of His Imperial Majesty to the government in its present make-up; and the demands of the country for an executive endowed with public confidence. Let the Monarch decide how he wishes to direct further internal policy—along the path of ignoring such desires or along the path of reconciliation; choose, in the second instance, a person possessing public sympathy and charge him with the formation of a government. Without the solution of this cardinal question, we will not get off this point anyway. Personally, I am in favor of the second alternative—the selection, by His Majesty the Emperor, of an individual, and the charging of this individual with the make-up of a Cabinet which corresponds to the wishes of the country.

I. L. GOREMYKIN: This is quite a different aspect of the issue. We may return to this later. Now I ask A. V. Krivoshein to state definitely: Is he in favor of, or against, the adjournment of the Duma?

A. V. KRIVOSHEIN: I have repeatedly expressed myself against a lengthy Session and have not changed my view. But, in the present situation, the resolution of the question of adjournment must come from the Monarch; it must come after the report of *that* Council of Ministers which His Majesty will choose, depending upon his decision about the direction of future policy. The will of His Majesty the Emperor is sacred to us and will be carried out by us.

I. L. GOREMYKIN: I am continuing the poll on the question of adjournment, which I have put. In order that there be no misunderstanding, I repeat: We are only voting on the interruption of the Session until November, not on the final adjournment of this particular Duma. (Addressing himself to the Navy Minister): Your opinion?

I. K. GRIGOROVICH: I am for adjournment, after the passage of legislation on the Refugee Conference.

P. N. DUMITRASHKO (Vice-Minister of Communications): I, also.

A. I. NIKOLAENKO (Vice-Minister of Finance): I, also.

S. D. SAZONOV: It seems to me that the point of view just formulated by A. V. Krivoshein cannot be bypassed by the Council of Ministers without discussion, and must be conveyed for information to His Majesty. Personally, I am in full agreement with it. It crystallizes all that we have been circling about and dodging for many days now.

P. N. IGNAT'EV: I, too, join with A. V. Krivoshein. No matter what we promise, we will not be believed. Everyone expects changes and a redefinition of policy.

P. A. KHARITONOV: The formulation of the problem, as offered by A. V. Krivoshein, corresponds fully to the present political situation. I fully agree that all our declarations will not help a bit. One must decide the matter of one or another course of internal policy and choose men who will be able to execute it.

I. L. GOREMYKIN: It follows that the question of adjournment of the Duma must be postponed until the ministerial portfolios are distributed, and the monarch's prerogative of choosing ministers is limited?

A. V. KRIVOSHEIN: I am ready to agree to a simultaneous adjournment of the Duma and a change of Cabinet.

PRINCE N. B. SHCHERBATOV: Yes, really, it is time to stop marching in one spot. Dissatisfaction in the country is increasing with threatening rapidity. Everyone is waiting for one or another slogan. One must determine future internal policy, and one must call new people for it. It is our duty to request His Majesty to end this uncertainty and speak the decisive word.

I. L. GOREMYKIN: This means, in the opinion of some of the members of the Council of Ministers, that the decision on the question [of adjournment] should be transferred from us to His Majesty the Emperor.

PRINCE N. B. SHCHERBATOV: Yes; the question is so important

and so pregnant with consequences that it can be decided only by the Monarch.

PRINCE V. N. SHAKHOVSKOY: The reasons that I have heard have convinced me that it is necessary to compromise with public opinion on the issue of the government. Otherwise the crisis will drag on and fatally complicate the internal situation; therefore I, too, agreeing with the opinion of A. V. Krivoshein, am in favor of a change of the Cabinet, but with a simultaneous adjournment of the Duma.

A. V. KRIVOSHEIN: To develop my thought further, I would put it this way: We, old servants of the Tsar, take upon ourselves the unpleasant duty of adjourning the Duma, and, at the same time, firmly state to His Imperial Majesty that the general internal situation of the country requires a change of Cabinet and of the political course. His Majesty's decision on the basic question, in one or another way, will also decide the personal composition of the future government.

I. L. GOREMYKIN: Well, who are these new people? The representatives of the factions, or members of the administration? Do you intend, at the same time, to nominate desirable candidates from a particular camp to the Emperor?

A. V. KRIVOSHEIN: I, personally, do not intend to nominate anyone. The make-up [of the new government] should correspond to the political course chosen by His Majesty. Let His Majesty the Emperor invite some particular person and charge him to determine his future collaborators. Any other procedure is impossible.

I. L. GOREMYKIN: It is therefore considered necessary to present an ultimatum to the Tsar—the resignation of the Council of Ministers, and a new government.

S. D. SAZONOV: We are not presenting, and we do not intend to present, an ultimatum to His Imperial Majesty. We are not rebels, but as loyal subjects of our Tsar as Your High Excellency. I beg you very sincerely not to use such terms in our discussions.

I. L. GOREMYKIN: I withdraw my words. This is not the time to become personal. This means, ultimately, that the Council of Ministers has come to the conclusion that the Duma must be adjourned and that, after our fulfillment of this task, a new Cabinet should be appointed in accordance with the desires of the Progressive Bloc.

PRINCE N. B. SHCHERBATOV: When I speak of a change of policy and a new Cabinet, I am not following the Duma and the bloc, but my own inner conviction, which is based on my evaluation of the general political situation. The whole country desires a change of the Cabinet, and I join it.

A. A. POLIVANOV: The plan of action is a correct one, I think—the Duma to be dismissed by the existing Cabinet, and His Majesty the Emperor to be requested, immediately after this, to call on a new executive, corresponding to the wishes of the country.

I. L. GOREMYKIN: I take upon myself, without any hesitation, the responsibility for adjourning the Duma, as I am convinced that this measure is necessary to calm the country down and to organize the defense. But I do not find it possible for myself to press on His Majesty the Emperor people who are unacceptable to him. As I said earlier—perhaps my views are archaic, but it is too late for me to change them.

PRINCE N. B. SHCHERBATOV: The issue is not one of pressing particular people on His Majesty the Emperor. We have no right to do this. The question is a different one: to unite the cabinet on a course to the right or to the left, and to end the present uncertainty. The decision of this question is fully the monarch's. It is in his power to choose both the direction and the people whom he will entrust with carrying it out.

I. L. GOREMYKIN: Very well, we will convey all this to His Majesty, and he will not wish to change anything. Then what?

S. D. SAZONOV: Then each one of us, having fulfilled his duty as a member of the Council of Ministers, will obtain his freedom of action and will personally convey to His Imperial Majesty his own view of the general political situation and of the consequences which stem from this view.

A. D. SAMARIN (who had come to the meeting toward the end of the debate): Is it proper for us to say to His Majesty the Emperor: "Change the government and appoint new people?" What reason do we have for such a declaration? I would find it difficult to underwrite a reference to the desire of the whole country, for there has been no questionnaire and no one knows the true desires and yearnings. The Duma cannot be considered as expressing the opinion of all Russia; highly different, and even irreconcilable demands concerning the make-up of the new Cabinet, based on party considerations and interests, are expressed in her own midst. And if we, personally, are demanding a new government, then it is my profound conviction that we have no right to transfer the whole burden of this decision to His Majesty the Emperor and thus make more difficult his already very difficult situation; and all this at a time when it is our duty to help him, with all our strength, to resolve the emerging crisis. We should submit to His Majesty the fundaments of a political program which corresponds, in our view, with the changed circumstances of the internal and external situation; and report to him, at the same time, that there is no real unity in the Council of Ministers in its present make-up—a unity which is particularly important in view of present developments; and that, therefore, we are petitioning for the creation of a different government, which should replace us, and which would be enabled to bring the proper program into being. If such a declaration were approved in principle, it would be our duty to name an acceptable person, for abstract statements about public confidence do not mean anything in substance, and are simply a propagandistic trick. And, if His Majesty the Emperor rejects our common petition, then it remains for each one of us to act in accordance with his own conscience and his understanding of his duty as a loyal subject of his Tsar and a servant of Russia.

I. L. GOREMYKIN: And what is your opinion about the adjournment?

A. D. SAMARIN: It seems to me that we should take this act upon ourselves, in order to relieve His Majesty the Emperor and our successors.

In conclusion the Council of Ministers favored the point of view of A. V. Krivoshein, with the amendment of A. D. Samarin: namely, to accomplish the adjournment of the Duma in the nearest future (in a nice way, having agreed with the Presidium and the leaders about passing the unfinished government legislation necessitated by the demands of wartime) and, following that, to submit to His Majesty a petition for a new Council of Ministers.

I. L. GOREMYKIN: All of today's arguments will be conveyed by me, in detail, to His Majesty the Emperor. Whatever His Majesty will deign to order I will carry out. Let us see what happens.

I. L. GOREMYKIN: As long as His Majesty the Emperor has not replaced us, we have to go on with current business. I hear rumors that, at the forthcoming *zemstvo* assemblies, it is planned, on instructions of the Konovalov assembly, to discuss the Moscow resolutions. What information does the Minister of Internal Affairs have about this?

PRINCE N. B. SHCHERBATOV: Quite right; in the majority of the *zemstvo* assemblies one must expect such issues to arise, in the spirit of the Moscow City Council. As far as town councils are concerned, we have already decided not to protest formally against this. I think that the same attitude should be taken towards the *zemstvos* —that is, to observe through one's fingers, but not to answer.

I. L. GOREMYKIN: Our measures can be anticipatory, and not only *post facto*. The Ministry of Internal Affairs disposes of governors who could warn the chairmen of the assemblies of the undesirability of political declarations.

PRINCE N. B. SHCHERBATOV: One should not adopt different policies for similar matters, for town and *zemstvo* self-governments. I would consider it hardly proper to exert pressure on the leaders of the nobility through the governors, in this case. It could place them in a difficult position and damage their prestige. These are men who are very useful in local life, and one must support them in every way.

P. A. KHARITONOV: Because of the general nervousness in the country, we had decided not to protest formally the resolutions of the town councils. This conclusion, it seems to me, still remains in force and is quite applicable to the *zemstvo* assemblies.

PRINCE N. B. SHCHERBATOV: I expressed myself in this very sense to the representatives of the bloc, when the question came up during our conversation. They agreed that the present situation is quite tense and that one should be particularly careful in dealing with the organs of self-government. They insisted on the necessity of replying to declarations from the provinces.

A. D. SAMARIN: One should wish for far fewer political resolutions in the provinces. Various arguments and discussions about resolutions only hasten fermentation in various obscure spots. Hence, I would consider it useful to point out to the leaders of the nobility, in confidence, the undesirability of permitting the formulation of political questions at *zemstvo* assemblies during the war, at least from the point of view of maintaining calm in the country.

I. L. GOREMYKIN: Yes, and I think that one should explain that the silence of the government, in answer to all this chattering, is not a sign of consent. The Minister of Internal Affairs [Shcherbatov] should, in general, display far more energy.

A. V. KRIVOSHEIN: I agree with A. D. Samarin. The repetition of one and the same thing, moreover from various God-forsaken little corners, only creates agitation. The resolution of the Moscow City Council is sufficiently vivid and definite not to require repetition in a thousand different ways.

PRINCE N. B. SHCHERBATOV: Very well, the Ministry of Internal Affairs will show more energy; it will send out a very stern circular, and the very next day it will be in all the newspapers. There will be resounding screams about pressure being put on local self-government, and so forth. Ultimately, the resolutions will still be voted, and the only result of the circular will be that they have a more bitter tone.

I. L. GOREMYKIN: Why put it in writing when it can all be done verbally? There is enough time for that before the opening of the assemblies.

A. D. SAMARIN: One must take care, of course, that the instructions to the leaders of the nobility do not get into the newspapers.

It was decided that the Ministry of Internal Affairs should exert verbal pressure on the leaders of the *zemstvo* assemblies.

Again, discussion on the state of the press. The military authorities do not want to do anything. Government insistence accomplishes nothing.

A. V. KRIVOSHEIN: This is a sore spot requiring strong medicine. There are huge numbers of newspaper articles which are absolutely impermissible in content and tone. The country is being revolutionized before the very eyes of all the authorities, and no one wants to interfere with this outrageous phenomenon. After all, we are now fighting the greatest war in all history. The fate of Russia is at stake, and we march around in one spot. Apparently, both the military censorship and the Chief Administration of the Press are blind. Is it really possible that the Council of Ministers has no way of forcing these subordinate institutions to discharge their duties intelligently and conscientiously?

P. A. KHARITONOV: You heard, after all, how Frolov referred to the directives from Headquarters at our last meeting . . . What do you suggest be done? Even though Headquarters personnel has changed, the old spirit has apparently remained.

A. A. POLIVANOV: As I have had the honor of repeatedly reporting to the Council of Ministers, the essence of the problem lies in the fact that military censorship, like all other institutions of the Russian Empire, must be guided by law; and political censorship is not provided for in the law on military censorship.

PRINCE N. B. SHCHERBATOV: Well, what can the Chief Administration of the Press do when all the largest centers, in which all the more influential and widely distributed organs are published, are located outside its jurisdiction? They are either within the theater of operations or under martial law. In these forbidden areas—among them, Petrograd—the imposition of fines and the closing down of newspapers lies outside the power of the Minister of Internal Affairs.

A. V. KRIVOSHEIN: There can be no division of authority in matters which concern the well-being of the whole State. And this well-being categorically requires the maintenance of calm in the country, in the name of its defense and of the continuation of the war on which the very existence of Russia depends. It should be equally clear, both to civilian and military officials, that the present agitation in the press in not helping to calm the spirits of the population and to focus their attention on the struggle against the enemy. Everyone, on every corner, reads the newspapers. The sharp change in the tone of the press which has occurred lately, after some quiet, is agitating the public. We have spoken here, for instance, of the danger of political meetings in the Duma. But it meets rarely, and all kinds of speeches are made in it. On the other hand, the newspapers instill into the mind of the reader, every day, various thoughts and moods, depending on party interests. It is necessary to regard the issue of the press not from the points of view of the various ministers, but from that of the State as a whole. And one should come to a general agreement, in order to establish such procedures and such measures as are necessitated by the exceptional times we are living in. Why is it that one sees no initiative on the part of the head of the Chief Administration of the Press? It is his duty to be the guardian of general State interests in this matter.

S. D. SAZONOV: The post is now actually empty. The present head of the Chief Administration possesses many virtues with the exception of one—suitability for his post.

PRINCE N. B. SHCHERBATOV: What can the head of the Chief Administration do, when the master of the fate of Petrograd— General Frolov—does not wish to listen to anyone, not even the Council of Ministers?

A. V. KRIVOSHEIN: The whole tragedy of our time, our tragedy and that of Russia, the root of universal discontent and irritation —lies in this. Everyone talks about unity and about accord with the nation, and meanwhile the civil and the military authorities cannot agree and have not been able to work together for a whole year. The Council of Ministers discusses, requests, expresses desires, submits wishes, submits demands—and the gentlemen generals spit on all of us and don't wish to do anything. Such a Frolov should be wiped off the face of the earth in twenty-four hours, so that the other Frolovs take heed and not ruin Russia.

A. A. POLIVANOV: Give concrete instructions to the military censorship. Which tendencies in the press are disastrous to Russia?

A. V. KRIVOSHEIN: What kind of instructions can there be about such a question, in which one should be guided by one's patriotic feelings and by one's love for one's suffering motherland?

S. D. SAZONOV: Our Allies are horrified by the licentiousness which reigns in the Russian press. In this licentiousness they see very frightening auguries for the future.

I. L. GOREMYKIN: I am again forced to ask the Minister of Internal Affairs [Shcherbatov] to pay the most serious attention to the urgent necessity of taking the most decisive measures, in his Ministry, for the cessation of outrages in the press; and to get together with the proper military authorities about joint activity in this respect. I hope to see His Imperial Majesty in a few days, and I will report to him on the desirability of putting pressure on Headquarters. I will ask the Emperor for categorical instructions, in order to end this impossible situation.

After the discussion of a few minor problems they dispersed in a very nervous state. The crisis is fully posed. Something is awaiting us or, as Ivan Longinovich [Goremykin] likes to say, "Let's see what happens." Well, I really do find myself in the midst of historic events. I cannot say that one can take it lightly, when everything wavers before one's eyes and falls apart and, on top of it, the Germans are pushing right along, unembarrassed by anything.

XVI

The Meeting of
2 September 1915

—————◆◆◆—————

THE CHAIRMAN OF THE COUNCIL OF MINISTERS [Goremykin] has been to the Tsar's Headquarter in Mogilev, with a report on the date of adjournment of the Duma and on the further course of policy. The morning of his departure I told I. L. Goremykin that he's not going off to see the Emperor at an easy moment. Usually stingy with words, this time he answered me in the following way, which I noted.

[I. L. GOREMYKIN:] Yes, it is hard to vex the Emperor with the tale of our disagreement and the weak nerves of the Council of Ministers. It is in his power to choose one or another course of action. No matter what his order, I will carry it out at any cost. My task is to exonerate the Tsar from all reproaches and discontent, at my expense. Let them accuse me and curse me—I'm already old and I will not live long. But while I'm alive, I will fight for the inviolability of the Tsar's power. The whole strength of Russia lies only in the monarchy. Otherwise there will be such a mess that everything will be lost. First of all, one must conclude the war, instead of occupying oneself with reforms. There will be enough time for that after we chase out the Germans.

I. L. Goremykin returned from Headquarters on the 1st of

September with an Imperial order to release the Duma for its autumn vacations not later than the 3rd of September, and for the present Council of Ministers to remain in its present make-up, at its post. When the situation at the front permits, His Majesty will personally summon the Council of Ministers and will decide everything.

By the beginning of the meeting, the Ministers had apparently already been informed of the decisions brought back by the Chairman, and this was reflected in their mood and in their discussions. In order to characterize what follows I will begin with my epilogue:

The crisis is at hand. Terrible nervousness. I have often seen the Council in an informal situation, but nothing like this has ever happened during meetings. S. D. Sazonov was particularly upset and virtually hysterical by the end of the meeting. When I. L. Goremykin was leaving the room, having adjourned the meeting, the Minister of Foreign Affairs [Sazonov] announced: "I do not wish to say goodbye to this madman, or to shake his hand." Then he walked towards the exit, staggering, so that I followed him to try to catch him if he fainted. Sazonov noticed nothing, and had the air of a man unconscious of his surroundings. In the anteroom he cried out hysterically, *"Il est fou, ce vieillard,"* and ran out of the building.

Polivanov was boiling over with bile, and looked ready to bite; he behaved quite indecently towards the Chairman. Krivoshein looked hopelessly sad and anxious. Ignat'ev, as he always does in difficult moments, was violently messing up his sparse hair. The sniper, Kharitonov, was silent most of the time, for some reason. The conversation was extraordinarily feverish, jumping from one point to another and inevitably returning to the adjournment and its consequences. It was most difficult, not only to catch characteristic sentences, but in some cases, to catch even the substance of the discussions. Sometimes I would stop writing. After all I am a man, not a machine! Well, what is to come? The lords fight but the heads which ache are the servants'! [1]

My notation began with the following:

A. V. KRIVOSHEIN AND OTHERS raise the general issue of the self-

---

[1] A Russian saying.

abolition of the government. Since the Special Conference on Defense, which is promoting public organizations, has come into existence, various public and other figures, and the *Zemstvo* Union headed by Prince L'vov, are stepping forth all over the place. In fact, this prince is virtually becoming the chairman of a special government; at the front they talk only of him and say that he saved the situation. He supplies the army, he feeds the hungry, he cures the sick, he establishes barber shops for the soldiers—in a word, he is some kind of an ubiquitous Miur and Mereliz.[2] But who surrounds him, who his collaborators are, who his agents are—no one knows. All his activity is uncontrolled, even though he is being given hundreds of millions from the treasury. One must either end all this or hand all power over to him. Irresponsible managers of important matters and of treasury funds cannot be tolerated. If one cannot take back from the Union what it has grabbed up to now, then, in any event, one must not widen its functions further. For example, the Special Conference on Defense intends to send a representative of the Union along with a government committee [which is being sent] to America for government contracts. This is highly undesirable, and gives to the committee a mixed character. It was decided to ask the Minister of War [Polivanov], in his function as Chairman of the Special Conference, not to confirm such a resolution.

I. L. GOREMYKIN: Address yourself now to the problem of the evacuation of Kiev; General Ivanov insists on it and Headquarters supports him. I must inform the Council of Ministers that its petition for a summoning of a military council with the participation of the government has been, temporarily, denied by His Majesty.

A. V. KRIVOSHEIN: To our deep regret.

I. L. GOREMYKIN: It was pointed out [by the Emperor and Headquarters] that it is necessary to send a special plenipotentiary to Kiev to carry out the evacuation, and concentrate the whole matter in his hands.

A. A. POLIVANOV: If the necessity of abandoning Kiev to its fate is recognized by Headquarters and confirmed by His Imperial

---

[2] The largest department store in Moscow.

Majesty the Supreme Commander, then it is not for us—poor, simple mortals—to discuss it. I think it would be most practical, and least harmful, to assign this difficult task to a committee made up of the representatives of the ministries under the chairmanship of the plenipotentiary.

I. L. GOREMYKIN: Senator Liubimov was mentioned as an energetic and efficient man.

A. A. POLIVANOV: Unfortunately, he does not come from there, and does not know the situation. Some preliminary measures have already been taken in Kiev, and it would be desirable for the plenipotentiary to be familiar with them.

PRINCE N. B. SHCHERBATOV: When we first discussed the possibility of the evacuation of Kiev, I sent Antsiferov, the head of the Chief Administration for Local Economy, there. He informs me that—because of the anomalous and contradictory orders of the numerous military authorities—panic, lack of purpose, and confusion reign in the city and threaten to complicate the whole matter unbelievably. He has been personally able, by means of his conversations and actions, to calm the *zemstvo* leaders somewhat, but the population as a whole is excited and ready to flee wherever they can. It is necessary to coordinate everything there and to concentrate everything in the hands of a sufficiently authoritative, experienced, local man.

A. V. KRIVOSHEIN: My soul is in agony at the thought that Kiev—the mother of Russian cities—is being condemned to the horrors of evacuation. But there is nothing to be done. There only remains for us to find means to soften the consequences of this evil. I, too, would prefer that the evacuation be conducted by a local man with the cooperation of the representatives of all ministries. He should be given unlimited authority and one should force the military authorities to obey him—otherwise no good will come of it.

A. A. POLIVANOV: I can suggest General Khodorovich. Even though he's not an ideal manager, he has known Kiev for a long time, and he has experience and sufficient prestige.

This candidate was found acceptable. It was decided to give instructions to the effect that everything should be moved deeper, further into Russia, depending upon the means of communications.

As far as the educational institutions are concerned, the instructions were that one should worry about the more valuable property, and that one should leave open the question of resuming instruction at the new locations—that this should be decided in each particular case, in conformity with the local situation.

I. L. GOREMYKIN: The question of the holy relics in Kiev is important. His Majesty the Emperor told me that they should not be evacuated, because one may be sure that the Germans will not dare disturb them; and if they do disturb them—so much the worse for the Germans.

A. D. SAMARIN: I must warn everyone that, in accordance with the orders of the Holy Synod, the evacuation of relics has begun.

A. V. KRIVOSHEIN: I don't understand how one can do that. It is, after all, a desecration of the relics.

A. D. SAMARIN: Everything is being done very properly. When one departs, one takes with one whatever is most precious. Abandoning Kiev, one cannot leave there that which is sacred, that which has been revered by the Russian people for centuries. I cannot believe that His Majesty the Emperor could express himself against the evacuation of relics. It is clear that the matter was not reported to him in all its aspects.

S. D. SAZONOV: If we abandon universally revered relics in Kiev, what a negative impression this will make on all Orthodox people! It is better to abandon anything else, but not the sacred.

I. L. GOREMYKIN: Is it a practical possibility to evacuate all the relics from the caves, where there are hundreds of remains?

A. V. KRIVOSHEIN: There is danger that, once they are moved from their place, the relics can get lost. This seems to me worse than their temporary abandonment into German hands. Superficial desecration will not desecrate the sacred.

A. D. SAMARIN: All these issues were weighed by the Holy Synod, who found it preferable to evacuate the relics. The issue involves only those most revered, and not all of them. The caves will not be disturbed. In general, the question has been thoroughly worked out, both as to principle and as to practice.

I. L. GOREMYKIN: In that case, let us not dwell any longer on this question. Let the office of the Orthodox [religion] solve it in its own way and take the responsibility on itself.

PRINCE N. B. SHCHERBATOV: I must call the attention of the Council of Ministers to the threatening situation which is being created by the overloading of the Alexander railroad with military freight. Smolensk and adjoining provinces are going without supplies because of the absence and impossibility of transport. Hunger threatens. Meanwhile, troops are being brought into the area and are making an already difficult crisis worse. The population is groaning. Its last stocks are being taken away from it, and are being paid for in some kind of scrip. The governors can do nothing, as it is not even considered necessary to forewarn them of the arrival of military units and military bases. Time and again there are cases: for example, approximately 11,000 soldiers were piled, all at once, into a settlement of 3,000 inhabitants. What can be done in such a case?

A. V. KRIVOSHEIN: Take decisive measures to disperse [such concentrations].

PRINCE N. B. SHCHERBATOV: I cannot give such orders. The Minister of Internal Affairs is a simple citizen and observer of customs there. And the customs are really very curious. The railroad is jammed; there are bottlenecks everywhere; it is impossible to get hospital trains through—but on the main tracks of one of the stations, there stands for days the train of one of our higher generals, named "the red-headed one," in order to distinguish him from the others, who is spending his free time in pleasant company. Of course everyone sees it and knows it. Outrage and irritation are universal. Well, now go ahead and try to maintain public calm.

A. V. KRIVOSHEIN: It is better not to dwell on the outrages of rear-echelon life. One can go mad from all this. Particularly with the awareness of one's own complete helplessness to fight against it. What a horrible impression this makes in these various places, and what consequences! Everyone knows that this general is one of the closest collaborators of Headquarters. And who is now in charge of Headquarters, who is our Supreme Commander? It is frightening to think of the kind of conclusions drawn by the suffering inhabitants, by the wounded soldiers, and by the whole mass at the front. What fatal times!

I. L. GOREMYKIN: His Majesty is now occupying himself with the problems of the rear area and of personnel. He knows all the inadequacies of its organization. With the help of Alekseev, who impressed me as being a very rational man, everything will gradually be worked out.

THE CHIEF OF CHANCELLERY [Lodyzhensky] reads out the paper submitted by the head of the Civil Chancellery of the Chief of Staff of the Supreme Commander, Prince Obolensky, concerning the refugee movement.

A. V. KRIVOSHEIN: With sorrow have I heard it, and its content I have not approved.

P. A. KHARITONOV: This paper is absolutely indecent in its tendentiousness and its misuse of facts. If one is to believe the author, everything is going well, everything has been foreseen, the military authorities are innocence personified, the movement [of refugees] is a spontaneous one and not created artificially, and so forth. It would be better if Prince Obolensky didn't tackle questions with which he is obviously unfamiliar.

A. A. KHVOSTOV: The Council of Ministers has repeatedly pointed out the terrible consequences of the system of devastating the territories abandoned by our army. Men are being driven away with whips, so it is difficult to speak of any spontaneous movement.

A. V. KRIVOSHEIN: In a conversation with me about refugees, [General] Ianushkevich told me openly that war proceeds by fire and sword, and that those who get in its way must suffer for it. Fatal for Russia as he was, I can understand that Ianushkevich could reason in this way, for the Lord has given him such an outlook. But, judging from everything, Alekseev is a man of a different kind, capable of seeing events from a broader point of view. How is it, then, that he takes no measures to stop the outrages? Is it possible that the Obolenskys and similar collaborators have had time to put blinkers on him, too?

PRINCE N. B. SHCHERBATOV: One cannot, as yet, notice any of the changes in the activities of Headquarters that were promised to us. Everywhere, the same old people are singing the same old tunes. It is necessary for the Council of Ministers to intervene, to call the attention of the proper people to the necessity, in the event of further retreat, of terminating the forced evacuation of the male population from the districts that are being cleared out. The men are followed by their women, their children, their junk, and their cattle. Additional millions will invade the interior of Russia, in order to empty it and to starve. If the Ianushkevich tragedy continues, it would be better to leave the population to the enemy; it is better that they die under the boot of the Germans than that they finally ruin the whole country, which is already groaning under the avalanche of refugees. One must explain to the military that the density of the population has limits, and that one cannot overstrain this string. It can break, and with it all the civilian authorities and Russia herself.

The other members of the Council, except for Polivanov, who did not open his mouth, expressed themselves in approximately the same tone. Again the painful question of the relations between [military and civilian] authorities, *oprichnina* and *zemshchina*, was brought up.

I. L. GOREMYKIN: I spoke at Headquarters about the refugee problem, but they do not want to change their views, as yet. His Majesty promised me that he would occupy himself personally with this problem and re-examine it in the light of the viewpoint of the Council of Ministers which I reported.

PRINCE V. N. SHAKHOVSKOY: Strikes have begun at the Putilov and the metal factories. The superficial excuse: the arrest of the elected representatives to the medical insurance cooperatives. The movement immediately took on a sharp character and was complicated by the submission of political demands. One can expect a further growth of the wave of strikes if one does not adopt anticipatory measures right now. It is particularly undesirable to bother the representatives to the medical insurance cooperatives. It is always easy to arouse the workers with such arrests and thus create conflicts which are then blown up into huge events.

A. A. POLIVANOV: If there are not going to be radical changes in the general situation, my thoughts about the future are extremely gloomy. At the last meeting of the Special Conference on Defense, the majority of public representatives expressed the conviction that the unrest at the Putilov factory (which sets the tone for the labor movement) is the beginning of a general strike in protest against the adjournment of the Duma. Everyone is expecting extraordinary events to follow the adjournment.

I. L. GOREMYKIN: All this is only intimidation. Nothing will happen.

PRINCE N. B. SHCHERBATOV: The Department of Police does not have, by any means, such soothing information as Your High Excellency. The testimony of all agents is unanimous, to the effect that the labor movement will develop to an extent which will threaten the safety of the State. It is on this basis that the Department of Police demanded that the military authorities make a number of arrests; among them, of a certain Sudakov, a very dangerous leader, who is playing the role of a mediator between the Mensheviks and the Bolsheviks.[3] Because of the present situation I have ordered him freed, and I have confirmed the necessity of particular caution in respect to members of medical insurance cooperatives. As for the reason for the labor disorders—which have gone as far as clashes with the police at the Putilov factory—the demands which are presented are: not to adjourn the Duma; to free the five imprisoned deputies of the Left faction; to increase wages by fifteen per cent; and so on. All these, of course, are only excuses to cover up the real aim of the underground leaders of the workers—to take advantage of the misfortunes at the front, and of the internal crisis, to attempt a social revolution and to usurp power.

S. D. SAZONOV: The picture presented to us is pretty hopeless. On the one hand, labor disorders which are apparently taking on an organized character; on the other hand, the totally extreme mood of the public groups concentrated in Moscow. It is said that, in the name of conducting the war to a victorious conclusion, members of the Duma, together with the *zemstvo* and the town conventions, are ready to proclaim themselves a constituent assembly. Everything, everywhere, is boiling, anxious, desperate—and in such a threatening atmosphere the adjournment of the Duma will take place. Where are we, and all of Russia, being led?

I. L. GOREMYKIN: I have the Imperial order to close the Duma not later than Thursday, the 3rd of September, which order will be carried out by me.

S. D. SAZONOV: But as everyone remembers, at the meeting on the 20th of August His Majesty listened favorably to our petition to decide about the adjournment of the Duma after it was discussed in the Council of Ministers and after we reported our conclusions.

---

[3] The two factions of the Marxist socialists.

That means that the Emperor has now changed his mind. It is important for us to know what caused such a sudden change.

I. L. GOREMYKIN: The Imperial will, once definitely stated, is not subject to discussion by the Council of Ministers. I request the Minister of Foreign Affairs [Sazonov] not to put such questions to me.

S. D. SAZONOV: We are not puppets, but men who bear the responsibility for governing Russia. If our mouths are to be shut on issues on which the fate of the State depends, then the meetings of the Council of Ministers are, in general, superfluous.

I. L. GOREMYKIN: All the considerations on the adjournment of the Duma, and on a change of policy, which have been expressed by the Council of Ministers, were fully conveyed by me to His Majesty. I reported to him all the different opinions in all of their detail. In answer to this came the order to close the Duma and to have all the ministers remain at their posts. What more is there to talk about, now?

A. A. POLIVANOV: The whole issue is: *How* did you report our opinions to the Emperor?

S. D. SAZONOV: And *what*, specifically [did you report]?

I. L. GOREMYKIN: I reported to His Imperial Majesty *in the manner* which was appropriate, and *that* which took place in the Council. I cannot allow myself to be addressed in such terms, and with such questions.

S. D. SAZONOV: But if our most loyal considerations were rejected, then may we interest ourselves as to what caused His Majesty to issue such a sharp order?

I. L. GOREMYKIN: Address yourself with this question not to me, but to His Majesty the Emperor. I am not required, and I find it unnecessary, to answer such questions.

S. D. SAZONOV: If I cannot get an answer here, then of course I will address myself to the Emperor.

A. V. KRIVOSHEIN: Our Chairman has informed His Majesty of all of our views. It is evident that our views and our understanding of the present situation are not shared by the monarch. He promises to talk with us when the difficult situation at the front is over. It remains for us only to wait, for it is not proper for us to demonstrate.

I. L. GOREMYKIN: I asked the Emperor to relieve me of the

Chairmanship of the Council of Ministers and replace me with a man better suited for the new conditions. In answer, His Majesty ordered me to remain at my post and to close the Duma. This I will do, no matter what.

A. V. KRIVOSHEIN: It goes without saying that an Imperial order cannot be put to discussion. But I do think that we have not only the right, but the direct duty, to foresee the consequences of the act about to be executed.

I. L. GOREMYKIN: His Majesty sees this question differently. I reported to him the fears expressed in the Council of Ministers, but the Emperor did not change his opinion. What else is there for us to discuss? Now, if there are disorders, one will have to act.

PRINCE N. B. SHCHERBATOV: From the point of view of further actions, I would like to ask for instructions from the Council of Ministers concerning the Moscow conventions.[4] The Governor, the Chief of the City Administration, and the Director of the Department of Police, all estimate the situation in Moscow as being very serious. Everything there is boiling, agitated, irritated, violently anti-government and expecting salvation only from radical changes. The whole flower of the opposition intelligentsia is gathered there, and is demanding power to direct the war to victory. The workers, and the population as a whole, are gripped by some sort of madness and are like gunpowder. An outburst of disorders is possible at any moment. Yet the authorities in Moscow have virtually no forces. There is one reserve battalion of 800 men, of whom only half are available, as 400 are taken up with guard duty in the Kremlin and other places. Then there is a squadron of Cossacks and, finally, two militia units stationed in the outskirts. All of these are far from reliable, and it would be difficult to order them against the crowd. There are no troops at all in the rural part of the county. Both the city and the county police are inadequate, numerically, to the demands that may be made on them. I must also note the presence, in Moscow, of about 30,000 convalescent soldiers. This is a wild band, not recognizing discipline, making scandals, clashing with the police (recently one of the latter was killed by soldiers),

---

[4] In 1915 the Union of the *Zemstvos* and the Union of the Towns were holding their conventions in Moscow.

freeing prisoners, and so on. Undoubtedly, if there are disorders, this whole horde will be on the side of the crowd. What would you suggest that the Minister of Internal Affairs do under these circumstances? To top it off, he doesn't have the fullness of authority in Moscow, as the military are giving orders there. How can I struggle against the conventions, which undoubtedly range beyond the limits set by law, but which can attract the crowd to their side at any moment and create an explosion? There are formal reasons for interfering, but what, in fact, can we do? In general, I cannot avoid repeating that both the *Zemstvo* and the Town Unions, which I found in full bloom when I took over the ministry, are a colossal mistake on the part of the government. One should not have allowed such organizations without a statute and without a determination of the limits of their functions. From a philanthropic beginning they have grown into enormous institutions with the most varied functions, in many cases purely governmental ones, and they are replacing many government offices. All this is done by usurpation, under the protection of the military authorities, who (as, for example, the redheaded Danilov) use them widely and give them enormous means. Some of the recent laws even refer to them as official institutions, but their personnel and their internal structure are not foreseen by law and are unknown to the government; in reality, they serve as a focal point for opposition elements and for various gentlemen with a political past, as well as for those who are dodging service at the front. It is impossible, now, to close these institutions down, primarily because they are working for the army. And from a political point of view, as well, such a measure would create serious complications. It follows that it is necessary to suffer them as an existing fact. One cannot doubt that their conventions will amount to a political demonstration, and perhaps even something worse. There will be heated speeches, provocative resolutions, and so forth. If one is to regard these conventions as assemblies defined by the Law of March 4,[5] and not as [official] institutions, one should demand

---

[5] The Law of March 4, 1906, dealt with the right of assembly. It was an amendment to the law of October 12, 1905. Both laws required official permission for any open-air assembly, and required the presence of a representative of the authorities: i.e., the police. The Law of March 4, however, made a distinction between public and nonpublic assemblies.

that they initiate a petition for permission [to convene], and one should send police representatives to the meetings. But I am convinced they will not ask any permissions of us, and will pose the issue as being that of a meeting of an institution officially recognized in law. The law does not provide for the presence of the police at such a meeting. What shall one do?

I. L. GOREMYKIN: Before my departure for Headquarters, you told me that police would be sent to the convention. Hence, basing myself on your words, I reported thus to His Majesty the Emperor, who approved it. If your declaration was incorrect, and if you have no such right [to send in the police], then I beg you to convey this for the information of His Majesty.

PRINCE N. B. SHCHERBATOV: I will send a report right away. The only course of action: to allow the convention in a building, between four walls, and to establish strict supervision [to see] that there is no contact with the crowd. If there is an attempt to go out into the streets, not to allow this; and, in the event of resistance, to take all measures foreseen by law, including the use of force. At the same time, one has to establish political censorship of the press, so that the discussions and resolutions of the conventions do not serve as subjects for agitation in the newspapers.

A. D. SAMARIN: It seems to me that one should avoid, in every way, open clashes with the conventions. After all, one should not forget that the *Zemstvo* and the Town Unions are not illegal organizations. The program of their activities was approved by the Minister of Internal Affairs in August of 1914, and envisaged only the evacuation of the wounded. At that time, only persons elected by the proper assemblies made up the Unions. Prince L'vov is the representative of the general *zemstvo* organization, which had its own funds, to the amount of nine hundred thousand rubles. What took place afterward is, in fact, nothing but the usurpative widening of authorizations and tasks without government sanction. In dealing with the Unions, it would be most correct to base oneself on the fact that their limits were foreseen at their origin and have not been

---

The latter are defined as consisting solely of members of a society or organization. A nonpublic assembly had the right to meet freely, "within four walls," without official representatives or permission.

officially broadened since. Remaining within these limits, the Unions can allow attendance at their conventions with the right to vote only to authorized elective representatives of the *zemstvo* and town self-governments. All other participants must be regarded as guests, as the public, or as those invited only for consultation. The meetings must be closed ones, without the participation of the press. One should immediately demand, for the sake of control, a list of permanent authorized members; and, in the event one discovers unauthorized persons, one should insist on their expulsion from the Union.

I. L. GOREMYKIN: One way or another, the Minister of Internal Affairs [Shcherbatov] is bound to take measures to see that the Unions do not evade supervision and that their conventions do not adopt tendencies which threaten the State order.

A. A. KHVOSTOV: A. D. Samarin's suggestion gives us a way out, since, by law, the presence of guests at a meeting gives us the right of police control.

A. D. SAMARIN: When the *Zemstvo* Union arose, comparatively few people took part in it, and they were all well-known. One can make it clear to Prince L'vov that this convention should be based on the same premises as the first one, and one could refer to the wartime circumstances, which do not allow assemblies with an undefined membership.

P. A. KHARITONOV: A. D. Samarin is a trifle mistaken. There has been no legalization of the Unions nor approval of their program by the government. In the abnormal atmosphere of the first days of the war, the representatives of the general *zemstvo* organization were received by the Emperor, who wished them success in their work of helping the wounded. Hence the legalization was an Imperial one, and not according to the Law of the 4th of March, which therefore does not apply to the case.

A. D. SAMARIN: But one cannot deny, after all, that the broadening of the tasks of the Union came about not *de jure* but *de facto*.

P. A. KHARITONOV: Yes, but the government has no legal basis for opposing this, as long as the Union does not have a strictly defined program and statute, properly formulated and properly confirmed. It is an organization which is *sui generis,* possible only in a wartime atmosphere.

I. L. GOREMYKIN: Moscow is under extraordinary police law.[6] If they cannot be convinced by words, then one must act. Police can be sent to the meetings on the basis of the extraordinary law. This law gives us the right to take any measures to safeguard order. And if the conventions begin to talk too much, then one can close them down.

PRINCE N. B. SHCHERBATOV: But exactly what is it that one can close down, if there is no officially permitted convention?

I. L. GOREMYKIN: The issue is not the interpretation of laws, but the safeguarding of State security. A meeting exists, and threatens to create trouble. It is the business of the authorities to stop outrages. The legal authorization for this—the extraordinary police law.

A. D. SAMARIN: It would be inconvenient to send the police to such a meeting. This would create a scandal and a parliamentary question in the Duma.

I. L. GOREMYKIN: It is the duty of the government to forestall public scandals. Parliamentary questions cannot be asked, because the Duma will not be in session. Outrages must be answered by decisive measures and not by superfluous politeness. Now is not the time to fuss over details.

A. A. KHVOSTOV: If the convention gathers without special permission, then only authorized representatives can be allowed in it. It is in this sense that we should present our demands, with all the consequences that derive from them.

PRINCE N. B. SHCHERBATOV: That is—if they do not obey the demands for the participation of only authorized representatives, then one should close down the convention. I have nothing against such a formulation of the issue.

S. D. SAZONOV: I expect nothing good [from this]. Even under normal conditions it would be difficult to arrange all this smoothly; and what about now, when it will all be taking place against the background of the adjournment of the Duma?

---

[6] *Chrezvychainnaia okhrana*, translated literally, "extraordinary protection," was a singular Imperial Russian institution, a form of martial law, exercised by the civil administration. It allowed the police to take all measures it thought necessary, on the excuse that public order was particularly threatened. It was widely used during the reaction which followed the revolution of 1905.

PRINCE N. B. SHCHERBATOV: This adjournment threatens us with one more convention. One hears of the intention, among the deputies, to go to Moscow in the event of adjournment and set up a second Vyborg there. What measures and actions should one take to deal with such an assembly?

A. A. KHVOSTOV: None, if the second Vyborg is as successful as the first.

S. D. SAZONOV: Well, one should not have any illusions on this score. Now, this convention will take place on a powder keg.

PRINCE N. B. SHCHERBATOV: Once the crowd is in the streets and undermines public order, its make-up becomes irrelevant. Here the methods of action are known. But what shall one do if the new *Vyborzhtsy* remain in a closed building and there engage in the redaction and discussion of a new Vyborg manifesto. What can the authorities do then?

I. L. GOREMYKIN: If they limit themselves to chattering, then let them go on with it. But, if their chatter threatens the safety of the State, then they should be dispersed.

PRINCE N. B. SHCHERBATOV: And what about the immunity of the deputies of the Duma?

I. L. GOREMYKIN: The immunity cannot serve as a shield for criminal acts. First, one should disperse them; then one can talk about immunity. In general, I call the attention of the Minister of Internal Affairs [Shcherbatov] to the necessity for acting decisively. This is not the time for formalistic doubts and considerations. One must stop the movement directed against the existing State order at all costs. When the war is over, then the question is different.

A. V. KRIVOSHEIN: All our discussion today has shown, with great clarity, Ivan Longinovich [Goremykin], that the difference between you and the majority of the Council of Ministers, respecting our views of the situation and on the course of policy, has become greater than ever recently. You have reported on this difference to His Majesty the Emperor; but His Majesty deigns to agree with your point of view and not with ours. Now you are embarking on a course of action which follows from the Imperial instructions given you; and, withal, the same persons who were arguing against the effectiveness of the policy you indicated remain your collaborators, by Imperial order. Forgive me this one question:

How dare you act when [even] the members of the government are convinced of the need for other methods, when the whole government apparatus which is in your hands is in opposition, when both external and internal circumstances are becoming more and more threatening every day?

I. L. GOREMYKIN: I will fulfill my duty to His Majesty the Emperor to the very end, no matter what opposition and lack of sympathy I encounter. I reported everything to His Majesty, and asked him to replace me by a more up-to-date person. But an Imperial order followed, and, in my understanding—it is the law. What will happen later? His Majesty the Emperor said that he will come in person and review everything.

S. D. SAZONOV: Yes, but then it will be too late. Tomorrow blood will flow in the streets and Russia will sink into the abyss! Why? For what? It is all so terrible! In any event, I want to declare out loud that, under the present circumstances, I do not take on myself the responsibility for your acts and for the adjournment of the Duma.

I. L. GOREMYKIN: I bear the responsibility for my acts and I am not asking anyone to share it with me. The Duma will be adjourned on the appointed day and no blood will flow anywhere.

A. A. POLIVANOV: That's a debatable question. Time will tell. But am I permitted to ask under what circumstances the adjournment will take place: that is, will it follow some government declaration to the legislative bodies, as we had said earlier?

I. L. GOREMYKIN: I do not find it necessary to be present either in the Duma or in the State Council, and I have no intention of making any declarations. This is fruitless and untimely.

A. A. POLIVANOV: That means you're moving toward a complete break with the Duma, if you do not even find it necessary to preserve the appearance of respect towards the legislative chambers which have been called to work by the will of His Majesty the Emperor.

P. A. KHARITONOV: The government has never appeared in the Duma at an interruption of a Session.

A. A. KHVOSTOV: I see no reason to create a precedent.

S. D. SAZONOV: That which has been done earlier is not binding. Now the times are as never before; now the issue is the fate of Russia.

I. L. GOREMYKIN: This statement is exaggerated and is based on nothing. If you wish to be present at the adjournment of the Duma, then go. I see no objection to it.

S. D. SAZONOV: Oh no! Thank you very much for the suggestion. I do not wish to take part in an act in which I see the beginning of the destruction of my motherland.

I. L. GOREMYKIN: In any event, the adjournment of the Duma will take place, and I will not be present. The question is closed. An Imperial order cannot be criticized by the Council of Ministers. I declare the meeting closed.

After these words, I. L. Goremykin stood up and left the chamber for his study.

On the 16th of September, 1915, a meeting of the Council of Ministers took place in the Imperial presence at the Tsar's Headquarters. I have noted down, from the words of I. L. GOREMYKIN, the following: "Everyone caught hell from His Majesty the Emperor for the August letter, and for their behavior during the August crisis."

Conclusion

———◆———

On the face of it, old Goremykin appeared to be right. The Duma was adjourned, reassembled, and readjourned a number of times, and nothing much happened. Certainly, the Duma and its fate did not seem to interest anyone outside society very much. And the issue which agitated the Council of Ministers above all others—that of the supreme command—agitated no one else. The Tsar commuted between Headquarters and Tsarskoe Selo. All that happend, beginning with the summer of 1915, was the notorious ministerial game of leapfrog. All the ministers who were in "opposition," except for Count Ignat'ev, were dismissed in the months that followed the summer crisis and their *démarche*. And Goremykin himself, who was not quite as ready to step down as he pretended to be, and who even used the influence of Rasputin to stay in power—he, too, was dismissed. But the choice of their successors was hard to explain. When A. N. Naumov, a rich land-owner, a conservative and leader of the provincial gentry, was appointed Minister of Agriculture in November, 1915, replacing Krivoshein, he was forced to point out to the Emperor that both socially and ideologically he was a comrade of Samarin and Prince

Shcherbatov, and "a more loyal subject than they I cannot be." [1]
And the sixty-six year old Prince N. D. Golitsyn, the last Chairman
of the Council of Ministers, appointed December 27, 1916, pleaded
with Nicholas II that he was ill, that in forty-seven years of service
he had never dealt with politics (most of his activity was with the
Red Cross during the war) and that "this cup should pass me by." [2]

And yet, if on the surface nothing seemed to change, the
majority of the Council of Ministers was also proved right—for,
seventeen months after their arguments and forebodings, the whole
government apparatus, still in stasis, was simply swept away. They
were right, but for the wrong reasons. The real reasons were stated,
with pain and understanding, by Zinaida Gippius. In her diary,
on February 25, 1917, when the revolution was under way, she
wrote:

It is interesting that the government shows no discernible signs of life.
One cannot understand where it is, and who, in fact, is managing things.
This is new. . . . The Prime Minister (I cannot even remember right
away who it is)[3] seems to be dead, [hidden away] in his apartment. . . .
Someone, somewhere, seems to be giving some kind of orders. Khabalov?[4]
Not even Khabalov. We are being choked by a gigantic corpse. That's all.
A strange feeling.

The Duma—it has assumed a revolutionary posture . . . the way
a trolley car assumes it when it is placed across the tracks. Not more than
that. The liberal intelligentsia have absolutely no communication or connection with the [revolutionary] movement . . . not even a contemplative-
sympathetic connection. They hiss: "What madmen! One must [do it] together with the army! One must wait! Now, everything for the war!
Defeatists!"

---

[1] *Padenie Tsarkogo Rezhima (The Fall of the Tsarist Regime): Steno-
grafischeskie Otchety doprosov i pokazanii . . . v Chrezvychainoi Sledstvennoi Komissii Vremennogo Pravitel'stva,* ed. P. E. Shchegolev, I (Leningrad, 1924), pp. 331 *ff.* Shchegolev's seven volumes, published in 1924-27,
contain all the interrogations of, and testimony before, an extraordinary
commission appointed by the Provisional Government to investigate all
the circumstances of the last years of the Tsarist regime.

[2] *Ibid.,* II, 251.

[3] The Prime Minister was N. D. Golitsyn.

[4] Khabalov was Commander of the Petrograd military district and of its
troops.

No one hears them. They are going hoarse without any purpose, in the Duma. And, with each moment, they seem to become less and less necessary . . .[5]

Not only the government, but society (nonrevolutionary by definition) was also helpless and paralyzed before the oncoming storm, for the simple reason that it neither wanted it nor understood its nature. The revolution, started by the masses of the population and expressing their desires and their opinions, swept away the Goremykins, the Sazonovs, and the Miliukovs, together and equally. It did so because none of these representatives of society had much of an idea of what the "people" wanted and what "popular opinion" was. When they had to face the people, when the revolution came, their reaction could be symbolized by the words of the classic liberal, I. V. Gessen:

I was in front of a solid shifting mass of human backs and chests. Human? Yes, of course, but the faces were, somehow, faceless, with wide-opened mouths, and the sounds coming from these [mouths] joined into a reverberating noise which pressed, physically, on one's ear drums. . . .

This was my first attendance at the ball of the revolution. . . . One had to break away from the established habits of life, and if such a denial of habits is difficult in itself, it was the harder now, for there was nothing to replace them. The situation became unstable, like quicksilver; one lost the feeling of confidence and of self-existence.[6]

The paralysis, then, had overcome those who were living in a world less and less real, and were slowly becoming aware of the fact. And hence their despair—for they neither knew the real world nor wanted to know it.

---

[5] Zinaida Gippius, *Siniia Kniga: Peterburgskii Dnevnik, 1914-1918* (The *Blue Book: St. Petersburg Diary, 1914-1918*) (Belgrade, 1929), pp. 75-76.
[6] Gessen, pp. 358-60.

Selected Bibliography

The purpose of this bibliography is to indicate the standard monographs on the prerevolutionary period and to provide a representative selection of memoirs and reminiscences, available in Western languages, by the various participants.

Buchanan, Sir George W., *My Mission to Russia and Other Diplomatic Memories.* 2 vols. Boston, 1923. Buchanan was the British Ambassador to Russia during World War I.

Chernov, V. M., *The Great Russian Revolution,* translated and abridged by Philip E. Mosely. New Haven, 1936. Chernov was the head of the Socialist Revolutionary Party.

Documents of Russian History: 1914-1917, ed. F. E. Golder, tr. E. Aronsberg. New York, 1927.

Golovine, N. N., *The Russian Army in the World War.* New Haven, 1931. Golovine was a Russian staff general during the war.

Gurko, V. I., *Memoires and Impressions of War and Revolution in Russia: 1914-1917.* London, 1918. Gurko was a member of the State Council and a high-ranking bureaucrat.

———, *Features and Figures of the Past: Government and Opinion in the Reign of Nicholas II,* eds. J. E. Wallace Sterling, X. J. Eudin, and H. H. Fisher; tr. Laura Matveev. Stanford University Press, Stanford, Calif., and Oxford University Press, 1939.

Kurlov, P. G., *Das Ende des russischen Kaisertums: persönliche Erinnerungen des Chefs der russischen Geheimpolizei.* . . . Berlin, 1920.

Levin, Alfred, *The Second Duma.* New Haven, 1940.

Miliukov, P. N., *Geschichte der zweiter russischen Revolution,* vol. I. Vienna, 1920.

Nicholas II, *Journal intime de Nicolas II,* tr. A. Pierre. Paris, 1925.

————, *The Letters of the Tsar to the Tsaritsa: 1914-1917,* tr. A. L. Hynes. London, 1929.

————, *Archives secrètes de l'empereur Nicolas II,* translated and edited by V. Lazarevski. Paris, 1928.

Nolde, B. E., *Russia in the Economic War.* New Haven, 1928. Baron Nolde was a well-known jurist in the Russian Imperial administration.

Paleologue, G. M., *La Russie des tsars pendant la grande guerre.* 3 vols. Paris, 1921-22. In English: *An Ambassador's Memoirs,* tr. F. A. Holt. 3 vols. London, 1923-25.

Pares, B., *The Fall of the Russian Monarchy.* New York, 1939.

Rodzianko, M. V., *The Reign of Rasputin: An Empire's Collapse,* tr. C. Zvegintzeff. London, 1927. Rodzianko was the President of the Duma during the War.

Savinkov, B. V., *Souvenirs d'un terroriste,* tr. B. Taft. Paris, 1931. Savinkov was a famous social-revolutionary terrorist; later prominent in the Provisional Government.

Sazonov, S. D., *Les Années fatales.* Paris. 1927.

Shchegolev, P. E., ed., *La Chute du régime tsariste,* abridged by B. A. Maklakov. Paris, 1927. This is a one-volume abridgement of the seven-volume collection on the fall of the old regime, edited in Russian by Shchegolev. See the Selected Russian Bibliography.

Shul'gin, V. V., *"Tage": Memoiren aus der russischen Revolution,* tr. M. von Reutern. Berlin, 1928. Shul'gin was a right-wing deputy to the Duma during World War I.

Sukhanov, N. (N. N. Gimmer), *The Russian Revolution, 1917: A Personal Record,* edited, abridged, and translated by J. Carmichael. London, 1955. Sukhanov was a Social-Democrat, a Menskevik active in the revolution.

Sukhomlinov, V. A., *Erinnerungen.* Berlin, 1924. The memoirs of the man who was Russian Minister of War until 1915.

Trotsky, L., *Our Revolution: Essays on Working Class and International Revolution: 1904-1917,* collected and translated by M. J. Volgin. New York, 1918.

Woytinsky, W. S., *Stormy Passage: A Personal History through Two Russian Revolutions to Democracy and Freedom, 1905-1960.* New York, 1961.

Zeman, Z. A. B., ed., *Germany and the Revolution in Russia, 1915-1918: Documents from the Archives of the German Foreign Ministry.* New York, 1958.

It would be virtually impossible, and not very useful, to list here all the Russian material that is available on this period. Only the major collections on the period just before and during the Revolution are noted.

Arkhiv Russkoi Revolutsii (Archive of the Russian Revolution), ed. I. V. Gessen. 22 vols. Berlin, 1922-37.

Byloe (The Past): 1917-1926, ed. P. E. Shchegolev.

Golos Minuvshego (The Voice of the Past), 1917-1923, ed. S. P. Mel'gunov. Moscow.

Golos Minuvshego na chuzhoi storone (The Voice of the Past in Exile), 1926-1928, ed. S. P. Mel'gunov. Paris.

Krasnyi Arkhiv. The chief Soviet collection of prerevolutionary material.

Padenie Tsarskogo Rezhima: Stenograficheskie Otchety doprosov i pokazanii, dannykh v 1917 g. v Chrezvychainnoi Sledstvennoi Komissii Vremennogo Pravitel'stva (The Fall of the Tsarist Regime: the Stenographic Records of the Testimony Given, in 1917, before the Extraordinary Commission of Inquiry of the Provisional Government), ed. P. E. Shchegolev. 7 vols. Leningrad, 1924-27.